Through the Poet's Eye

Through the Poet's Eye

The Travels of Zagajewski, Herbert, and Brodsky

Bożena Shallcross

Northwestern University Press
Evanston, Illinois

Northwestern University Press
Evanston, Illinois 60208-4210

Printed in the United States of America

10 9 8 7 6 5 4 3 2 1

ISBN 0-8101-1837-8

Library of Congress Cataloging-in-Publication Data

Madra-Shallcross, Bozena.
    Through the poet's eye : the travels of Zagajewski, Herbert, and Brodsky /
Bozena Shallcross.
        p. cm.
Includes bibliographical references and index.
    ISBN 0-8101-1837-8
    1. Zagajewski, Adam, 1945– —Journeys. 2. Herbert, Zbigniew—Journeys.
3. Brodsky, Joseph, 1940– —Journeys. 4. Civilization, Western. 5. Art. I.
Title.
    PG7028 .M24 2001
    891.8'547309355—dc21
                                                                    2001007515

To my husband, Dave Shallcross, whose presence made this book possible, and to Madeline G. Levine for her enthusiasm and encouragement

Is it lack of imagination that makes us come
to imagined places, not just stay at home?
Could Pascal have been not entirely right
about just sitting quietly in one's room?
—*Elizabeth Bishop*

Contents

List of Illustrations   xi

Introduction   xiii

PART ONE   Adam Zagajewski

1
Site Reading   5

2
Epiphany in Blue   19

PART TWO   Zbigniew Herbert

3
View with a Wayfarer   43

4
Passage to Rapture   63

5
Images of Darkness   **85**

PART THREE   Joseph Brodsky

6
Strategies of Disappearance   **103**

7
Empty Mirror   **123**

Afterword   **141**

Notes   **145**
Works Cited   **169**
Index   **181**
Acknowledgments   **191**

Illustrations

Figure 1. Jan Vermeer van Delft, *Girl Interrupted at Her Music (Music Lesson)*, circa 1660, oil on canvas, 38.7 × 43.9 centimeters, New York, Frick Collection, page 23

Figure 2. Torrentius (Jan Simonsz van der Beek), *Still Life with a Bridle*, 1614, oil on canvas, 52 × 50.5 centimeters, Amsterdam, Royal Museum, page 78

Figure 3. Kasimir Malevich, *Black Circle*, 1913 (1923–29), oil on canvas, 105.5 × 105.5 centimeters, Petersburg, State Russian Museum, page 93

Figure 4. Kasimir Malevich, *Black Square*, 1913 (1923–29), oil on canvas, 106.2 × 106.5 centimeters, Petersburg, State Russian Museum, page 139

Introduction

Le poète est celui qui regarde.
—André Gide

Through the Poet's Eye is an excursion into a territory informed by the intensive and dynamic interplay of the visual and the verbal as it occurred during travels undertaken by three Eastern European poets. These poets—Zbigniew Herbert (1924–98), Joseph Brodsky (1940–96), and Adam Zagajewski (born 1945)—are, of course, best known for their verse. Yet each of them also wrote some of the most original essays of this century. It is this prose—remarkable for its cross-cultural complexity and interdisciplinary richness—that constitutes the analytical material of the present volume.

The point of departure of this book consists of the travel experiences of these poets who, for various reasons, journeyed to the West (both during and after communism). Each undertook his journey under circumstances quite different from the others: Brodsky was exiled from the Soviet Union with no prospect of return; Zagajewski left Poland without any intention of making his home in France; and Herbert, unwilling to emigrate, nonetheless made extended visits abroad. While living in the West, they all became intimately acquainted with Western culture. Whether encountering visual masterpieces in the formal environment of a museum or strolling through sinking Venice—considered by Brodsky "the greatest masterpiece our species produced"[1]—each poet created, in his own fashion, an essayistic testimony which connected him to the stream of European culture.

I do not propose here a comparative examination of the interrelationships among the three authors, although I discuss certain analogies when pertinent. Instead, I inquire into that which is particular to their essay writing: a revelatory perception of the visual arts. As attested to in their essays, a correlation exists between the sensory experience of travel and an epiphanic perception of the visual arts. This correlation informs an epiphany's dynamic nature, for epiphany is itself a brief passage shaped by external and internal forces. Therefore, I define the three travelers' parallel experiences with art as epiphanic travels. What I describe here as epiphanic journey is, in sum, a dynamic and intensive moment of insight and motion produced by the interdependence of movement and works of art. Such epiphanies can be blissful or bleak but are always endowed with a "transfiguring perceptual power," a power that goes beyond transforming travel and can transform the traveler's world and life.[2]

Zagajewski, Brodsky, and Herbert blend observations of their surroundings with an eye toward human artistic achievements. Traditionally, travel opens the self to enlightening experiences, but in the case of epiphanic travels such viewpoints are taken further than one would normally expect. In the modern era, when being "on the road" has become a veritable way of life, these poets from "the other Europe" transform travel, through their art, from a common and often utilitarian necessity into an intriguing meditation.[3]

For decades during the Communist regime, these poets were disinherited and isolated from Western culture. This deprivation, most acutely pronounced in Herbert's poetry, did not reduce the poets' needs to mere dreams of traveling abroad at the time when such travel was impossible. According to Stanislaw Baranczak's interpretation, disinheritance is an irrevocable state of mind.[4] However, in the essays written by Brodsky, Herbert, and Zagajewski one observes that disinheritance is not necessarily irreparable. Their parallel moments of vision speak of the

poets' intense union with works of art and of their spontaneously recovered connections with the Western culture from which they had been
excluded. In fact, the more alienated they were from value-bearing de-
posits of that tradition, the more intense their encounter with them was.

In their longing for the West's forbidden fruit, they traveled to its
artistic sanctuaries, not to restitute the aesthetic utopianism of moder-
nity and its religion of beauty but to observe art for themselves in its
natural setting and to embrace the rich visual heritage of such places.
Their travels resulted in their inner transformations. It was G. W.
Goethe's description of a voyage to the roots of culture in his *Italian
Journey, 1786–1788* as introducing his spiritual renewal that established the foundation for such journeys. I would indicate yet another,
much older layer of tradition that informs such an experience: the
medieval poets' view of a journey as a spiritual quest. The peregrinations
of these three contemporary wanderers from Poland and Russia, although not necessarily therapeutic and devoid of religious objectives,
are instead raised to another level of meaning. They speak of the
present-day human condition of being on the road and, especially, this
condition's impermanence.

Travel allowed them to see everyday life and its seemingly insignifi-
cant and particular aspects preserved in the regional cuisine, the art of
tasting wine, architecture, and urban planning. If art spoke to Herbert of
the menacing chaos of history, its very existence reflected creative efforts
taking shape in the stable if disorderly environs of the artist's atelier.[5]
Only a firsthand knowledge of the surroundings could give special insight to Brodsky contemplating the constant attempts and failures at
preserving Venice, whereas the nuanced colors of the stone used to build
Romanesque and Gothic churches in France reminded Zagajewski of
the concreteness of medieval architecture. Affected by and preoccupied
with History, its tragic conflicts and bloody battles, they also found during their travels history written in the lower case, the marginalized history of patient labor and overlooked particulars of the quotidian. As
students of art sensitive to its domestic settings, their approach is close to
the Annales, the French school of historical thought.

They were, on the other hand, discriminating in their choices and,
in accordance with their own philosophies and aesthetics, frequently did
not accept or remained indifferent to the art of critical acclaim, whether
it is the *Mona Lisa* by Leonardo da Vinci or recent architectural trends.

Motivated either by their learning or by their desire to influence the existing canon by the sheer force of their personalities, they favored or rejected the standard measure of beauty. Refuting at face value the canonical significance and elitist prestige of the art produced in the Western Hemisphere, they were able to turn their travel experience into a valid dialogic encounter with another culture. For them, art was a privileged tool for gaining insight to the true or hidden nature of reality as well as an effective vehicle to resist otherness.

The experiential energy so characteristic of epiphany recalls the question central to the discourse on modernist epiphany in works of fiction. In his classic study *Epiphany in the Modern Novel,* Morris Beja characterizes epiphany as a "sudden spiritual manifestation . . . being out of proportion to the significance or strictly logical relevance of whatever produces it."[6] The idea that trivial things produce epiphanies owes much to the prose of James Joyce and other modernists. I find compelling evidence, at least in the material I have studied, that countermands this prevalent view: the incongruity between the cause and effect is not necessarily true for all epiphanic events, and is especially not valid in the case of artistic epiphanies, which originate in visual masterpieces. In fact, these epiphanies can be intimately connected to art that stimulates them, and in proportion to that stimulus. According to our society's hierarchy, well-crafted artworks do not belong to the category of things trivial. Therefore my inquiry postulates that correlation, more often than not, prevails over irrelevance.

Furthermore, it is not a coincidence that artistic epiphanies are experienced while these poets are on the road. Their arrival in a foreign land and the temporal suspension of everyday life at home, fraught with its habits and concerns, prove to be important catalysts for the unfolding of their vision. Travel, understood as motion and the successive change of one's surroundings, acts as an agent that anticipates the epiphany's occurrence and creates the right psychological and aesthetically receptive frame of mind. It also shapes the epiphany's dynamic nature. Thus, the epiphanies that I have grouped together in this volume have a progressive character that counters their traditional reading as crystallized instants. This feature of the epiphanic moment is additionally supported by the progressive structure—which I address in detail—of the artworks that stimulate the epiphanies in question. By exposing the dynamic aspect of epiphany, I engage in its counterreading as stasis and employ the concept of motion in terms of the passage. My use of the category spans from kinetic motion (be it a passage through a foreign land, a city, a museum, or any other interior) to the passage understood in terms of a powerful rush of emotions, which usually constitutes the moment of revelation. Furthermore, the passage is conceived in terms of the artifact's inherent form—its progressive structure to be followed by the epiphanist. And, finally, I reconstruct many intertextual passages, which are employed to mark a shift from one type or aspect of representation to another.[7] This understanding of the phenomenon not only expands the established discourse on epiphany but also allows the grasping of its connection with travel and other forms of motion.

Another important aspect of my understanding of epiphanic travel stems from its metaphysical rather than strictly religious attributes, though the proximity between certain epiphanies and theophanies is not always clearly defined. Significantly, most of the biblical theophanies occur in transit (for example, Saint Paul's illumination on the road to Damascus), and in my reading I point to certain vestiges of this archetypal pattern preserved in artistic epiphanies.[8] Yet, I would like to emphasize that my conception of the epiphanies' spiritual meaning is clearly posited against any *traditional* religiosity. Rather, these are metaphysical moments of perception conditioned by movement and informed by images. When qualified only in terms of intensity and brevity, these instances of insight may oscillate toward a vision, a wider phenomenon usually less dependent on the sensory experience than epiphany. In fact, some critics such as Martin Bidney bring epiphany closer to a vision by stressing the intensity of epiphany more than its other qualifying features.[9]

The originality of the authors' approach to travel writing lies in their creative interpretation of the journey—which they experience in an intensely visual manner—as a metaphysical journey. Their views are sustained through the creative capacity to transform the mundane aspects of the world they observed into a sublime vision. For it is noting the successive changes of place, in conjunction with that peculiar state of the self focused on the outside world, that allows travelers to view their own particular reality in fresh ways, and also serves as a means of stimulating their creative energies.

Although in this book I propose a reading of Herbert's, Zagajewski's, and Brodsky's travel essays based on the centrality of their revelatory experiences, it is not a case of perfect balance, nor is it intended to be, for as often as they tend toward agreement, there is much in their distinctive voices that sets them apart. Instead, my inquiry rests upon and gains relevance from the crucial fact that these are the only writers in our contemporary literature whose travel sketches are developed into tropes for gaining epiphanic access to the nature of eternity and the finality of death.

It is not without special significance that these authors are first and foremost poets endowed with a visual sensibility,[10] apparent in their desire for either the objective or the objectless vision. Connected to their fascination with material objects, these inquiries are heightened by their individual means of expression. The staple of their poetic craft is quite obvious in their descriptions of various artifacts as coloristically imitative (Herbert); as oscillating between nominalism and lyricism (Zagajewski); or as evoking the near-mystical vision of the objectless preworld (Brodsky). Although the examination of the inner relationship between their poetry and essays is beyond the scope of this book, the conviction that their respective travelogues and poetry complement and comment on each other underlies my investigation.

There are other correlations between the epiphanic travels as related by these writers.[11] It is not by accident that Brodsky, Herbert, and Zagajewski, writers who opposed totalitarianism, should introduce the narrator as a solitary wanderer, a *flâneur*, for whom the act of seeing is his basic modus operandi.[12] In their separate accounts, alone in crowds of tourists, they celebrate the primacy of visualization, the capacity which, in turn, prompts their epiphanic insight.

The volume is organized in a simple, forthright manner. The main line of my interpretation follows a trajectory of epiphanic instances that ranges from the blissful to the bleak, and from an intense identification with a work of art to the negation of such union. In each of its three parts, I first focus my attention on the "circumstantial evidence": the poets' traveling abroad as an experiential beginning, which sets the groundwork for their epiphanies. Next, I analyze the individual epiphanic process itself and the epiphanized works of art, utilizing a variety of interdisciplinary readings.

I offer selective readings from the following books: Adam Zagajewski's *Solidarity, Solitude: Essays by Adam Zagajewski; Two Cities: On Exile, History, and the Imagination;* and *Another Beauty;* Zbigniew Herbert's *Barbarian in the Garden* and *Still Life with a Bridle: Essays and Apocryphas;* and Joseph Brodsky's *Watermark.* Other travel sketches by these writers, some of them never published in book form, are also treated. These readings in turn are tied to Jan Vermeer van Delft's *Girl Interrupted at Her Music,* Johannes Torrentius's *Still Life with a Bridle,* and Kasimir Malevich's *Black Square* and *Black Circle.* Many other visual works also come into play as an integral part of *Through the Poet's Eye.*

Through the Poet's Eye

PART 1

ADAM ZAGAJEWSKI

1

Site Reading

To stare at some inexplicable old stonework,
inexplicable and impenetrable,
at any view,
instantly seen and always, always delightful?
—Elizabeth Bishop

Multitude, solitude: equal and convertible terms for the active and fecund poet.
—Charles Baudelaire

Travel Schemes of a *Flâneur*

During the turbulent 1980s, when the initially triumphant Solidarity labor union was crushed, and with it the hope of a nation struggling under the yoke of communism, it would seem natural for Polish writers to respond directly to the plight of their country. Many did, and did so forthrightly, while others, the poet Adam Zagajewski among them, were torn between two contradictory impulses: unanimity with a society in which they had roots, and an unfettered solitude elsewhere. Zagajewski made his choice: his solitary position was a condition necessary for creation, and in 1981 he went to Paris.

Yet the desire *not* to participate must have been difficult for the poet, particularly in light of a Polish poetry burdened with the Romantic myth of artist as noble flag bearer. The dilemma of political activism (the Deed) versus creativity (the Word) was shared by most Polish Romantics and was acutely felt by Adam Mickiewicz, whose choices frequently indicated the total incompatibility of these two options.[1] Similarly, Zagajewski, once a member of the New Wave movement,[2] became reticent in the early 1980s, although he wrote essays, most notably those collected in the volume *Solidarity, Solitude.* He also recognized his own desire to escape responsibilities imposed by society's misfortune to enter what he found to be much more personally rewarding: the epiphanic world of art. The critic Adam Kirsch characterizes this domain as his "zone of solitude" and points to *Solidarity, Solitude* as the turning point in his development.[3] In that respect, it is hard not to agree with Kirsch's evaluation of *Solidarity, Solitude,* which almost in its entirety pays tribute to history as it pertains to a certain collective thinking, with the one notable exception of "Flamenco," an essay which takes as its premise a solitary union with art.

This is not to suggest that Zagajewski in "Flamenco" advocates any misanthropic estrangement from the demands of society and history, but simply that he searches for a different path for individual expression. Precisely because of this essay's crucial role in Zagajewski's growth as a thinker, Kirsch's further argument that a separation of "things not conditioned by history" according to what genre the poet writes in ultimately falls short.[4] To be sure, Zagajewski neither consigns his defiance of history solely to verse, nor does he limit his essays thematically to deliberations on politics and society. Instead, what can be stated about his stratagem, which deliberately mixes genres and topics, is far more complex.[5] In his essays, the opposition between history and the self on the one hand and revelation and the quotidian on the other are not treated from the point of view of aesthetic escapism. His method— particularly evident in his book-length essay *Another Beauty*—is represented through a deft interweaving of such disparate elements as memoir, art criticism, autobiographical and travel sketches, and aphorisms, with patches of poetic diary stitched in. I shall discuss later in this chapter the new sense of mission and solitude that it evokes.

Another Beauty insistently attests the author's complete withdrawal from partaking in any political activity, which for him clearly belongs to the concerns of the past. Zagajewski does not repudiate whatever efforts he brought to bear in using his art to engage in political causes, but he redirects its tenets toward a different challenge. In fact, his expression of a sense of belonging to the human community is one of the new directions and responsibilities he uses in his search for a totality (*całość*). Although the volume extensively explores the private and the familiar territory of the narrator's past, it also speaks of his inner struggle to reach out to the world of beauty created by others. This act, balancing the writer's spiritual pursuit, evokes transcendence on a small, intimate scale and comes nearer to the ineffable transcendence of God.[6] As a milestone in his development, Zagajewski's most recent volume of essays harks back to "Flamenco," the first recording of an illumination in Zagajewski's prose writing, an illumination achieved in large part as a result of his observing Jan Vermeer's "other" pictorial beauty. Even the Polish title of the volume— *W cudzym pięknie*[7]—speaks of its author's dialogic project and his absorption of the world's cultural heritage. Czeslaw Milosz was the first to notice Zagajewski's natural capacity to resist cultural deprivation,[8] which was an almost inevitable fate for generations of Poles who grew up under the Communist regime and were shaped by its uniform system of education and propaganda. Years later, in his brief note on *Another Beauty,* Milosz observed that the poet's development directed him to embrace a new type of involvement:

> As a poet and as an essayist, Zagajewski has the feeling of partaking in something huge, that is, in the constantly growing region of the completed works, in which the emotions, thoughts, and experience of mankind are preserved. His self-conscious *passivity,* that is, an *action of absorption* [italics mine] gradually broadens from Gliwice and Cracow to the landscapes, architecture, and painting of Italy and France.[9]

In the act of contemplation, the poet accepts as a primary value the enriching presence of works of art which he has encountered in various parts of the world. Zagajewski's receptiveness in embracing other cultures—inasmuch as that culture is represented by works of art—has rather distinct ramifications for his earlier work, his poem "W cudzym pięknie" ("Another Beauty") providing a clear example.[10]

What separates Zagajewski from many other writers who follow the same path of solitary reflection is his attachment to the visual aspects of his passages. To emphasize the pensive nature of his strolls, I would claim—by redefining Montaigne's distinction between the passage and the essence—that Zagajewski treats his passages as the means of reaching the essence of reality. This insight, as we shall see in chapter 2, is sometimes associated with his epiphanic rapture.

Like Brodsky and Herbert before him, Zagajewski is an avid walker. From his boyhood in the city of Gliwice to his days as a student in Cracow (a particularly picturesque city which welcomes solitary strollers), Zagajewski never outgrew the habit—more precisely, the *need*—to explore the world, for the better part on foot, forsaking almost all other means of conveyance. Yet, as his essays give ample proof, the writer does not solely subordinate himself to impressions inspired by the environment alone but is selective, striking a balance between the experience of his physical sensations and the inner ruminations they induce. In this manner, Zagajewski, in his role as wayfarer, never seems to lose himself in Dante's dark woods.

By comparison, Herbert cultivates a more casual approach to his site readings: at the outset, he is more prone to simply "loaf around"[11] without engaging in any prearranged plan. Only later, moved by either time or his mood, does he actively visit some place of interest in a highly methodical and purposeful way.[12] Brodsky, the third poet in our constellation, represents yet another approach, immersing himself totally in his environs, as if he were its organic and mobile part, a curiously benign eye that absorbs all that it sees. For all their differences, however, these three peregrinators share one element: their solitary wanderings are a deliberately chosen form of meditation, which belongs to the literary and philosophical tradition spanning from Jean-Jacques Rousseau to Walter Benjamin.

The relationship of movement—the physical act of walking and how it stimulates the imagination—prompts me to examine what conditions Zagajewski's insight gained on the road, and how this insight is articulated. Let us then take a look at the origin of the image of a *flâneur,* which—as he states in *Another Beauty*—goes back to the 1960s. During this period, Zagajewski, a philosophy student at Jagiellonian University in Cracow, began to indulge in long, solitary strolls within the city and its environs. The essay abounds in the information on what strikes him as pertinent to his own growth as an artist and encompasses both the banal and the sublime, the dreamy and the beautiful—the extremes which he finds best exemplified in one passage through Cracow.

As though exasperated by the city's ambivalence, he writes: "This city is beautiful. It's not a beautiful city."[13] *Another Beauty,* which reconstructs the mental meanderings of its writer as he peruses Cracow's familiar cobblestone streets, is in this respect as revealing and elevated a portrait of a city, of its *genius loci,* as were Leopold Bloom's ruminations on his native Dublin. In his essay, Zagajewski takes us through a concentration of largely neglected architectural masterworks confined within medieval walls. A sense of order prevails in the city's Magdeburg type of urban planning. Since its rigid symmetry was altered only partially at the end of the nineteenth century, Cracow has maintained a coherent structure, which gives Zagajewski, the *flâneur,* a sensation of totality: "The narrow medieval streets leading to the Old Market, the shifting perspectives, the nervous rhythm of the rooftops—all joined to form the blood vessels of a living, organic system" (67–68). Given its cramped space, picturesque plazas, and winding lanes, the city is indeed particularly conducive to pedestrian traffic. And as Zagajewski attests, there is much to see and delight in; from the narrow-shouldered, sixteenth-century buildings decorated with polychrome motifs to the scenic outskirts and furthest point, Kosciuszko Mound, he is there to guide us every step of the way:

> From Kazimierz I set off for St. Catherine's Church; I turned up on narrow Skałeczna Street towards the Church on the Rock, glimpsing en route an ancient wall surrounding one of Kraków's many monastic gardens. . . ; then I walked along the dark, captive Vistula towards Salwator Hill. I crossed the ugly, Austrian part of Wawel Castle beneath Franz Joseph's dark brown barracks and passed the student boathouse; the Norbertine convent rose in front of me, with its gentle Toscan silhouette. Once I reached the convent, I turned right and headed down a path by the Rudawa, steering left of the august hill of Gontyna. . . . I hit my favorite path right afterward, and I struck out toward the Kosciuszko Mound. (72–73)

This was the poet's route for years, taking him through the most visually pleasing parts of Cracow to the green summit of the hill that offered an unobstructed panoramic view of the city. The two perspectives, from within and without,[14] provide him with an opposing range of thought, and when combined, result in the complete optic knowledge of the city and add to his sense of wholeness. The alternating changes in vantage point from the city seen up close to the city observed from afar have an undeniable effect on his aesthetic pleasure and the limits of his cognition.

An instructive example in just how Zagajewski plays off these two points of view and, subsequently, evaluates their resulting images is given in the passage of the book regarding his visit to the Church of the Franciscans. Its Gothic walls are decorated with art nouveau stained-glass windows by Stanislaw Wyspiański. Commenting on the main piece in the series, the multicolored window entitled "God Father—Come Forth!" (196), Zagajewski examines the impact his vantage point has on his perception of this work of art. As he approaches the masterpiece created at the end of the nineteenth century, his perception of the stained-glass window changes accordingly. From the nearly abstract configuration of bright colors reminiscent of a tree, the shape seems to shift as he draws closer, turning into a bird, then shifts again, settling at last into a fantastic figure who appears to be delivering a speech (195–97).

As in a Rorschach test, the writer reads various images into one obscure configuration of forms. The conclusion is irrefutable: Zagajewski's understanding of the image depends on the distance between himself and the work as he observes it. To achieve a clear vision of this complex configuration with its confusion of flamelike lines, the beholder cannot be too close or too far away from it. The work's fluid form, not at all immediately discernible, offers a clear image of itself only when one stands in the right spot, just a few feet away. There, the image exerts its powerful pull and cannot be mistaken for any other image. Thus the viewing of Wyspiański's stained-glass window permits the narrator to apprehend the phenomenon of a parallax view, which can show an object in various guises and, depending on the location of its beholder, fools the eye.

Is this exercise a lesson in relativism or agnosticism? Certainly, Zagajewski is indifferent to the ramifications of either category. Instead, he uses the peculiarities of his vision to broaden his optic knowledge, which, in turn, allows him to grasp the multidimensional aspect, or the whole, of an object. This faculty is necessary to his absorption of a work of art, and in addition, it initiates a certain active-passive stance, whose near-mystical characteristics serve to underpin his contemplation. Thus this parallax vision coalesces with his idea of totality, which is also central to his thinking. Reminiscent of Rainer Maria Rilke's *Weltin-nenraum,* Zagajewski's sensation of unity as the overcoming of dramatic dichotomies present in life and the world may unexpectedly occur to him during a university lecture, a solitary walk, or, most obviously, in those moments when he quietly reflects on the nature of art itself.

A Classifier versus an Accidentalist

Topography displays no favorites; North's as near West.
More delicate than the historians' are the map-makers' colors.
—Elizabeth Bishop

Elizabeth Bishop's belief that "topography displays no favorites"[15] would hardly find a proponent in Zagajewski. For him, topography and one's perspective go hand in glove, as if locale or one's point of departure and return exist only in one's subjective consciousness. His essayistic topography is a map of his past fascinations, an ever-expanding territory which he gladly visits again and again, less for nostalgic reasons than to find its new aspects and explore its deeper meanings.

Nothing better illustrates this interrelationship than his choice of perspective: a bird's-eye view which embraces the whole and marginalizes the particular. This preference for the overall view we have already witnessed in his observation of Cracow and its environs from the heights of the Kosciuszko Mound. It is a choice that gains more significance (and grandeur) when it is supported by his poetry. "Before me, Cracow in a grayish dale," he writes at the start of his early poem "A View of Cracow."[16] Another earlier poem, "A View of Delft"—an ekphrasis of Jan Vermeer's well-known canvas[17]—also testifies to the appeal that the representation of unobstructed urban panoramas has to him. And in *Another Beauty* we read: "A bird's eye-view reveals the city's petty secrets, secrets that would be difficult to detect from street level. The view from above resembles a confession, the town admits its venial sins—but not its true, cardinal misdeeds, you have to look for these elsewhere, in memory and forgetting" (13). This type of access to reality's more obscure aspects ascertained from the vantage point from above implies a position of authority, if not supremacy in face of the object of observation. As the narrator considers his cognitive privileges from on high, he is simultaneously challenging the assumptions granted to a wayfarer. Furthermore, as Elżbieta Kiślak observes, the view from above serves as a means of obliterating history, whose visible traces are more apparent at close range.[18]

In his obsessive search for the total meaning offered by the encompassing view, the narrator may occasionally leave the realm of art and culture for nature. In his essays collected in *Two Cities,* Zagajewski uses two diametrically opposed figures and their respective philosophies to address the phenomenon of nature. One of these figures is an accidentalist who observes reality from above and afar. This figure, a somewhat disoriented political immigrant from Eastern Europe, narrating both the title essay "Two Cities" and "Spring Thunderstorm," struggles to understand better this new, unfamiliar civilization west of the Vistula. Certain experiences he endures have their counterpart in Zagajewski's own life as he had lived it in the 1980s. Unlike the traveler who is central to *Another Beauty,* the accidentalist, as I name him, is not Zagajewski's alter ego. The second figure, whom for my purposes I regard as a classifier, observes reality through a microscopic lens. In "Essentialist in Paris," Zagajewski gives this role to the prominent man of letters Ernst Jünger. The methodical mind of this German writer strictly classifies the complex whole of the world according to a scientific system. Both characters represent completely different approaches and, by implication, their opposing ontologies: the accidentalist gravitates toward the absurd, whereas the classifier is drawn toward a more ambitious and inclusive encounter with the whole universe inasmuch as it is structured and collated systematically.

Zagajewski's manipulation of these two contrary figures and their antipodal approaches—approaches that nevertheless coexist within the same collection of essays—goes beyond simple summation of their obvious differences. Rather, the author scrutinizes in depth both the deficiencies and the strengths of these two cognitive methods and does it for a reason. For him, what is important is the question of whether their synthesis is at all plausible. Synthesis, totality, wholeness, entirety— Zagajewski employs all those terms repeatedly to connote the sense of unity that is fundamental to his thinking. Their roles reflect the same dilemma, albeit on the higher level; that is suggested in my analysis of two contradictory points of view.

Zagajewski's preference for the overall view, such as that from an airplane where vast vistas virtually swallow what can hardly be discerned by the naked eye, is evidenced in this passage:

> I have been living in the West for a few years now. I am constantly invited to congresses, conferences, and lectures. When flying, I always try to get a place by the window and I look greedily—I cannot tear my eyes away from the surface of the earth. Forests like green lace, cities like beads, the pastel colors of spring fields.[19]

Because the meaning of the world is either unattainable or made obscure for this Eastern European émigré, the vantage point given from the bubble of the airplane window allows him to see more clearly the surface and gives him hope that he would recognize, however fleetingly, its ultimate meaning: "What is the world? Is it orderly or chaotic? Streams wind haphazardly through lazy meadows, mountains give way to plains, the ocean is light blue and mute (125)." The traveler is in search of accurate direction, untrammeled by obscure, confusing, and misleading signs. Surveying the surface of the world, he reads as if it were a map, as though whatever imprints and traces to be found on it should be perceived as a systematic group of markers and guideposts mirroring the world: "I looked at the slabs of sidewalks, as if expecting to find *a map on them, a blueprint, guidelines* [italics mine]. But the sidewalk, polished by the soles of thousands of diligent pedestrians, had nothing to tell me" (128–29). A sidewalk, which for Zagajewski is an unerring if common part of the Parisian cityscape, ceases here to be a bearer of truth. Behind this struggle to find the meaning lies a strong conviction that the purpose of existence is never readily apparent, but is interwoven into the surface of things as in a tapestry. The type of vision on which the observing narrator relies is for him a matter of utmost importance, for it conditions what he views as a cartographic pattern created by various natural forms. Yet, mapping the visible even from an advantageous viewpoint does not remove obstacles presented by sheer inexpressibility:

> In the airplane I did not know how to think, and it was not fear that was paralyzing me but passionate interest: it seemed to me constantly that one of these times I would understand the *meaning of this map* [italics mine], that the barely visible church steeples, wooded strips, riverbeds, and

country roads would finally speak to me, because they clearly had something to say. (136)

Through his eyes, the landscape undergoes a change and becomes
an open-ended, three-dimensional semiotic system reflecting a dynamic
and confusing view of reality. A map—ordinarily, a static representation
of reality schematically reduced to two dimensions—is transformed into
an actual part of the world. In Zagajewski's description, it is as though a
huge transfer sheet were laid over the countryside, endowing the natural
flora with the shapes of letters which promise the imposition of order on
the whole land, about which, however, he has not a clue. As José Rabasa
notes, "The map functions as a mirror of the world, not because the
representation of the earth has the status of a natural sign, but because it
aims to invoke a simulacrum of an always inaccessible totality by means
of an arrangement of symbols."[20] Hence, the total image is not available
and in "Spring Thunderstorm" Zagajewski is only recording the attempt
at grasping this wholeness: "And between these cities the airplane and I,
by the window, staring at the cuneiform writing of forests, fields, and
villages, deciphering the *secret meaning of this real, meaty map* [italics
mine] of Europe" (136). Imposed on these images of the world is an art-
ful cartographic design which organizes the very fabric of reality's visual
concreteness. By blurring the separation between the actual landscape
and the map—a method which allows him to grasp both surfaces—
Zagajewski has to negotiate his basic ambivalence in understanding
reality: either it is too diverse in its gravitation toward total meaninglessness, or stability and order can be distilled from the chaos of its actuality.
How the writer resolves this dilemma I discuss in the following chapter,
but at this preepiphanic stage the itinerant essayist finds himself caught
between the poles of chaos and order.

If one follows Zagajewski closely, there is a category of travelers who
journey not to experience pleasure but to discover for themselves the
meaning hidden in the rich alphabet of natural objects. Zagajewski
believes such travelers succeed in their clearly stated objective, for they
know how to decode the rich alphabet of things. And one such outstanding example is Ernst Jünger, whose capacity to discern the order of
the world never ceases to fascinate Zagajewski, even though his skepticism finds much to fault with the limitations of Jünger's approach.
While in Paris as a Nazi officer, he "took long walks and looked . . .

noting, like a traveler in a strange country, his favorite trees—the Judas tree, for example—and also rare minerals and insects."[21]

Paris—the city where God is revealed to Rilke in images of poverty and sickness, and where a tree communicates total meaninglessness to Sartre—speaks to Jünger in a language which serves to systematize species. Part of Jünger's appeal is explained by Zagajewski in his description of the German writer as "someone who has touched the sense of the world, someone who has *seen* the order of the cosmos" (181). He is the initiate to whom the higher sense of the universe was revealed but who does not know what to do with this insight, or at least fails to address it in his writing.

This happens much to our loss, Zagajewski insists elsewhere, for we are less apt to be aware that "human life and objects and trees vibrate with mysterious meanings which can be deciphered like cuneiform writing. There exists a meaning, hidden from day to day but accessible in moments of greatest attentiveness, in those moments when consciousness loves the world."[22] As we come to recognize the confidence of the narrating voice, the self-assuredness in his realization of reality's coded essence, the path leading to an illuminating transformation is open. Is our chaotic condition then an inescapable predicament?

The Envoy of Mr. Zagajewski—Traveler

You must change your life.
—Rainer Maria Rilke

One of the answers is given ten years later, in *Another Beauty*. Standing before Wyspiański's elusive masterpiece in the dark interior of the Church of the Franciscans, the writer contemplates God's gesture, signified by a raised hand in the archetypal act of creation, so frequently depicted in Christian iconography. It is this image that prompts God's message that Zagajewski intuits. Reinvent yourself, change your life, He seems to command the viewer. Although God is a living presence, and not a force merely intimated by the beholder who conjures His words, the source of the message remains debatable. We do not know for sure whether He is God who speaks or God who raises His hand in silence. How does the meaning of His message come through? It is my belief that the source of the message remains deliberately unspecified, so we do not know whether for Zagajewski God in Wyspiański's stained-glass window represents the Logos or the iconic God. I would not stress this ambiguity if it did not directly relate to the type of Zagajewski's creative imagination, whose roots—in my estimation—are both verbal and visual.

At this juncture, Zagajewski interjects a message to change oneself which points to more than a vague spiritual orientation leading to an inner renewal. Rather, what appears to be a suggestion for change Zagajewski takes in *Another Beauty* as an ethical command, compelling the reader to go on a pilgrimage to distant lands and visit old churches such as those found in France. In this message of several pages, Zagajewski invites the reader to journey west, out of Poland, to Paris, then on to the south of France. (I should add that *imaginary* travel is also permitted by the author.) Because the sites he recommends are largely limited to examples of the Romanesque and Gothic styles, he broadens the scope, taking in whatever catches his eye. But it is the churches that hold the greatest fascination for him, and it is the churches that he suggests the reader visit.

And what does such a pilgrimage to France's old houses of worship promise the reader besides an enriching intercultural encounter? In what way does this choice differ from other acts of cultural obeisance? In his belief that only the visual arts can offer us a unique experience, the narrator prepares his reader: "Take a look at the squat little Romanesque churches that conquered the stony hamlets of the Ile-de-France. They're usually closed, but that's all right, it's enough to view them from the outside and be moved by their stocky silhouettes" (199). The promise of what awaits us inside, both in its architectural wonders and ornamental decor is denied; but Zagajewski takes stock and settles for what he sees outside, commenting on the churches' unidealized organic and earthy beauty. We are moved far away from Wyspiański's masterpiece, but the journey comes to a full circle when the writer sees a reflection of the Polish artifact's majesty and violet color in a lavender field in Sénanque.

Travel is the interaction of sight and motion, hence the preponderance of verbs in his message connoting the acts of seeing or moving. The dominance of the eye over the other senses conjoins with the physical effort of walking, and we are indeed participants in the journey the narrator wants us to take, for the traveler implied in this message is a rather strange creature, seemingly devoid of all physical attributes but eyes to see and feet to walk.

Yet it is the narrator's distinct voice that goads and cajoles us, presses us on with utterances punctuated with frequent imperatives: "do a lot of walking," "you'll note," "stop by," "observe," "take a trip," "drop by," "make your way," "you must get to know." For all its prodding, however, the voice is never strident. We are instead shepherded by a connoisseur confidant in his own powers—confidant that what moves him will move us. Ringing with amiable certainty, these imperatives do not pound on the reader with the monotony of a march. Vibrating with a nuanced allure ("you'll like it"), caring advice ("bring good shoes"), gentle persuasion ("you will note with surprise"), and seductive suggestion ("shiver from faith and yearning and even desire" [199]), his voice, slow but never tired, reaches the crescendo when he evokes the spires of the Chartres Cathedral. By then, of course, the reader is caught up in his enthusiasm and the cadence of the long sentences, which slows down the dynamics of the message, speaks to his receptivity.

A feeling of conviction and of gratitude for what only the realm of art can offer permeates the message. The reader's journey goes quite beyond what one can expect from organized tourism. The progression of images and movements in Zagajewski's message brings a total—and *total* is the operative word here—and nearly miraculous transfiguration of reality:

> Go for a walk in the rain, in the drizzle of a warm September day—rain's not hard to come by in Paris! Take the side streets and the broad boulevards. In a while, if you're patient and watchful, you'll note with surprise that in this gifted city even damp sidewalks trampled by pedestrians become long strips of canvas, reflecting, as in the atelier of Pisarro or Monet, the sky, the clouds, the rooftops and the fickle chimneys of old apartment houses. Their shapes will be slightly off-kilter, fanciful, wavy, and wet—but you'll like it, you, who could draw only with triangles and straight lines! (199)

Inanimate objects pulsate with life and energy and are subjected to a startling metamorphosis: works of art take on human characteristics (the Sainte-Chapelle, for instance, transforms into a peasant woman who speaks in a dialect), while other, more commonplace fixtures, such as the Parisian sidewalks, mutate into refined artifacts. The remoteness of a place or an object signified on the map becomes palpable and concrete in Zagajewski's rendering.

Again, I must reiterate that the writer does not describe in his text the canonical and static beauty of these objects but the qualities he invents in them. What do these processes promise? Perhaps only that one who witnesses reality in the constant process of transformation can more easily face the challenge of his or her own renewal. For the writer's "paved solitude" within the city, as Nathaniel Hawthorne memorably described this state, also undergoes transformation. Both observing and isolated by his own volition from the crowd, the writer partakes in the moments of "unique intoxication from the universal communion."[23] Like Baudelaire's lonely *flâneur* in *The Parisian Prowler,* although luckily deprived of his splenetic mode, he reaches through his imagination and art a union with humanity.

Is there anything else that Zagajewski's exhortation suggests? The answer is determined by the way he conceives his envoy's ultimate goal: "You'll see works of art so finished, so full that they offer more than mere momentary pleasure. They give you something you can keep, something that shapes your very spirit—forms, enchantments that remake reality itself" (199–200).[24] Promising renewal, Zagajewski's envoy espouses neo-Platonic ideas merging beauty with ethical values and, far from any adherence to the religion of beauty, also injects in them a new creative energy. The invented and transfigured beauty of artworks in turn reinvents reality. The text offers a positive direction—the contemplation of art promises to uplift the individual from an otherwise indifferent, callous world: "you'll make the journey in mind and experience a little beauty (since you'll find ugliness, vulgarity and evil wherever you are, even without my advice)" (*Another Beauty,* 201). Zagajewski presents a fascinating verbal-visual possibility here: his word, mediating between the reader and the arts, transfigures the image of art as well as that of the entire visible world. Chaos thus is an escapable condition, for one can find sureness and ethical order only in art, because the world certainly does not have it. Yet Zagajewski in his approach to art goes beyond understanding its function as merely therapeutic. His empathic descriptions of works of art inevitably hark back to his spiritual union with the pictorial world in what I call the epiphany in blue.

2

Epiphany in Blue

I'd give the whole of Italian painting for Vermeer van Delft.
—Pablo Picasso

"New York, New York"

In art—more precisely in literature, but certainly not confined to it—
one's experience of an epiphany can either encompass the stark vision of
an apocalyptic end of the world (as it occurs in Bruno Schulz's luminous
short stories), or it can embody a sudden recollection of the past (as it
does in the most memorable type of retroactive epiphany in Marcel
Proust's seven-part novel). In the purest sense, however, an epiphany
stands for the highest, albeit the briefest, cognitive and spiritual moment in one's life, conceived as an intense manifestation of reality's
essential nature and intuitive grasp of the truth. Scholars widely differ
on any exact definition of the term, but what most agree on, and what
provides for us a common ground for discussion, is the unpredictable
suddenness of the vestment of its appearance.

Adam Zagajewski is a fervent adherent of such sudden and intense encounters. What distinguishes him from other epiphanists, particularly in the field of literature, is the fact that his epiphanic imagination is sparked by the visual arts, mostly representational painting and architecture of the past. The artworks that inspire his epiphanies serve to link those elusive events with the poet's philosophy of the objects themselves. Zagajewski's epiphanic insight is object related, and phenomena or situations of an ephemeral nature do not inspire his ecstatic states of mind.

In *Another Beauty,* Zagajewski venerates the artistic epiphany's "majestic clarity" (31) and describes other piercing moments as "inspiration's flame," "exaltation," and "ecstatic" or "dazzling revelation." Here I quote one of his poetic variations of this fleeting but blissful state of mind in Clare Cavanagh's lucid translation:

> This moment, mortal as you or I,
> was full of boundless, senseless,
> silly joy, as if it knew
> something we didn't.[1]

Stimulated by the sight of a French Romanesque church, the poet's revelatory moment is classic in its brevity and the purity of its emotional outpouring. But Zagajewski as the subject of these feelings is also aware of the aftermath of such moments of bliss: "Our spiritual life is shaped by alternating currents of exaltation and demystication" (*Another Beauty,* 30). Preoccupied with this discontinuity he often speaks of alternating states whose changes are registered on various levels of his consciousness. For example, if the initial phase in his narrative happens to be a radical departure from everyday consciousness into an epiphanic ecstasy, the state that follows leads to a painful awareness of his solitude. My introductory characterization should not necessarily suggest the writer's sense of mood but rather define his frame of mind and thus determine his desire for a more unified perception of time and reality.

What interests me in his ever-changing emotional makeup is the way those alternating states of consciousness are linked to the writer's epiphanic sensitivity. His passage from the ordinary state of mind to illumination, I view as the *mouvement,* a sweeping onslaught of emotions rich in their all-encompassing diversity. (Understood as an emotional change, its scope is extended here to include a kinetic passage, the actual motion undertaken by the narrator.) Such a release of spontaneous emotions may not necessarily result in any permanent frame of mind.[2] Temporal and emotional changes experienced by Zagajewski defy any static state of consciousness, which usually is a result of religious illumination or conversion. Under Zagajewski's pen, those transformations ensue, as we shall see, in a fusion of his contradictory emotions and assumptions regarding reality.

The narrator of Zagajewski's essays, caught in the state of cognitive blindness, faces reality and perceives it as obscure and chaotic. When an epiphany occurs, his sudden recovery of insight grants him an impression of harmony. Yet, what the dual vision of blindness/insight and chaos/harmony suggests is far from the actual complexity of the process as it occurs. For the greater his blindness, the more sensational and effective is the restorative potential of his insight. Unaware of that blindness and failing to exercise a deeper awareness of the self, Zagajewski retrieves his epiphanic discernment vis-à-vis the work of art and thereby becomes conscious of his limitations. Regardless of whether the sudden moment of recognition occurs by virtue of Velázquez's or Rembrandt's paintings, it always manifests a new meaning of reality.[3] This interdependence appears with various degrees of explicitness in most of the epiphanic events related in his essays. One such epiphany, governed by his restored insight, takes place in New York City. Though the location seems to be purely coincidental, it becomes a meaningful fulcrum for the whole experience. But why New York?

One can ask whether Zagajewski belongs to those outsiders who actually admire that large, prodigious metropolis. The written account of one of his numerous visits to the city—"Flamenco," from his first volume of essays, *Solidarity, Solitude*—vigorously probes this query. It is clear that he has membership in that club of writers who share with Albert Camus their ambivalent feelings about New York.[4] In "Flamenco," the reader follows Zagajewski as he wanders its grim and gritty streets, observant but not at all restful, in the speculative manner of Rousseau's countryside sojourns. Instead of contemplating his surroundings, Zagajewski feels that the city throws him into a state of uncertainty and confusion. He is unable to absorb the frantic, maddening pace of the urban reality. New York City oppresses his senses with its noise, traffic, and aggressiveness. However, the city's disconcerting impact is instrumental in establishing the nature of the relationship between everyday events and the poet's calling.

Among the root causes for the pervading sense of chaos is the city's street-grid planning, introduced early in the nineteenth century, in a much quieter time and before the era of motorization. Today, the grid plan allows the invasion of traffic into every street. Unlike other major metropolitan areas of the world, New York offers no respite from the intrusion of urban reality, no sleepy plazas or tranquil cul-de-sacs. Other than its parks, it is difficult to find in this busy metropolis a quiet corner, unless one steps inside a restaurant, a business club, or a museum. It is the last that offers the kind of refuge Zagajewski craves. Yet, even as he enters the Frick Collection, the poet-essayist has no inkling that he is about to experience a significant change in his feelings.

Besides the much-sought quietude he has at last found, another component seems to prompt the epiphany: the character of the building itself. The Frick, as it evolved, is more than just a small-scale museum, for it combines what used to be the private home of a steel magnate and his personal art collection. This double sense of privacy, which pervades the premises, makes the crossing of its threshold memorable. The Frick's indoor garden with its water fountain hard by the vestibule calms the nerves against outside disturbances. This, in addition to its exquisite holdings, makes the Frick a unique sanctuary indeed. While meandering through its various galleries, Zagajewski stops in front of one of the Vermeers hanging there and at once experiences a sudden jolt.[5] The canvas which causes this ecstatic impulse is Jan Vermeer van Delft's *Girl Interrupted at Her Music* (see figure 1).

As a result of this remarkable encounter, Zagajewski proceeds to record the exact moment, describing the seventeenth-century masterwork and his ecstatic reaction to it. Such a unity of ekphrasis and epiphany is frequently employed by Zagajewski.[6] In this instance, he evokes all the emotions constituting an epiphany in one unified instant: the suddenness, intensity, and bliss generated by the painting are combined with his impression of unanimous whole where the emotional configuration culminates in a glorious union between the epiphanist and the epiphanizing work of art.

The sensation comes to him unexpectedly and passes just as quickly, as if the observer and the figures he observes in Vermeer's painting paused briefly in their separate tasks to take stock of each other: "All of a sudden, I felt how reality stopped for an instant and froze in harmonious motionlessness."[7] Although he depicts the initial stage of the meta-

Figure 1. Jan Vermeer van Delft, *Girl Interrupted at Her Music (Music Lesson)*, circa 1660, oil on canvas, 38.7 × 43.9 centimeters, New York, Frick Collection

morphosis in terms of a frozen moment, its entire trajectory actually defies any static sensation and is construed as a change-inducing occurrence. In an immeasurable flash, he experiences a total transformation of his vision that culminates in his seeing the entire world from a different perspective: "Before that it had been naked, aggressive, agitated, everything was possible, all questions were open, nothing was obvious or certain, pretty or ugly—simply enormous, growing, mobile, without order. . . . Suddenly there is tranquility, in me and in all of New York" (163). Although Zagajewski perceives this metamorphosis through a language of emotions, it is a direct result of his aesthetic contact with an artifact. Therefore, he does not keep its pictorial aspects at bay; on the contrary, he gives the reader the full sense of his visual pleasure. Curiously, the effect is not rendered solely through his ekphrastic power but through his desire to become unified with the painting. With the exception of describing the color and light of the canvas, he does not slavishly duplicate the details of the painting in his narrative. The ekphrasis is minimal: "A blue tablecloth, next to it the little girl and her mandolin, the music teacher" (162), and, a few lines down, a notation of the chairs painted by Vermeer. The description then turns into a very specific interpretation of the painting underscoring the magic-working of the color and light, which envelop the objects in *Girl Interrupted at Her Music.*

This spareness on the writer's part does not suggest any weakening of his power of observation, nor does it imply that his verbal skills are subservient to the visual illumination he has experienced. Rather, his focus is on what he considers essential in the painting and how that gave rise to his epiphany. In that regard, he feels no need to depict at length every detail of the painting, which was reworked anyway.[8] Thus by concentrating on the luminous qualities of one of the canvas's colors, he intensifies the effect of his chromatic interpretation.

From Saura to Huxley

The most important, most extreme, and most incurable dispute is that waged in us by two of our most basic strivings: the one that desires form, shape, definition, and the other, which protests against shape, and does not want form.
—Witold Gombrowicz

The urban framing of Zagajewski's epiphany represents only a small part of the conceptual setting carefully depicted in "Flamenco," an essay which otherwise is a mélange of meditation, recollection, and sensual experience. The text begins in an unassuming, straightforward manner, so typical of many such an adventure: "One day I went to the movies" (151). The day happened to be dreary; the movie was Carlos Saura's *Carmen.* Structured by the flamenco's rhythm, which organizes and directs the chaotic emotions of its protagonists, the film's narrative—in Zagajewski's rendering—introduces all the major components that find their place later in his epiphany at the Frick. It is clear that Zagajewski interprets the film in a way that both prepares the account of his euphoric experience and articulates the main tenets of his aesthetics. Musing over the dialectical pattern of harmony and chaos, the poet extends those ideas into an opposition between form and formlessness. If we follow Zagajewski, the notion of form, an integral part of his thinking, is present in "Flamenco" through dance and rhythm, both of which express its rawest core.

And what is form according to the poet? As he attests in his essay, form can be any dynamic, albeit clearly structured, ontological moment that resists the void. Form is something that happens, or, to paraphrase Heidegger, "comes into being." In Zagajewski's concept, form struggles with chaos as in "a mortal embrace" (156). This perennial battle between form and formlessness—unmistakably reminiscent of Witold Gombrowicz's philosophy[9]—presents the main reason Saura's film, evoking the conflict between passion and rhythm, jealousy and order, stimulates Zagajewski's meditations. Form thus is a force based on will and can be directed against destructive elements in life (such as jealousy, which is at the center of the film). As I have already mentioned, he does not necessarily comprehend those principal elements in terms of pure contradiction. Avoiding a schematic, dualistic philosophy, the poet allows for a dynamic link to exist between them: "form feeds on chaos" (156). In the essay, Zagajewski's meditations on form and chaos are directly followed by his epiphanic leap into an opposite frame of mind. Consequently, the chaos he experiences in New York becomes a point of reference for his vision of Vermeer's painting as informed by a blue harmony.

Zagajewski defines *epiphany* as an intense moment of insight by referring to William Blake's concept of the "open door of perception."[10] As if to underscore and reaffirm his own epiphanic perspicacity, Zagajewski returns a number of times in "Flamenco" to Blake in comments such as this: "If one were to open wide the doors of perception . . . we would have to be silent and remain in eternal mute wonder" (160). And yet, Zagajewski's attitude toward Blake's belief oscillates from the wish to be enlightened to the certainty that the door of perception would indeed open uncharted territory for him.

The scope of "Flamenco" extends from the polemical analysis of revelatory instances to the account of one such moment offered by Zagajewski in support of his argument. As I see it, that argument is a rebuttal of the premise at the center of Aldous Huxley's essay "The Doors of Perception." In that essay, Huxley describes his experiment with mescaline. Seduced by the drug's visionary effect, the author finds the heightened intensity of his consciousness comparable to the visions recorded by a number of artists and mystics. Coincidentally, the artist whose work Huxley initially considers the most exemplary is Jan Vermeer, whom he describes as "trebly gifted with . . . vision."[11] In Huxley's evaluation, this painter perceived the human figure in quiet repose in the manner of an object in a still-life painting. This is precisely why Huxley could not accept Vermeer's painterly vision in its entirety. For him, the Dutch master represents his figures as being too contemplative and not active enough to manifest fully their "essential Not-self" (39). The lack of selfhood in the human figure leads Huxley to the conclusion that "the doors of Vermeer's perception were only partially cleansed" (39). The paraphrasing of Blake's axiom has the ring of a verdict; and yet, dismissed by Huxley as a less-than-perfect example of a true vision, it is Vermeer's art that inspires Zagajewski's epiphany in blue.

In what I view as Zagajewski's counterreading of Huxley's discovery, the exploration of pure perception stimulated by chemicals is simply out of the question. For Zagajewski, the role drugs play in inducing a vision is replaced by numerous other causes, art being the primary catalyst. For him an epiphany produced by a work of art deepens perception (without the artificial help of drugs); it opens wide the door of perception by virtue, in this particular instance, of Vermeer's artistry. In a characteristic turn of thought, Zagajewski, a thinker no less inclined to speculation than Huxley, does not view the perceptual opening toward reality as entirely advantageous: "It is impossible to live in the open doors of perception, the world is too rich and garish" (161). In other words, the outside danger that chaos would pervade and alter our senses is quite real (as shown in the New York City episode), and one needs to develop a system of defense against it. Again, according to the poet, art can fulfill that role and distill unlimited possibilities of pure perception. Sorting out the "garish" excess, one gradually achieves the true essence of a thing.

Zagajewski's meditations on form are immediately followed by an epiphanic occurrence, which results in his leap into an opposite state of mind. To negotiate between his extreme feelings of ecstasy and monotony, of the world's harmony and chaos, Zagajewski recalls the image of the ever-changing sky: clear or overcast, blue or covered with formless clouds. Those visible manifestations of contradictory motions allow him to recognize the fundamental unity of the universe: "I know that

God would have to be both form and formlessness" (166). God is the unifying principle of oppositions, the nostalgic echo of Cusanus's idea of divine entity as *coincidentia oppositorum*. Consequently, the differences existing between the accidentalist's and the classifier's approaches are solved on the higher level, although in the manner reminiscent of deus ex machina.

The Blue Bliss

> *Whether slick light sharp high bright thin quick sour new and*
> *cool or low deep sweet thick dark soft slow smooth heavy old*
> *and warm: blue moves easily among them all, and all pro-*
> *foundly qualify our states of feeling.*
> —William Gass

Jan Vermeer's *Girl Interrupted at Her Music* shows a corner of a quiet interior where, to the left of the picture, a shaft of light filters through a mullioned window. Hard by this window is a table with two chairs. Seated on a third chair, farther to the right, is a young woman. An elegantly dressed young man leans toward the woman and is shown handing her a letter. Somewhat distracted, she takes it from his hand, yet her gaze is directed elsewhere—outward, toward the viewer. This domestic interlude in the life of a Dutch woman alludes to two of Vermeer's persistent themes—letter reading and music making. How-ever, in the picture, none of those activities actually takes place, for the young woman is *about* to read the letter, her gesture implying that she has *just* put aside her musical instrument. Thus the painting catches a transitional act, representing no more than a brief instance when the woman puts aside one occupation to indulge in another.

In his ecstatic perception of Vermeer's *Girl Interrupted at Her Music*, Zagajewski draws our attention to the Dutch master's palette. The one color that has a particular effect on him is blue, which, incidentally, was one of Vermeer's favorites as well. As his paintings in toto attest, Ver-meer's palette is distinguished mainly by his judicious use of blue and yellow, two colors which normally have contradictory effects on paint-erly compositions. The interaction of those opposite colors, combined with their calculated distribution on the canvas, brings a chromatic balance to Vermeer's works. The same can be said regarding the yellow and blue used in his *Girl Interrupted at Her Music.* In it, yellow is used to depict the light as it is reflected on the wall to the right of the painting, while blue, which appears in the center of the canvas in smaller swathes (the tablecloth, the pitcher, the back of the chair, and even the music notes are blue), is picked up in a paler hue on the man's cloak.

Zagajewski's admiration of Vermeer's choice of color is analogous to a perceptual pattern formulated by Marcel Proust, also a champion of Vermeer. The French writer admonishes us not to concentrate solely on Vermeer's themes and to avoid the temptation of linking them with other Dutch paintings of the time. Instead, Proust's advice is to "isolate the particular impression that his color produces."[12] It is obvious in his statement that Proust's thinking goes against the grain of the traditional theory of color, which stipulates that pigment serves only to enhance form. That approach is codified, in part, by the eminent art historian Bernard Berenson's conjecture that the principle of subordinating color to all other elements of composition is a matter of aesthetic imperative: "In all the varieties of visual representation and reproduction of objects that are assumed to be outside ourselves, and of images flitting through our minds, colour *must* [italics mine] necessarily be the servant, first of shape and pattern, and then of tactile values and movement."[13] Color, though quite versatile in Berenson's assessment, is destined by him to play only the minor role of an attribute in representing objects.

Emancipated from its traditional subservient function, the color blue in Zagajewski's epiphany is not used simply to define or highlight a few objects on Vermeer's canvas; rather, its silvery tones act to bind each element into a monochromatic, harmonious whole. As such, it also permeates the senses of the epiphanist, whose "blue pleasure of existing" ("Flamenco," 162) is expressed through that color. Zagajewski speaks of the sudden encroachment of the color blue into the world. The blue pigment spreads freely outside the canvas: "the world . . . put on a blue robe" (163). During his illumination, the epiphanist fancies himself an impassioned dyer who colors the world blue. But the metamorphosis extends the color blue beyond the boundaries of reality, for Zagajewski performs a further chromatic transformation, which transcends it into eternity. Wassily Kandinsky, as superb a theorist as he was a painter, believed that blue represents transcendence and takes the beholder on a pursuit of the infinite. That seems to be particularly true for Zagajewski.

Yet for all the searing power it holds for him, the writer, nevertheless, balances the blue tonality of his vision by referring to Vermeer's light, which he sees not as ordinary but as a "fraternal and wise" (163) light. That heavenly emanation, which envelops and unifies the objects in the painting, is a major component in the epiphanic transformation of reality that occurs to him at the Frick. The laws of physics do not apply to that sensation of unity, Zagajewski observes, thereby implying a certain level of metaphysics. He compares the light to the soft blue "ocean's interior" (163), a simile that anticipates his reading of Vermeer's interior as an alternate reality. The color blue in sacred art signifies a heavenly place of happiness, and it is that serenity that is reflected in the epiphanic bliss related by the poet. Blue as orchestrated by the author in "Flamenco" is not simply a coloring of his ecstatic awareness of the change, nor does it give voice to the blue of melancholy or grief: it rather speaks the language of a happy consciousness.

One Work, Two Titles

Most of the mental conditions induced by the color blue are explored in depth by William Gass in his book-length essay *On Being Blue*. In it, he ascribes to that hue a vast array of sublime and erotic values: his broad approach allows him to speak in one breath about transcendence and phallic allusions.[14] One might venture to ask whether Vermeer's painting could be subjected to a similar interpretation, and, if so, what the sexual undertones of the painting are. So far, Zagajewski's interpretation of the color hints at no such meaning. It is not from Vermeer's use of blue that the sexual innuendo emanates but rather from the painting's representational ambiguity. Even the fact that in Zagajewski's writing Vermeer's painting bears two titles, *The Music Lesson* and *Girl Interrupted at Her Music,* is suggestive of a telling duality. For him, they are not variations on the same theme but indicators of two completely different readings of the canvas. In "Flamenco," he calls the painting *Girl Interrupted at Her Music,* whereas in his poem "Homeless New York," he refers to the same painting as *The Music Lesson.*[15]

The painting's semantics can indeed be understood in two very different ways, depending how its subject matter is interpreted through the ambiguity inherent in the titles. The problem has to do with the understanding of the man, the girl, and their social functions. Does the man fill the role of music teacher, as Zagajewski suggests, or suitor? Could he be both? If he is the girl's music tutor, the title *The Music Lesson* would be appropriate. If he is her paramour (his elegant cloak and intimate gesture corroborate this supposition), what he hands to her is a love letter and not a music sheet. In so doing he thereby interrupts her lesson, and so the second title seems more relevant. The girl's apparent lack of shyness and vulnerability, coupled with the fact that she receives the gentleman in her private unattended room, confirm the reading of the encounter as an erotic scene.[16] If we accept that version, the beholder becomes a voyeur, a role which does not fit at all in Zagajewski's elevated experience.

This is not to suggest that the poet, in his reading of the painting, is unaware of its iconographic puzzle, despite the fact that he uses the more suggestive title in the description of his epiphanic event. Rather, he perceives the man as the neutral figure of a teacher (and not as someone whose desire violates the boundaries of domestic stability) and his female counterpart as a "little girl" (162) for a reason. By overlooking the scene's erotic subtext, Zagajewski does not necessarily impose a prudish stance on the reader. His avoidance is necessary to soften and sublimate any dramatic tension connected with love. Zagajewski wants to circumvent, at all cost, the sense of anxiety inherent in such an interpretation. Thus, his coherent reading of the canvas's scene as completely elevated and serene is at parity with his epiphanic revelation of the color blue.

"Home, Home Again"

> *I lost two cities, and lovely ones. And, vaster,*
> *some realms I owned, two rivers, a continent.*
> *I miss them, but it wasn't a disaster.*
> —Elizabeth Bishop

The traditional Polish pattern of political emigration and exile was abolished for the second time in this century in 1989, when Poland held its first free election since the prewar period. During that unexpected turn of events, Zagajewski, the émigré poet, became an expatriate who continues to live in the Paris suburbs. His permanent address in Courbevoie is one of three addresses he uses: he moves to Cracow for the summer and to Houston in the spring to assume his teaching responsibilities at the Creative Writing Program at the University of Texas. With this kind of lifestyle, which his profession imposes upon him, Zagajewski can be justifiably viewed as a perennial transient in search of a home. The fact that he has already developed an affinity with Paris, whose liberty he celebrates (not without irony) as "a just city . . . tolerating poets"[17] seems to be threatened by his other difficulties in settling down. Portrayed by a critic as pursuing a "deeper understanding" of the world,[18] Zagajewski articulates this quest together with his need for a spiritual homeland. The high expectations he had before his return visit to Lvov, the town of his birth, after many years of absence, only reinforced his ever-present feeling of alienation: "I found foreignness in my home town. I found foreignness within me" (*Another Beauty*, 59). This conclusion intensifies his universal feeling of not belonging. Nycz comments that this confession, though it confirms Zagajewski's negative self-knowledge, also speaks of a "positive realization of his own actuality."[19]

Although my reading is not intended to be biographical, I would concede the possibility of such an interpretation to shed some light on what caused Zagajewski's acute sense of isolation and uprootedness. By his own admission, history interceded more than once in his life in ways that deprived him of what Milosz would call a "native realm," with which he could entirely identify: "During my childhood, History governed ruthlessly, with an iron hand. At its command, my family had to resettle in the West; History shaped my schooling, my youth, my university education in Cracow, and even my poetic beginnings—rebellious, contrary."[20] Taken by his parents in his early infancy from Lvov (which ceased to be a Polish city due to the Yalta agreement) to Gliwice (the German city, which by virtue of the same agreement, ceased to be German), Zagajewski grew up in a family and milieu where everyone longed for Lvov and kept their distance from Gliwice. In one characteristic instance, he writes that Gliwice was "the worse one of the two. Smaller. Unpretentious. Industrial. Alien."[21] This combination of nostalgia and separateness could have prevented his developing any meaningful attachment to Gliwice; consequently, this experience predetermined his need to seek his spiritual home elsewhere, either in Cracow or

Paris. The realization that what he was looking for was indeed "a city of the imagination" (*Another Beauty*, 15–16) came only late.

Standing before *Girl Interrupted at Her Music*, Zagajewski becomes cognizant of a different feeling: the usual reserve existing between himself and the outside world has been abolished. Seduced by what he sees on the canvas, the writer believes that he has found a perfect world in Vermeer's painting and thus begins to renegotiate the condition of his alienation. His first impression is fed by an overpowering desire to identify with this work of art. He expresses a craving to settle into the painting's realm: "I was as happy as if I could move into Vermeer's painting and live in it forever" ("Flamenco," 163). Vermeer's painting, the archetype of the ideal reality for Zagajewski, awakens his short-lived desire to exist within its universe, according to its rhythm and order.

Schopenhauer observed that certain works of art can inspire the beholder to seek a complete identification with their "other beauty," to use Zagajewski's words. If this general rule is true, then, one may ask, which properties of *Girl Interrupted at Her Music* created the writer's brief but overwhelming desire to belong? Or, was the painting as an epiphanic agent entirely irrelevant to his emotionally charged epiphany?

The answer to the latter question is no. With the exception of two cityscapes *The Little Street* and *View of Delft*, Vermeer's oeuvre is represented only by interiors, mostly inhabited by women. These appealing interiors are studies in tranquil domesticity, enclosed by walls, windows, and heavy curtains. It is my opinion that this sense of the home as a private shelter is best epitomized in the painter's *Woman Holding a Balance*. This work evokes the image of a pregnant woman holding in her hand a scale on which she is weighing gold while some pearls are lying on the table. Pearls, which grow in the safety of a shell, do not serve here merely as a prop but also as a commentary reminding us of the woman's pregnancy. She represents an enigma beneath whose calm countenance a new life is growing.

In sum, beholders are first invited to let their eyes roam the painted interior, then to contemplate the woman's inner life. This passage in many of Vermeer's paintings could be understood as a "journey into the interior,"[22] which is extended into a journey into the painted figures' consciousness. I would like to emphasize the notion of the progressive structure of Vermeer's painting if only to suggest that it parallels

Zagajewski's own emotional passage. The "homeward/inward" passage prompts Zagajewski to enter into the painted interior and feel at home. This interior that one can live in only imaginatively nevertheless deepens his need for a real connection. The will to linger in this state of mind is irresistible: "How I would like to stay in this painting. Remain in its form" ("Flamenco," 163). But the all-pervasive feeling of dislocation, which is the natural mode of existence for the writer, returns ever more powerfully: "Suddenly I realized I can stay neither here nor there forever, permanently; neither in the great chaotic city nor in the painting. When I am in one, I yearn for the other" (164). However, for Zagajewski there exists other means of abolishing the distance. One possibility is indicated in his endowing the furniture in *Girl Interrupted at Her Music* with the property of intelligence, for how can one feel alienated in a realm where objects can relate to one's consciousness?

Gazing Objects

Zagajewski's object-related epiphanies cannot be understood fully without an inquiry into the nature of objects. For example, in *Another Beauty,* the narrator's eye constantly mediates between his mind and the environment that informs his perception of objects. His wandering eye captures the fleeting moment and presents what he sees as if it were a still-life painting: "An orange lay on the table. The shrieks and laughter of children rose from the courtyard below. It was four in the afternoon" (105). In this description, reminiscent of haiku in its simplicity and its three syntactic units, the orange and the table (probably the two most popular objects in the still-life genre) exist separately from their immediate surroundings, of which we know nothing. Although the children's cries break the silence of the afternoon, they serve to accentuate the solitariness of these two objects. Nevertheless, the objects delineate each other and are indispensable for each other's appearance: the pedestal and the centerpiece. Here, with a Brancusi-like minimalism, Zagajewski creates an elemental image of things.

Prone to the minimalism suggested by this description, Zagajewski resists the temptation of describing objects in detail. The reader learns little about the particulars of their surfaces because they usually do not constitute their thingness.[23] By limiting information regarding the objects' distinguishing features, the writer shifts our attention from their surfaces to their essences. On the other hand, he tends to evoke details only if they are meaningful.

Preceded by his interest in classical music and jazz, his introduction to the world of the visual arts was initiated by his fascination with objects which he cites in "Two Cities":

> I showed more feeling for objects than for people. I was drawn by steel constructions, the wrought-iron balustrades of nineteenth-century bridges, the Gothic roofs of hundreds of small cities, the rhythm of balconies and windows, ladders and stairs flying in a July sun. I was a late constructivist, an unconscious epigone of currents from the twenties. I kept wanting to admire things and their rhythms, as if I did not know that even things are tired, indifferent, and sad; objects, too, had survived the war, administered death, become declassed and degraded. (42)

As this passage illustrates, the writer's sensitivity toward the visual aspects of things precluded their utilitarian and purely material functions. Instead, he looks at things, by his own account, with the eye of a constructivist, of an artist. Zagajewski's acquaintance with the visual arts was informed by real things and their plasticity.

In his specific understanding of the artist as a creator of objects, Zagajewski focuses on the objet d'art with the same scrutinizing intensity as Rilke did in his probing into the mysterious side of things. The objects' hidden life, particularly pronounced because Zagajewski reinforces their link with the still-life genre, is an alternate ontological proposal to the normality of human existence, as in the poem "Morandi":

> Even at night, the objects kept vigil,
> Even as he slept, with African dreams; . . .
> Even as he slept, deeply, as only creators
> can sleep, dead-tired,
> the objects were laughing, revolution was near.[24]

Never interested per se in the mere appearance of things, Zagajewski instead creates in his poetry correlative objects in which he imitates their external attributes in a limited way while inquiring about the mystery locked inside.[25] Acknowledging the formative role Herbert's poetry played in developing his approach toward objects (*Another Beauty*, 129), Zagajewski ruminates in his essays on the "poetry of objects" (129), of both the objects' aura and essence. Cognizant of the objects' darker enigmatic side, he may occasionally withdraw from penetrating their mystery, satisfied by merely proclaiming its inevitable presence: "The simplest/apple inscrutable, round."[26]

Yet, true to himself, Zagajewski is preoccupied more by the notion that the entity of an object lies in its enigmatic existence. In *Another Beauty,* he adds probably the most illuminating comment to date regarding this phenomenon: "(things) dwell with us, seemingly tamer than the friendliest dog or cat. But we never see them whole, they always hold a certain mystery, a side we can't see, and for them this is perhaps their key, their root, their heart, their core" (127). The writer would have us believe that we do not live in a world of things devoid of communication. In this regard, his approach opposes one of existentialism's main tenets that denies the possibility of authentic contact, even claiming that a gaze turns another person into an object. But if we follow Zagajewski, objects, although impenetrable, are familiar, and can soothe one's sense of solitude and create an intersubjective realm. How does Zagajewski propose to achieve such an intersubjective connection with things? Certainly not just by retextualizing the concept of the objects' faithful presence. Rather, he suggests a means of visual communication between objects and human beings.

A major influence regarding the link between Zagajewski's epiphanies and the unattainable essence existing in objects was the philosophy of the Polish phenomenologist Roman Ingarden, one of Edmund Husserl's students and an original thinker himself. According to the writer, in his attempt to describe objects as faithfully as possible, Ingarden was able to grasp their essential structure and succeeded in investigating them in depth without marring their thingness. This phenomenological ability turned Ingarden—at least in the eyes of his students—into a demiurge, a powerful conjurer of forms and matter: "All he had to do was trace the shape of a chair with his hand, like a painter, and the chair stood there before us" (*Another Beauty,* 127), one of his ardent followers claims. Zagajewski, who attended several of Ingarden's lectures and was otherwise fascinated by the myth of the philosopher, accepted the validity of Ingarden's creativity in his own skeptical fashion. For him, Ingarden brought things into existence by presenting them either from a new perspective or on the spur of the moment.

The equation of the philosopher's and the painter's vision, as formulated by Zagajewski, is more than a celebration of their creative insights. It articulates an unlikely affinity between their respective activities as well as their verbal and visual expressions. Thus, the old divide between the intellectual and the artistic spheres can be overcome. It was Edmund Husserl who observed in his letters to Hugo von Hofmannsthal that "The artist, the 'observer' of the world, . . . conducts himself just like the phenomenologist."[27] But the strongest argument regarding this affinity comes from Husserl's pen when he claims "the phenomenological view is also closely related to the aesthetic view in the 'purer' art" (113). As we shall see, Zagajewski combines both outlooks: he is at once a poet who describes objects with phenomenological precision and a phenomenologist who sees the objective world's essence. Or, according to his own definition: "The poet is the philosopher's older brother" (*Another Beauty*, 32).

Zagajewski qualifies the materialization of objects as possessing both poetic and plastic characteristics; thereby he parallels the phenomenologist's knowledge with that of the artist's métier. On this foundation, he builds an equation of ideas, objects, and words based on intentionality. Zagajewski, the former philosophy student, expresses this conviction in a casual manner, in a language completely devoid of philosophical jargon:

> I can't write Kraków's history, even though its people and ideas, trees and walls, cowardice and courage, freedom and rain all involve me. Ideas as well, since they cling to our skin and change us imperceptibly. The Zeitgeist chisels our thoughts and mocks our dreams. I'm intrigued by all kinds of walls; the space we inhabit isn't neutral, it shapes our existence. Landscapes enter our inmost being, they leave traces not just on our retinas but on the deepest strata of our personalities. Those moments when the sky's blue-gray suddenly stands revealed after a downpour stay with us, as do moments of quiet snowfall. And ideas may even join forces with the snow, through our senses and our body. (*Another Beauty*, 20–21)

Such a blending of inner life with immediate experience, or, if you will, the ontological status of ideas with world of things, is an acceptable phenomenological approach. The same premise is also present in Zaga-jewski's poetry, where objects and human beings exist in an intersubjec-tive relationship, in what the poet perceives as the momentary solidarity of people and things:

> A moment of quiet covenant
> in the Egyptian museum
> in Turin; people and things, . . .
> we watched one another, the old and young
> of one world, mute and imperfect.[28]

In the poet's view, even an ancient dagger preserves the mortal tremor of the body it once pierced. Grasped intuitively and immediately, artifacts crowded in display cases are endowed with the capacity to observe what observes them—the Sunday crowd of tourists in the museum. From this visual reciprocity, recounted in his poem "Covenant," emerges one of Zagajewski's strongest arguments against the traditional division be-tween objects and the self. Zagajewski is also probing this separation by reversing the seen-seeing dichotomy.

The bond between the seeing eye of the self and an object gains addi-tional significance with the inversion. From Zagajewski's perspective, the eye of the self is no longer the only observing participant of the visual exchange because the so-called inanimate object is capable of returning the gaze. This shift of the objects' role does not necessarily imply a change in their natural condition by means of an imposed personifi-cation. It is rather a recognition of their hidden life, which phenomenol-ogy attempts to describe. Relevant to this phenomenological presump-tion, Zagajewski's observations of those instances which evoke objects as gazing entities are particularly astute when he takes into consideration the visual arts. The works of art observe reality from their hitherto unknown "other" side and become witnesses of human existence: "The quiet pupil of things, unreined / glittering with blackness."[29]

In *Another Beauty,* Zagajewski reconstructs the point of view of yet another female figure of Vermeer's, his *Young Woman with a Water Jug,* at the Metropolitan Museum of Art in New York.[30] In the painting, the woman is placed closer to the viewer and slightly off center; she is shown standing as she rests one hand on an open window frame while grasping with the other a silver water jug from the table. The writer endows this young woman with limited perceptual abilities; though she is granted the sense of sight, details escape her eye and she hears only silence. Her acute awareness of her predicament leads the painted subject to a realization of her ekphrastic status:

> She looked towards the window attentively, as if expecting an answer or sign. She grasped the window frame with the fingers of her right hand, just to be sure. The daylight was both blurry and intense. She couldn't make out any details. More than this—it was absolutely quiet, as if the city's streets were padded with a thick layer of snow.
>
> Finally, she understood: I'm only a figure in a painting by Vermeer. (119)

I would like to return once more to Huxley's supposition that the Dutch master's figures possess the same calm and static quality as objects. Huxley's concept coincides with Zagajewski's interpretation of what I refer to as the ekphrastic status of the woman. In her dual role of a verbal representation of pictorial creation, she is able to recognize the ontological ambiguity of her oscillation between existence as an object and as a being endowed with at least a degree of consciousness. However, Zagajewski makes her ignorant of the title of the painting she is a part of and does not disclose the title to the reader. The title of the canvas, *A Young Woman with a Water Jug,* which he alludes to, is beyond her knowledge. Only the reader can bestow on her her full identity.

With this in mind, let us take a look at another of Vermeer's paintings as retextualized by Zagajewski in his poem "Bezdomny Nowy Jork" ("Homeless New York"). In it, an exchange of looks between a young woman and her beholder is replaced by a different kind of visual activity.

> Vermeer's painting "The Music Lesson"
> becomes a lens, a blue eye,
> which is looking at the city
> with tenderness.
> Could God look otherwise
> at mad and imperfect cities?[31]

In the poem, a prime example of the reversible modes of sight, the poet uses Vermeer's picture as though it were the eye of God turned outward to the viewer. If God is immanent or all-encompassing, as this reading implies, His immanence is not defined in the pantheistic sense but is contained within the framework of a painterly vision.[32] The question mark at the end of the sentence bespeaks the hesitancy in the poet's voice. Though the correlation between the masterful work of art and his sudden illumination gains a metaphysical justification, the ultimate meaning of this illumination remains—as in most modern epiphanies—indeterminate. If this utterance were to confirm the supernatural manifestation, the line would read roughly in the following manner: "God looks at the cities in this way." The biblical prophet's certainty, however, is not bestowed on the epiphanized poet.

It is critical to our understanding of the nature of Zagajewski's epiphanies to connect them with his remarks regarding the objects' existence. For epiphanies to occur, they require reciprocity between the inner world of the poet and the objects he encounters. They ensue from the moments of accord between these two participants (traditionally irrevocably split) of the epiphanic event. The moment of inception here is the moment of a happy union between epiphanist and artifact.

The brief instances of the objects' magical materialization, described by the writer as *intense* moments of being, are closely related to his epiphanies sparked by artifacts. This connection becomes even more apparent if we compare both the writer's description of his suddenly recovered epiphanic insight and his characterization of Ingarden's eidetic vision. In each case, Zagajewski writes of seeing in objects both their essence and their full visual materiality, a type of eidetic vision which privileges intuition and which we should distinguish from any form of realism. To articulate such perception, Zagajewski resorts to lyricism, the language that can express such ideas as "a strange state of bliss, almost a trance" (*Another Beauty*, 128). Immediacy, intensity, and ecstasy combined with intuitive grasp of the pure essence of objects are the elements which constitute both his epiphanic and his phenomenological visions. Thus both forms of vision serve to define each other.

PART 2

ZBIGNIEW HERBERT

3

View with a Wayfarer

I have never lost the spirit of a wanderer.
—Zbigniew Herbert

Although Zbigniew Herbert is considered one of the most prominent
Polish poets of the twentieth century, his essayistic achievement is no
less noteworthy; as such, it is marked by a map and topography which
correspond to certain regions in western and southern Europe that he
visited. After his collection of essays entitled *Barbarian in the Garden*—a
compilation of reflections on his travels to Italy and France—the poet
published separately a handful of essays on his travels to Crete and
Greece.[1] This was followed by his second essay collection, *Still Life with
a Bridle,* in which Herbert narrowed his scope to the northern region of
Europe, to Holland in particular, an area he had explored several times
before. Herbert's journeys present a complex undertaking meant to
create from a rather beaten path a "journey of his own" that takes into
account his imaginative sphere.[2]

Pilgrimage to the Garden

In *Barbarian in the Garden,* Herbert's travel routes pass through museums and cities, encompassing both the history and the contemporaneity of western Europe. His wandering eye registers various views and perspectives, whether from a bus, a window, or the top of a Gothic tower. He juxtaposes open and airy panoramas against the backdrop of the narrow winding streets of a medieval Italian town. Everyday details, cityscapes, and landscapes enveloped in vibrant colors fill his travelogues with a broad array of sensory data.

On one level, the narrator's itinerary includes artistic sanctuaries such as the cave paintings in Lascaux, the Greek temples in Paestum, the Italian and French Gothic cathedrals, and Sienese architecture decorated with early Renaissance frescoes. His renderings of these places glow with the passion he obviously feels toward them.[3] Yet, on another level, his descriptions of such pivotal moments in western European history as the destruction of the Cathars and the Templars hold his first impression in check. This oscillation between the contemplation of art and wanton acts of carnage constitutes a deliberate link in Herbert's essayistic strategy. In his approach to art, Herbert does not isolate art from its historical, social, and economic context, which also includes his own involvement in the particulars of his travels. Rather, he shows art in its natural connection with the rich and varied texture of life, and thus blurs the clean division imposed between them by traditional art history.

In Herbert's approach, works of art do not simply represent autonomous artistic entities isolated from exterior forces, but function as a reflection of and response to history or society's various needs, whether they serve the purpose of magic or reinforce other nonaesthetic notions. Herbert also ascribes to art a sort of reverse logic by blurring the distinction between the order of art and life. While such cultural habits as wine tasting and eating truffles are elevated to forms of art, the carved limestone at Paestum feels as warm as human flesh, and in Athens, the Acropolis is surrounded by the smell of onion. According to the author of *Barbarian in the Garden,* artifacts are living objects, endowed with bodily attributes. Their organic character liberates them from their strictly aesthetic status. Herbert employs in his art discourse an apocryphal type of vision, which prompts him to include the lost sounds and smells, the incremental touches of history crucial in changing accents between the central and the marginal meanings.

This characterization of art in terms of its supraaesthetic qualities does not exhaust all the aspects of Herbert's critical perspective. To do his art criticism full justice, one has also to look closely at his epiphanic perception of works of art.

Based on nonaesthetic forces, the status of the work of art reflects the narrator-traveler's approach as he acts as an enabler of sorts, someone who links an evanescent moment brought upon him by an artifact with his own contemplation of it and the suggestive events that gave the piece resonance. This interaction of object and event is enacted in *Barbarian in the Garden,* where Herbert's desire to visit Lascaux Cave and observe on its walls the oldest known frescoes of humans, is counterbalanced by his experience at Montsegur, where his gaze focuses on the ruined city walls, witness to a siege.

In *Barbarian in the Garden,* Herbert overcomes the familiar travails of modern travel by clothing his narrator in the garb of a pilgrim and by opposing this stance to the conveniences of organized tourism. Herbert uses in his construing of the narrator's persona in *Barbarian in the Garden* certain elements of pilgrimage inasmuch as his journey west is informed by the pursuit of knowledge. Intellectual and spiritual stimulation is thus the driving motive in his pilgrimages to Paestum and Senlis; and it is at these two sites that Herbert attempts to interweave his travel observations with art.

It is instructive to note that Herbert himself never uses the term *pilgrim.* The renowned critic Andrzej Kijowski, who pointedly entitled his review of *Barbarian in the Garden* "Pielgrzym" ("Pilgrim"),[4] views the narrator as shaped along the lines of a pilgrim in two fundamental ways: humility and a capacity for rapture, both of which he exercises consistently throughout his narrative. Both virtues, which I connect with Herbert's epiphanic perceptivity, Kijowski argues are necessary in the emotional makeup of every pilgrim.[5]

As any standard dictionary informs us, a pilgrim was one who simply journeyed abroad, through alien lands. In the twelfth century, the original meaning of *pilgrim* as an alienated wayfarer conflated with the strictly religious practice of visiting sacred places.[6] At that point, the word *pilgrim* began to encompass the universal meaning of one who passes through life as an exile from one's homeland, or in search of it, or, indeed, in search of a higher intellectual or spiritual goal. Herbert not only presents his pilgrim as humble and in awe when confronted with a masterpiece but also intersperses with those transcendent moments his thoughts and feelings pertaining to the journey itself. As befitting a pilgrimage, his simple means of conveyance are combined with a clearly defined route, destination points, and a sense of mission. Invariably, it is this last that supplies the real nourishment, as is borne out in his sketch "The Acropolis and the Little Soul," which I consider programmatic for his travel objectives.[7]

> Since I was chosen—I thought—without any particular merits, chosen through the game of blind chance, I have to bring meaning to this choice, take away its fortuity and randomness. . . . It means to live up to this choice and to make it one's own. To imagine that I am a deputy or representative of all those who did not succeed. And as becomes a deputy or a representative, to forget oneself, to strain my whole sensitivity and capacity of understanding, so the Acropolis and Mona Lisa would be repeated in me, obviously, according to the standard of my limited mind and heart. And, what I understood about them, I could deliver to others.[8]

What is notable in this passage is that Herbert plays with the double meaning of the word *wybór* (choice) as "selection" and "election." The distinction in the original Polish is finely nuanced, but for the English reader what is important is that Herbert, privileged to travel abroad, wears the mantel of a representative of all those he has left behind. Like a religious pilgrim, who represents his entire community, he feels humbled yet strengthened by his clear sense of mission and duty. Though Herbert's travel experience is seldom referred to in the larger context of the political situation at home, "roots always precede routes," as the anthropologist James Clifford succinctly notes.[9] And, obviously, Herbert is not blind to his good fortune. For indeed, communism for the most part banned travel to the West, a prohibition which was relaxed only after Khrushchev's famous speech condemning the excesses of Stalinism in 1956. Nevertheless, access abroad remained restricted to a certain extent, thus causing among many Poles, rather predictably, a longing for things foreign to a degree verging on hunger.[10]

  Herbert's critical remarks on what has become the institution of tourism create proper perspective for his travels as pilgrimage. The focus of tourism on mass appeal, its prescribed travel routes, and almost automated consumption of art and culture is an answer to those who need an easy and passive form of entertainment. The commercialization of the arts in museums and archaeological sites turns tourism into one manifestation of mass culture. Tourists dutifully respond to art but, deprived of spontaneity and lacking spiritual awareness, do not actively engage in any artistic discovery.[11]

As one might expect, Herbert's critical assessment of the tourist trade leaves little to recommend it. Photography in particular draws the poet's ire, for in his estimate, the camera obstructs the immediacy of perception, falsifies memory, and offers a cheap substitution for reality. Once in Siena, Herbert compares the apathetic guides to accountants, because they do not stimulate a single spark of emotion in the tourists' "mechanical eye."[12] Evidently, Herbert does not accept the notion of the tourist who carries and clicks his Kodak as a contemporary *homo ritualis.*

The Stones of Paestum

His pilgrimage to Paestum, an archaeological site known for its three Greek temples, one of the oldest in existence, is preceded by a liberating act of mental ablution: "One must be free: forget the photographs, diagrams, guides and lectures on the immaculate clarity and loftiness of the Greeks."[13] Though overburdened by erudition, Herbert selects what information he finds pertinent in fully understanding the objects around him and writes an essay entitled "Among the Dorians," in which he utilizes his experience of various phenomenal aspects of Paestum: only touching the old stones of the Doric temples gives him intimate knowledge of their material existence.

Herbert's otherwise acute sense of perception denies the most obvious aspect of the ancient architecture: the buildings are *not* intact. In his nostalgic reading, the Greek buildings transcend fragmentation solely on account of their inner stylistic logic: "Even the most decayed are not assemblages of crippled fragments, a confused heap of stones. Even the half-buried drum of a column or a separated capital maintain the completeness of their art" (27). Yet, the artistic wholeness of the temples is not entirely unproblematic. Nature and time had washed away more than their original bright colors, for the temples' status has been reduced to mere stage decoration. They seem artistically coherent, but they have lost their original function as a shrine, and this irrevocable secularization represents the most critical outcome of the visit in Paestum. To appreciate fully this aspect of Herbert's cultural critique as articulated in "Among the Dorians," we should investigate the interrelationship between the original totality of these buildings and their present status.

Herbert's essay on the Doric architecture presents the problem of simultaneously seeing the buildings in Paestum and working out their verbal representation. On the one hand, he rejects their fragmentation by using a synecdochal argument, for the existing parts evoke the whole. The synecdochal concept, combined with the buildings' stylistic integrity, seems to suggest a wholeness of what has been destroyed. On the other, he compares the Doric columns to a "charred forest" (29). These statements indicate that both wholeness and fragmentation permeate this site. Such qualities create a certain representational inconsistency, which calls to mind yet another form of duality inherent in Herbert's depiction of Paestum.

Indispensable to the representation of ruins is the opposition between negative and positive space. As in Barbara Hepworth's sculptures, to use a modernist example, sculpted stone constitutes positive space, while what has been carved out from it connotes negative space. In Herbert's description of the ruins, however, negative space is shifted from its traditional role of defining the destroyed material to a completely different dimension. Although aesthetically speaking, Paestum represents for him a perfect material wholeness, its negative aspect stands for the spiritual dimension that has vanished. For Herbert's understanding of a work of art as organically united with its supraaesthetic functions, this is a very serious lack. The Greek temples were inseparably wedded to their religious purposes, and their present negativity speaks of the absence of the rituals once performed on the sacrosanct altars of Paestum. Therefore, a sense of spiritual loss pervades this site. "What is a temple without mystery?"—asks the narrator only to reply promptly—"The skin torn off a snake, the mere surface of the mystery" (28–29).[14]

Only in part the intrusive presence of tourists gives the visitor an incentive to act retroactively, to call for the restoration of the value of what is sacred. It is, rather, the desecrated sanctuary that motivates him to suggest the most improbable remedy. Tourists, he says, should "bring an ox and slaughter it in front of the altar" (29). This impassioned thought is followed directly by the quotation from Homer depicting Thrasymedes and Peisistratos performing an animal offering in book 3 of the *Odyssey*.[15] This passage reenacts the lost spiritual wholeness and pointedly serves to illustrate how far-reaching is Herbert's concept of the organic character of works of art. Only through a full reenactment of past rituals, the writer suggests, can the temples' negative dimension be filled in.

By juxtaposing an authentic religious act to tourist behavior, Herbert reveals the depth of the cultural and spiritual divide which exists between ancient and contemporary cultures. In this respect, Herbert's "Among the Dorians" anticipates the postmodernist discussion regarding cult objects taken out of their original context, in particular, the Native Americans' sacred objects displayed in museums' profane space.[16] This contradiction between museum value and cult value, as indicated by Walter Benjamin, has turned in Herbert's account into an insoluble dilemma.

On several occasions Herbert makes it clear that the distance he keeps from the crowds visiting museums—and the resulting solitude—are the most desirable, if not prerequisite, conditions for his journey. In Ermenonville (Jean-Jacques Rousseau's resting place), while passing streams of cars, he observes not without irony, "I am the sole pedestrian."[17] The tourists' "tight herds," as he puts it, are to be ignored. Armed only with a notebook and a sketch pad,[18] he appears to be a traveler from another era. Caught between the implied Scylla of Communist-ruled society and the Charybdis of consumerism in the West, the pilgrim stubbornly undertakes a journey of his own.

The Pilgrim and the Tower

Negotiating the spheres of history and culture, art and religion, Herbert's pilgrim often challenges himself with a physical feat to test the limits of his endurance. In one characteristic instance, the wanderer observes, while looking up at the Church of Notre Dame in Senlis, that "a Gothic cathedral relates not only to eyes but also to muscles" ("Memories of Valois," 171). He realizes that it took centuries of human labor to build cathedrals and feels compelled to respond with his whole body to the physical effort which these buildings imply.

Senlis is the site of the Church of Notre Dame, formerly a cathedral, in the French region of Picardy. With its soaring spire, which measures 256 feet from the ground, the thirteenth-century church stands as one of the finest examples of the Ile-de-France Gothic style. The church's lofty height represents to the visitor a physical challenge and he resolves to climb its tower. But he also admits to the feeling of the sublime: "The call of Gothic is as irresistable as the call of mountains" (171).

It is significant that Herbert uses the motifs of ascent and descent as the salient figurative devices in his account of climbing the tower. His brief report of this adventure is organized according to the contradictory rhythms of ascent and fall, salvation and damnation, as if he had assimilated the medieval iconographic program that decorates the tympanum of the Senlis cathedral into his own thoughts. Another remarkable feature of his ascent is the dramatic interplay of light and darkness in the winding stairway: punctuated by sudden flashes issuing through narrow openings in the thick walls, the gloom is offset only intermittently. Sculpted gargoyles and monsters enhance the drama and exultation of the ascent. The profusion of sculpture in the narrow gallery, which the narrator compares to a stone avalanche, demonstrates the integration of sculpture into architecture, which, for him, facilitates the transformation of the church into an organic whole. The grass, lichen, and yellow flowers which grow in its crevices, combined with the sculpted bestiary, effect the transformation of the structure.

Before he reaches the summit, his effort in climbing becomes as dangerous an undertaking as it was for medieval pilgrims in their respective journeys:

> It is a vertical crevasse. Sometimes I walk in total darkness clinging with both hands to the wall: sometimes the steps become loose stones. . . . The stairs end. In front there is a wall in which I must find a grip. If it were more slanted, it would be a typical overhang. I climb vertically, fighting for balance with my entire body. Finally an open platform—the end of ascent. Blood pounds in my temples. (171–72)

At the top of the spire, the vast sky and distant fields greet the exhausted climber: "I am high on a stone gorge which opens to heaven" (171–72). However, he compares his way down the stairs to a descent into hell: it is long but devoid of any detailed observation. The trek represents the reverse image of ascent, which the narrator likens to flight. This unusual foray is structured as a unified physical-spiritual endeavor, reflecting the sculpted images of heaven and hell as depicted on the church's door, and as such, adds yet another layer of meaning to the notion of pilgrimage in *Barbarian in the Garden.*

The Enigma of Arrival

We are not so badly off, if we can
Admire Dutch painting.
—Czeslaw Milosz

At the very end of his first volume of essays Herbert introduces a different notion of a journey. "I rush towards death" (180), he states in "Memories of Valois." From this existential awareness of human finality stems the conceptual foundation of Herbert's second essayistic volume, published nearly thirty years later. Numerous differences separate Herbert's earlier travel essays from those written in the 1980s and 1990s. These differences, of a conceptual, generic, and thematic nature, clearly indicate that Herbert's second volume takes as its point of departure— often negative—his first volume.

In counterpoint to *Barbarian in the Garden,* whose narrative is a collage of critical art discourse, historical inquiry, and travelogue, which includes street scenes, entertaining exchanges with the citizenry, and numerous other details of the locale, in the first part of *Still Life with a Bridle*—entitled "Essays"—not a single individual is represented. Even Herbert's passionate critique of tourists is gone. In this respect the reader is confronted with a disquieting absence and silence. "Apocryphas,"[19] the second part of *Still Life with a Bridle,* is composed around a few fictional characters; however, they are destined to die, and their stories fade like mere ciphers on a crowded tapestry. "Apocryphas" also includes historical figures who once populated the low, horizontal landscape of Holland.

The narrator-traveler in "Essays" experiences Dutch architecture and paintings in a solitude and silence which reveal his meditative mood. A casual chat in a restaurant with a waiter, a few words exchanged with a local farmer, or, in lieu of voices, a glimpse of a human face registered by the narrator's eye in a museum—all the rich texture of life indispensable in travel writing and mastered so lovingly in *Barbarian in the Garden* is scrupulously eliminated from Herbert's second volume.

Holland is here presented to the reader as one enormous and rigorous *nature morte*. The consistency of this excluding gesture indicates that Herbert is shifting emphasis away from what is considered the norm of travel writing to a completely different representational and cognitive mode. By carefully eliminating his contemporaries, with their own concerns and affairs, he aims for an effect evoked by their absence. And it is primarily by means of this absence that the author creates a representation analogous to the visual genre of still life. Whereas in his first volume, Herbert skillfully frames his essays on the visual arts and historical sketches using the genre of travelogue, the generic design of his second collection is different.

Only "Delta," the first chapter of the second volume, belongs strictly to the genre of travel writing, whereas the remaining essays take the reader on a historical journey to seventeenth-century Holland. Even in his sketch on tulipomania, Herbert blends historical material with lyrical ekphrasis of old engravings with tulips. All subsequent essays in *Still Life with a Bridle* transcend this project and are developed more informally. They are more idiosyncratic—inasmuch as they describe the author's self-revelatory experience with Dutch painting—and evoke his personal and unbridled taste. The author concludes these essays with the parablelike "Apocryphas," which entirely transcends his experience of being on the road and welcomes the reader to the realm of imaginative writing.

The moment of arrival to a new or unknown place is charged with special meaning in Herbert's universe. The rites of passage in *Still Life with a Bridle* are as smooth as the road leading his car to the open and flat Netherlands, with only a few bumps registered by the traveler. He admits that he experiences a "gentle" feeling of alienation, a state which causes his eyes to notice readily "objects and banal events that do not exist for the practical eye."[20] Surrounded by the unfamiliar, he perceives numerous details of buildings and streets: "the color of mailboxes, tramways, different shapes of copper doorknobs, knockers on doors, stairs always winding in a dangerous way, wooden shutters whose surface is crossed by two straight diagonal lines, a big 'X' and the four fields of these big 'X's alternately filled with black and white, or white and red paint" (7). The final image of the crosses in this inventory is informed by a geometric discipline that pushes it to abstraction and obliterates the distinction between the order of life and the order of art.

In *Still Life with a Bridle,* the wayfarer's perception, however keen, is extremely selective. Unlike his counterpart in *Barbarian in the Garden,* this traveler is shaped almost entirely as a disembodied mind. Striving to achieve an extreme economy of description, he limits his eye to certain tangible objects only, and excludes human presence in any of its countless manifestations. In "Delta," Holland reveals itself to the speaker's "other eye" in a way that is simultaneously elliptical and palpable, both intensely visual and still. The country is seen in terms of its abundant artistic heritage. For instance, the town of Veere gives him the aesthetic impression of a drawing with "deceitful decorations of an idyll," and its antique shops are compared to "huge still lifes" (6). These images dominate "Delta" and create a pure, yet rigid interrelationship between the narrator and the country alien to him. Through this perceptive stratagem Herbert effects a unity of representation of Dutch culture in its focus on visual thingness, as "the kingdom of things" (9). Holland becomes here its own visual heritage: the country is identified with its Golden Age culture, with painting as its crowning achievement. In so doing, his familiarity with the Dutch visual tradition helps the Polish writer to domesticate Holland's contemporary reality for himself, to adapt more readily to its novelty.

The visual attraction of Dutch cities, taken for granted by their citizenry and unnoticed by their "practical eye" (7), becomes richly engaging and informative for the Polish author's "other" eye. His sideward glance, as it were, thus gives him an unexpected advantage. His sense of sight itself may not be better than that of the local inhabitants, but, endowed with the special insight of a foreigner, he sees differently and as if from a distance. The paradox of such a view is highly valued by Mikhail Bakhtin, who observes that "in the realm of culture, outsideness is a most powerful lever in understanding."[21] Hence Herbert's otherness and his willingness to voice his frequently subversive notions about Dutch culture render his position privileged. Strikingly, Herbert questions the widely accepted conception of Dutch art as realistic to create his own subjective vision.

After projecting his position as an outsider-insider, Herbert reinforces the understanding of Dutch culture in his narrative as fundamentally visual by claiming that "painting in Holland was omnipresent."[22] He also qualifies his first visual impressions of Holland: it resists his verbal account and remains "difficult to describe" ("Delta," 4). Herbert eventually creates a cognitive tension in his narrative between the two perceptive modes: he considers the visual to be superior to its textual counterpart. Such a belief corresponds with long-established notions of Dutch art as primarily appealing to the eye. A critical account of this approach to Dutch painting was given by, among others, Sir Joshua Reynolds, in his eighteenth-century *Journey to Flanders and Holland:*

> One would wish to be able to convey to the reader some idea of that excellence, the sight of which has afforded so much pleasure: but as their merit often consists in the truth of representation alone, whatever praise they deserve, whatever pleasure they give when under the eye, *they make but a poor figure in description. It is to the eye only* [italics mine] that the works of this school are addressed.[23]

The mundane elements in Dutch paintings—what he calls "the naturalness of representation"[24]—supposedly preclude Reynolds from offering an interesting verbal reflection. Herbert views the verbal-visual tension quite differently. The erudite Polish poet, unlike Reynolds, an admirer of Dutch art, believes that descriptive capabilities are unequal to intense visual perception: "A literary description resembles the laborious moving of heavy furniture, it develops slowly in time while the painterly vision is sudden, given like a landscape seen in the illumination of lightning."[25] But, as we will see, Herbert views the essential inadequacy of verbal description, confronted with the sheer abundance of images awaiting translation into words, not exclusively in terms of the supremacy of images over words. Not surprisingly, Leonardo da Vinci established a hierarchy of arts subordinated to painting. As a painter, first, he naturally considered painting the highest form of artistic expression. Herbert, both a poet and an art connoisseur, relies only on words, and yet in his own parergon he too gives primacy to vision as the most efficient means of perception. Because of its potential, sight is designated in *Still Life with a Bridle* to be an emblem of authorial self-consciousness.

As Bogdana Carpenter remarks, though against Herbert's objections, the poet articulates his visual experience quite eloquently.[26] What then compels him to establish a parergon whose sole purpose tends to undermine the results of his own presentation? On one level, Herbert reintroduces here a few of the most important moral imperatives of his ethical system: authorial virtues of modesty and control of his craft, and humility and restraint, glorified in his poem "Old Masters" and best incarnated in the paintings of medieval artists.[27] (In Herbert's reading of anonymous medieval painting, the aesthetic and the ethical coexist as a whole.) On another level, however, he is using a traditional rhetorical device of the inexpressible well established in Polish literature. In Adam Mickiewicz's *Pan Tadeusz,* for example, "no words can tell" the taste and smell of *bigos,* the Polish national dish. By the same token, no words can describe Dutch painting. Herbert's account of Dutch painting in terms of its resistance to description not only privileges the visual mode but also strengthens it through rhetorical device. It is also possible to see Herbert's dissatisfaction as resulting from his sense of failure as a translator of one medium into another and as an imitative artist.

The Self and the Mirror

Both *Barbarian in the Garden* and *Still Life with a Bridle* take as their point of departure the epistemological purpose expressed in Goethe's dictum "Wer den Dichter will verstehen, muss in Dichters Lande gehen" ("Who wants to understand the poet should go to his land"). In applying this idea to painting, Herbert is careful to stress the importance for Dutch seventeenth-century painters of their immediate surroundings. Some of these painters—Vermeer, Hals, and Rembrandt, to cite three of the more popular names in the canon—never traveled farther than their own backyards. They never went to Italy, a virtual must for any serious student of painting at the time, nor even to any neighboring countries. Such a lack of travel experience lent their art an authentic focus that would have otherwise faded: "They remained faithful to the trees, walls, clouds of their homeland, and to their native towns" ("The Price of Art," 35), Herbert says. He continues his defense of their attachment to home by praising "this provincialism by choice" (35) for giving them a unique creative energy.

Because place is also integral in Dutch art as "an accurate epitome of visible reality ("Delta," 45). Herbert makes the examination of this reality the justification for his voyage. Unlike his previous journeys to

Holland, during which he only devoured "paintings, books, and monuments" (3), this time he intends to be an "ideal traveler." As such, he compares the order of art with the order of things—"monuments, books, and paintings with the real sky, the real sea, and real land" (4). Fully aware that the Dutch painters, like none before or after, created a faithful image of their country by incorporating its landscape, architecture, people, interiors, animals, and so forth, Herbert's clear objective is to examine how their art and their world *reflected* each other.

In considering the fact that Dutch art since the nineteenth century has been viewed, regardless of genre, as realistic (Schopenhauer, for instance, regarded Dutch still lifes as the highest realization of objective art), the narrator expresses a great deal of skepticism. At the center of his doubt lies the nature of Holland's landscape. Constantly wrested from the sea and ravaged by other forces of nature, it has undergone innumerable changes over the centuries. Thus, an accurate identification of painterly locale—as Henry James made so bold to attempt—was, and is, impossible.[28]

Herbert's other difficulty in pinpointing any exact location matching the landscape of a particular painting lies in the fact that Dutch artists occasionally treated the rule of mimetic topography in a rather cavalier fashion. Verisimilitude of the landscape in every detail was not an absolute imperative for them. For example, in Herbert's account, the Church of Saint Pankras as depicted by Jan van Goyen in his *The View of Leyden* was moved by the artist from the center of the city to its outskirts. Fidelity to place, therefore, was sometimes expedient only insofar as it conformed to the rules of composition.

In "Delta," the traveler is aware that his goal of comparing the real land and its reflection in seventeenth-century Dutch painting is almost impossible. Yet, driven by an insistent desire to reach "the heart of Dutch landscape, the inside of Holland" (9), he succeeds in finding by chance an unspoiled countryside, untouched by time and the elements: the valley between the river Lek and the river List. The memory of this green valley, to be taken later "on the journey like a talisman" (9), plays an important function in Herbert's preparation for his study of Dutch painting. Its pure beauty gives him both a natural framework and a point of reference (reminiscent of pilgrims' talismans) indispensable to his pursuit. It is, after all, the only unchanged part of Holland, identical to the real landscape that was seen by his "collective hero, the Dutch bourgeois of the seventeenth century" (8). Only after understanding the level of the physical world as mirrored in past art is the writer well equipped to take his journey of the eye.

In his reflections on representation of reality in Dutch painting, Herbert plays masterfully with a variety of mirroring surfaces. On the most obvious level, he remarks on the mirroring functions of the canvas of an illusionistic painting, the eye, with its ever-present shine, or even a drop of water. And, in the final analysis, Herbert's own text reflects all of these mirroring agents. Surprisingly, reflections on the surfaces of larger bodies of water, including the sea and Amsterdam's many channels, are not registered by the writer's otherwise perceptive eye. He favors minia-ture mirroring objects over those of more monumental dimensions.

In meditating upon Jan van Goyen, his favorite landscape painter, Herbert asks: "What emerges from fog and rain, what is reflected in a drop of water?" The answer comes in the form of van Goyen's *Landscape with Objects,* "a painting so small it can be covered by the hand. . . . The picture does not hang from the wall. This shred of the world was placed in a glass case, to make one bow over it" ("Delta," 16). Displayed like some icons in the Eastern Orthodox Church, van Goyen's painting inspires a reverential attitude. It is but a fragment of the world, as if unframed and existing beyond the canvas,[29] and its perfect trompe l'oeil works here like magic. This mode of visual deception, which the Dutch painters mastered, impels the author to believe for a moment that art is at parity with nature and nature at parity with art.

Van Goyen's miniature painting is an illusionistic wonder that re-flects the world like a drop of water and simultaneously exists as part of the same world. And in fact, both a drop of water and a miniature painting are synecdoches; the former recalls the image of water as a primal element, and the latter suggests the visual totality of the world. The logic of part for whole, however, does not entirely explain Herbert's thought regarding the miniature mirroring surfaces. He needs a means to embrace a larger reality. A static map, for example, is one vehicle for achieving his aim: "Here in Holland, I had a feeling the smallest hill would be enough to take in the entire country: like a huge map that one can bring closer or move farther from the eyes" ("Delta," 5). As a mortal, he possesses a severely limited, fragmentary knowledge, yet he can grasp the meaning of the whole through its various parts. Totality of knowl-edge, however, is "reserved only for the highest beings" (5). It is on this absolute level that Herbert introduces the ultimate and supreme mirroring surface—"God's eye" (5). It contains "the enormous magnitude of the world and the heart of things" (5), reflecting and uniting both the visible and the invisible.

The likening of God's eye to a mirroring surface is a mystical concept that first appeared in Jakob Boehme's writings. The seventeenth-century German mystic conceived the idea of divine wisdom as an anthropomorphic eye that mirrors all creation.[30] According to Boehme, the whole of creation is organized visually as a system of mirrors that reflect each other. The supreme mirror of God's eye is reflected in increasingly lower levels of the universe, of which the visible reality of this world is the lowest. In Herbert's essay there are two specific images which link his comments with Boehme's ideas. One is God's eye as creation and the mirror in which God's eye sees itself, and the other is the heart of the infinite world, also reflected in God's omniscient eye: "Here in Holland, I had a feeling the smallest hill would be enough to take in the entire country. . . . It was not at all a feeling accessible to lovers of beauty, or purely aesthetic. It was like a particle of the omnipotence that is reserved for the highest beings: to embrace the limitless expanse with its wealth of detail, herbs, people, waters, trees, houses, all that is contained only in God's eye—the enormous magnitude of the world and the heart of things" ("Delta," 5). Herbert evokes both the totality and the essence of the universe to convey more adequately the emotional and spiritual aspects of his perception of the Dutch landscape. Because he is perfectly aware of the uniqueness of such perception, he is quick to draw a sharp distinction between the aesthetic experience and his near-mystical encounter with the Netherlands.

But let us return to Van Goyen's painting. This work compared to a drop of water becomes, in essence, a minute floating mirror constituted by its luster, convexity, and roundness. Equally brilliant, convex, and round are the small mirrors depicted in the early art of the Netherlands, when boundaries between Flemish and Dutch art were still undefined, and later, when Dutch art emerged distinctly as a school of its own. This type of mirror appeared in Jan van Eyck's signature masterpiece *Portrait of Giovanni Arnolfini and His Wife, Giovanna Cenani,* and later in Quentin Metsys's *The Banker and His Wife,* and yet again in Hans Memling's *Madonna with a Child.* By likening Jan van Goyen's landscape to a mirroring drop of water, Herbert seems to allude to this rich visual tradition in Dutch art. As his essays unfold, the recurrent motif of a mirror becomes an intricately elaborated leitmotiv that informs the essays' poetics and is elevated to the role of a cognitive and aesthetic principle. In this double function, the motif of a mirror is entirely devoid of any narcissistic meaning that could be associated with the authorial ego, or with any ironic introspection such as that evoked in Herbert's earlier poem "Mr. Cogito is examining his face in the mirror." Rather, the essays offer a universal, cognitive perspective, and in this respect they constitute a radical departure from Mr. Cogito's self-analysis.

Journey of the Eye

Antinomies inform the creative universe of both Herbert's poetry and his essays.[31] His essays, though, are also permeated by a certain contrariness, of which the writer is fully aware: "It should be honestly confessed: we have a strange liking for presenting follies in the sanctuaries of reason, and we also like to study catastrophes against a gentle landscape."[32] The inner *esprit de contradiction* is for Herbert a particularly creative impulse that causes occasionally startling shifts from visible reality to the metaphysical dimension. Accordingly, one and the same phenomenon can be for the writer a source either of earthly joy or of spiritual experience.

Just as the author strives to experience the landscape of Holland in as unmediated a way as possible, he also attempts to become familiar with its light. The essay "Delta" consists of a minute description of the weather throughout one day, including cloud formations and the various hues of light. With seventeenth-century Dutch landscapes in mind, the narrator shows a keen interest in the subtle changes that occur above and beyond the skyline: "What is the light of Holland, so luminous for me in the paintings but absent in immediate surroundings?" (17) he asks in another attempt at comparing images as reflected in paintings with their original settings. He goes on to explain that the visible world is in constant flux, its terrain having undergone innumerable permutations over time and its transitoriness reminiscent of J. M. W. Turner's canvases. For Herbert, however, the immediate experience—as phenomenologists would have it—of this disembodying effect caused by the heavenly elements is not the last word on the subject. The narrator describes a storm until "the spectacle was finished. The sky was clear. The wind stopped. Faraway lights went on and off, and all of a sudden without warning, without a breeze or anticipation, a huge cloud the color of ash appeared, a cloud in the shape of a god torn apart" (17). Obviously, in this description the final phase of his experience goes far beyond the gathering of meteorological data. Rather, a different sort of realization dominates his direct sensual experience. Within the abstract form of a cloud he finds the figure of a god inscribed. Yet how arbitrary is this image? What does it allude to, if anything?

Herbert's observation of the weather—undertaken to establish another point of reference in his study of Dutch landscape painting—turns out to have a transcendent spiritual dimension. Herbert refers here to a certain visual tradition in painting. For example, in Phillip Otto Runge's painting *Die Ruhe auf der Flucht* (*Repose during the Flight*), a billowing, tattered cloud shaped like God is depicted in the foreground of an otherwise serene sky. In this respect, the dramatic immediacy of the writer's experience becomes an interesting case of perception, much in the spirit of Ernst Cassirer, according to whom our perception is informed by a coherent system of symbols. To say that Herbert inherited certain cultural forms of perception from the visual arts would be only an overly general conclusion and would ignore Herbert's persona and his own sensitivity. As a poet, essayist, and thinker, Herbert remains skeptical, never trusting one source alone, and is demonstrably eager to see the opposite side of the spectrum, the other side of the story. Hence, his empirical inquiry into the appearance of the Dutch sky is complete only when he observes in its clouds a glimpse of a higher presence.

In a similar instance, Herbert claims that unlike his mentor, the French Romantic Eugène Fromentin—whose book *The Old Masters of Belgium and Holland* is his only guide through the country[33]—he is not inclined to ponder ephemeral matters. Rather, he celebrates the tactile and discernible beauty of a Gothic wall of the Knights' Hall in the Hague, which is for him "like a fabric: perpendicular, taut, without any decorations, tightly woven with thick yarn and a narrow, stringy, pitchy warp. The scale of colors is contained between ochre and umber with caprate added. The tint of the bricks is not uniform. From time to time a fawn-brown appears like a half-baked roll or the color of a fresh, crushed cherry, then again a mysterious violet covered with glaze" ("Delta," 8). At one pole, the writer venerates the Gothic brick wall in all its tactile earthiness; at the other, walls may stimulate in him emotions quite distinct from his admiration of the basic material that went into their construction. This multilayered perceptive faculty becomes most apparent on an occasion in the small town of Veere, where he comes across a "thickset and smooth" historical building. Though it is overshadowed and hardly visible, he sees its facade as "a sculpture of God without a face. It emerges from the night similar to a rock growing from the ocean; not a single ray of light reaches this place. A dark mass of primordial matter against the background of night's blackness" (6). He articulates this dark revelation in a double negative: God is deprived of a face, and light is not shed on his appearance. The presence of the invisible—unlike that of the experiments with Dutch light—turns out to be more direct. The building is not merely compared to God but represents him. Herbert does not intend to characterize his direct experience of the sacred embodied in the simplest architectural form as conditional. Instead, his usually cautious attitude is overcome, and he collects data from both sides of reality, not just that which is empirically observable. As a result, the meandering of his "empirical" eye is complemented by discoveries of the "inner" eye, and the perceptive energy renewed with each journey of the eye develops into an unending process crowned with his epiphanic encounter with Torrentius's dark canvas.

4

Passage to Rapture

My friend, blood shaking my heart,
The awful daring of a moment's surrender
Which an age of prudence can never retract
—T. S. Eliot

As an essay writer, Herbert manifests two seemingly opposing beliefs about the nature of truth as concealed in works of art: first, that it can be reached through epiphanic bliss, and second, that truth—unattainable forever, or, at best, merely intimated—should be respected in the state of its permanent opacity. His understanding of truth allows him to convey a dramatic but firm belief in a certain metaphysical essence of the arts which can be neither entirely denied nor reconstructed in an objective manner. It is my contention that the mysterious truth, presented in an epiphanic rapture and conceived as a coded text, modifies Herbert's notion of the work of art as organically linked to its environment.[1] His epiphanic practice enhances the moment of perception and tends to disassociate (albeit temporarily) a work of art from its historical and social background. But to the heart of the matter—what is Herbert's epiphany?

Blissful or bleak, but always brief, Herbert's epiphanic moment of insight is not just a cognitive or sensory experience of art. With the exception of a few of his darker revelations, which are informed in terms of negative aesthetics and even gravitate toward negative theology, he does not give testimony in his work to any instances of theophany.[2] His metaphysical moment reveals a transcendence emptied of traditional religiosity. I view his epiphany, therefore, as an intense and ecstatic manifestation or realization of an otherwise ineffable truth, a realization that comes into being through the power of art.

Not every moment of viewing a beautiful work of art achieves an epiphanic character in Herbert's essays, and not every masterpiece, however well executed, can engender a revelation. What, then, makes an epiphany work? In spite of the brief and elusive nature of epiphany (as one of its proponents explains, it "passes, flames, and goes"),[3] I intend to establish what kind of art and artifacts contribute to this type of response in Herbert's essays. Critics tend to agree that the material aspects of epiphany are often irrelevant in comparison to the illuminating experience they engender.[4] It is my contention, however, that Herbert depicts such epiphanic instances as intimately connected to works of art that stimulate them. Further, it is not a coincidence that Herbert experiences his artistic epiphanies while on the road. Travel, understood as motion and the successive change of one's surroundings, shapes his reflection on the visual arts. For this reason, his epiphanic occurrences are generated by those masterpieces that are endowed with a *progressive structure of meaning*. Such grounding in the structure of the work of art differentiates Herbert's approach from an entire tradition of epiphanic writings.[5]

By the time Herbert uses epiphany as a perceptual mode in his travel essay "Labirynt nad morzem" ("The Labyrinth by the Sea"), it is already a long-established literary device of Romantic origin,[6] a device whose innovative character and experimental goals belong to the past. In comparison to modernist novelists such as Virginia Woolf and Thomas Wolfe, whose writings are characterized by chains of epiphanies, the Polish author relates his spiritual revelations much less frequently and with greater caution. His characteristic response to art remains enthusiastic and intense, occasionally even ecstatic, but the experience of an *Augenblick*,[7] in which the hidden semantics of an artwork in all its inexpressible depth are revealed, seldom is visited upon him. For comparison's sake, let us then first look at some of his non-epiphanic moments.

The Unbreakable Code

Herbert is particularly interested in gaining access to the mystery of a work of art, and in both his poetry and his travel narratives he explores the processes through which this happens. In his poem "Prayer of Mr. Cogito—Traveler," he glorifies the world whose artistic and natural wonders are accessible through travel. Enriching as they are, the traveler's encounters with works of art sometimes become quite problematic:

> —thank You that the works created for Your glory let me share a particle of their secret and I imagined in my great presumptuousness that Duccio Van Eyck Bellini painted also for me

> and also the Acropolis which to the end I never understood patiently laying bare before me its mutilated body. (12–13)

The unveiling of the mystery of the Acropolis has continuity in time, its duration coexistent with the duration of perception. However, the Acropolis never reveals its complete truth. *Satori* is beyond Mr. Cogito's ken. The attempt to grasp the ruins' deepest meaning is an unending perceptual process, something renewable with each journey of the eye. In this instance, Mr. Cogito waits, almost in supplication, for a glimmer of truth, and yet is conscious of his own limitations as a mortal being. The Acropolis—almost as attractive for Herbert as Mount Sainte-Victoire was for Cézanne, who never ceased painting the mountain—is also described by him in his essays "The Acropolis and the Little Soul" and "The Acropolis." In both instances, the ruins inspire the moment of rapture without illuminating insight. The direct contact with them, so much superior to looking at any reproduction, is rendered in a sensual and erotic way: "Where is this prevailing will of confrontation coming from, this passion pushing to a physical contact [with the Acropolis], this desire to put the hands, to unite bodily and then pull oneself off and walk away only to carry with oneself what? An image? A shiver?"[8] The mutilated body of the Acropolis submits itself to the gaze in an intimate manner reminiscent of the combination of the sudden spiritual vision and physiology present in Fyodor Dostoyevsky's and Thomas Mann's works.[9]

However, the sublimation of orgasm is not the source of Herbert's moments of illumination, as he speaks in those terms only once and qualifies the whole experience as the potential, the intimation, of the forthcoming encounter with the ruins.

As such, the verbal image of the Acropolis testifies to the fundamental epistemological difficulty that persists in Herbert's work; he evokes this dilemma in a more pronounced fashion in his essays, a genre more conducive for such speculation. These essays evidence his deliberate protection of the mysterious aura emanating from works of art and, even more poignantly, his enhancement of the mysterious in areas other than art.

How does Herbert pursue what is elusive and frequently sealed in a mysterious and indecipherable form? In one instance, speaking of Piero della Francesca's *Flagellation,* he simply acknowledges that it "will remain one of the world's most closed and obscure paintings."[10] In another episode, he undermines a whole school of research to indicate the supremacy of Gothic architecture because of its resistance to classification: "Naively I first searched for a formula which would explain the Gothic in its totality—its construction, symbols and metaphysics. But prudent scholars did not provide an unequivocal answer."[11] Because Herbert seeks definite and complete solutions, a rational scholarly method coexists with his intuitive approach. Both of the opposing approaches quickly reveal their weaknesses as critical methods, but both fit well with Herbert's predilection for antinomies.[12] His discourse, by embracing these two traditionally unreconciled responses, reaches a precarious equilibrium in their coexistence. To put it differently—the two competing forces of skepticism and metaphysical impulse, which are familiar stratagems in T. S. Eliot's work, bracket Herbert's critical persona. These ploys, as we shall see, are reflected in the opposition between a scholar's discipline and an artist's insight. In "Letter," the central text of his *Apocryphas,* this seemingly unbridgeable gap is discussed from Jan Vermeer van Delft's imagined point of view: "Our task [as artists] is not to solve enigmas, but to be aware of them, to bow our heads before them and also to prepare the eyes for never-ending delight and wonder."[13] By attributing the letter to Vermeer and addressing it to Anton van Leeuwenhoek, the seventeenth-century Dutch scientist, Herbert embraces the intuitive and the rational perspectives in one dialogic correlation. However, it is highly unlikely that Vermeer would not respect science and scientific progress; he clearly functions here as Herbert's mouthpiece.

I would like to take a closer look at how Herbert extends the presence of mystery outside artistic endeavors. For him it can appear in any cognitive undertaking. For instance, Herbert views the story of Alexander the Great's solution of the Gordian knot as an act of violence against mystery; Alexander the Great "murdered Mystery" by cutting the Gordian knot, he says.[14] Furthermore, Herbert develops a theory that explains the historical devaluation of this category. According to the poet's interpretation of the story, the importance of mystery gradually diminishes and thereby adds to an axiological emptiness in the sphere of history. Through this process, Herbert bridges his critique of culture with the central positioning of mystery in his discourse on art.[15]

Herbert's attempts at capturing mystery generate a rather fixed pattern. After encountering what he suspects is a mysterious truth concealed in art, the author makes an effort to unravel it by referring to existing scholarly interpretations. Except for developing his erudition, the net result of his rational pursuits is negligible or, at least, exposes the lack of an unequivocal solution among art historians. Only then, unable to find a convincing answer (a fact which, obviously, reinforces the sense of mystery), he assumes the role of a disseminator of mysteries. Yet in his self-appointed position of artistic mystagogue, Herbert frequently expresses disappointment and frustration at dealing with an unattainable truth. Such emotions underlie the portrait he paints of himself as a failed mystagogue in "The Labyrinth by the Sea."

This little-known essay, which describes his trip from the Greek mainland to Crete in the early 1970s, shares certain characteristics with *Barbarian in the Garden,* particularly in developing the speaker's sensual perception. Relating the expectation and realization of a great aesthetic adventure, the essay also includes the narrator's self-mocking attempt to decode an ancient script—an account which poignantly illustrates the insufficiency of a scholarly approach to explain satisfactorily the mystery.

The script, preserved on a clay tablet found on Crete, is covered with signs (some of them in the form of ideograms) arranged in a spiral pattern on each side. It remains undeciphered.[16] Known as the Phaistos disc, it may be understood as a *textual mystery* rather than a typical artifact, given that this form of hidden meaning plays a significant role in Herbert's discourse. As the story unfolds, we learn about Herbert's nearly obsessive desire to break the code of the script. His failure to do so is represented as a rather meandering nightmare. By employing the language of emotion and the subconscious, he ascribes to his mystagogic complex a deeply suppressed sense of self-control.

Herbert's passion for discovery in the world of art, or rediscovery which he hopes could eventually influence the existing canon, takes a characteristic turn in one of his brief notes on art dedicated to the early Renaissance fresco painter Altichiero. His profession as a writer suits him well for this task and allows him to take risks: "It happens often that great discoveries in the field of art history are the work of writers, not historians. This was, for instance, the case with the excellent Dutchman Vermeer, discovered in the nineteenth century by a French journalist and writer."[17] Curiously, the name of Théophile Thoré-Bürger, Vermeer's discoverer, remains unmentioned. In a parallel gesture, Herbert masks his own identity, using the pseudonym Patryk for his note on Altichiero. It is as if the revelation of the name and real value of Altichiero's art necessitated the obfuscation of another name. But who was Altichiero? The Encyclopaedia Britannica portrays him as the founder of the Veronese school and the most significant northern Italian artist of the fourteenth century.[18] So, even from this basic source we obtain scant information and a sense of distinctive hierarchy.

It is clear that for Herbert this nearly forgotten painter deserves reevaluation, which he nobly attempts to effect. For my reading, however, what is more significant is how Herbert structures his argument, which is meant to revise and bring Altichiero back to public notice. There are several themes in his comment that also appear in his reading of other artist's life and work, and thus make his discourse eminently characteristic. In his rendering of Altichiero, Piero della Francesca, and Torrentius, Herbert emphasizes the inexplicable nature of their creative processes, which take place in mundane circumstances, as well as the lack of knowledge about their personal lives—a lack made all the more enigmatic by the supraindividual and metaphysical character of what they created.

Herbert's desire to reevaluate the canon reveals more than a refined taste and style of discourse. As he admits, "I have tried my own strength, hoping that at last Altichiero would attain the deserved place among the most outstanding creators. And the delayed fame" (143). At the core of his evaluative task lies a sense of mission: to introduce less-popularized and less-ritualized images to the reader. Herbert's ideas transcend cultural dogma which could "freeze" the moment of vision granted by painting, and he conceives his writings on Altichiero and Torrentius as an act of cultural restoration. It would be difficult, though, to measure the popular success of Herbert's attempts to reclaim the artists who have unjustly fallen by the wayside, and even more difficult to ascertain the success of his role as this century's Thoré-Bürger.

Another attempt at breaking the code of mystery—this time concerning the text of Torrentius's life—is the lengthy, convoluted, and dramatic story told in "Still Life with a Bridle." Unlike the nightmare of the Phaistos disc, the episode described in that essay actually took place. As the story unfolds, Herbert's narrator makes a claim that there is no biographical information on Torrentius. His manner of reaching that conclusion is quite characteristic: at first, he looks for the necessary particulars only in various extant dictionaries and encyclopedias—an ultimately unsatisfactory approach in researching the seventeenth-century Dutch artist, who is represented by only a single canvas. After much searching, he finally encounters a monograph on Torrentius written by the renowned Dutch scholar Abraham Bredius and also finds other historical sources, among them *Observations on Painting* by Constantijn Huygens. In this classic study, Huygens, Torrentius's contemporary, includes a comprehensive survey of Torrentius's career and works.[19] Those sources, obviously, do not change Herbert's claims—enhanced by his eloquent phrasing—that the painter's life remains inaccessible. The level of inaccessibility changes, though. No longer stymied by a lack of scholarly sources, he nonetheless remains puzzled by the fragmentary and mysterious nature of the Dutch painter's biography. To give more substance to the artist's life as an "entangled knot of many threads," the narrator finds himself compelled "to make use of the terminology of magic" and to admit with animated certainty that "our hero escapes formulas, definitions, and traditional descriptions, as if his only ambition after death was to deceive" (92, 94). More important, the painter's life represents literary material whose meaning cannot be unveiled. Perhaps Herbert knew from the very beginning that Torrentius's life, preconceived in his narrative as a *hermetic cultural text,* was not to be decoded. However, the attempt to explicate it was a necessary tactic. This tactic established his life as an ineffable linguistic structure (though open for the kind of speculations on which Herbert thrives) to lay the groundwork for his next cognitive journey.

On this occasion, he undertakes an investigation of the emblematic text inscribed directly on the canvas *Still Life with a Bridle* painted by Torrentius. Before we begin our own inquiry, however, a word about the emblematic interpretation of Dutch art. As championed today by Eddy de Jongh, this analysis rejects because of its reductive tendencies the prevalent notion, popular especially in the nineteenth century, that Dutch art is realistic. Instead, it follows an older tradition of reading in the painting a hidden meaning which is alluded to in the form of a caption, motto, epigram, or commentary presented on the canvas. For contemporary scholars, it offers "a way to make the visible intelligible and the intelligible visible through a complex and richly organized conceit," writes Alpers, an adherent of realistic reading.[20] Torrentius's script makes indeed a perfect case for Herbert's emblematic interpretation.

After a prolonged reading of classic hermetic literature, and after probing the link between Torrentius and the Rosicrucians, Herbert concentrates with renewed energy on one item depicted in the bottom of the painting—a sheet of paper with a rather obscure couplet written in Dutch:

> What exits beyond measure (order)
> in over-measure (disorder) will meet a bad end.
> (101)

In a manner reminiscent of the Phaistos disc episode, Herbert approaches the poem as an arbitrary mystery, in spite of the fact that the gnomic poetry, to which the couplet belongs, usually represents some sententious maxim. Herbert's translation of the poem from Dutch into Polish seems to lead him, for some time, to understand the painting as an allegory of moderation, an interpretation not corroborated by the Dutch scholar Pieter Fischer. *Still Life with a Bridle* viewed as an allegory of restraint—an idea historically and iconographically feasible—would exist in perfect accord with the semantics of the bridle depicted in the painting. But Herbert fastidiously rejects this meaning for its "suspicious simplicity" ("Still Life with a Bridle," 101)—a reason which in itself reveals much about his methodology—and the ultimate meaning of the canvas remains open for never-ending interpretation. Thus the message which Torrentius chose to accompany his painting had, a few centuries later, reached a viewer endowed with insight and knowledge who took the time to fathom its meaning yet was careful not to jump to conclusions.

Herbert realizes the impossibility of breaking the code of the script, even though the couplet inscribed in Torrentius's painting seems an easy task. Why is he not content accepting the message at face value? In a gesture protective of the black tondo's gnomic poem, he explains that its mystery should be approached cautiously. Wary of a too literal interpretation, which "frightens away mystery" (101), the poet explores the other extreme—suggestiveness and ambiguity. Convoluted, or even perverse, as it most surely is, the whole argument betrays his desire to preserve and respect the aura of the mysterious, which, he feels, has long disappeared from our scholarly and critical understanding of the visual arts. By his firm and repeated assertion of the inexplicable, Herbert reaches the ultimate point of his cognitive journey: the point which I see as *reductio ad mysterium.*

Regardless of whether the medium under investigation is verbal or visual, Herbert usually conceives of the mysterious elements as a text. Therefore, speaking of Torrentius's still life, he confesses in a manner already familiar to the reader, "from the beginning I had the irresistible impression that in the motionless world of the picture something much more, and something very essential, was occurring. As if the represented objects combined in meaningful relations and the entire composition contained a message, *an incantation transmitted in the letters of a forgotten language*" (100 [italics mine]). This textualization of the painting's indecipherable message allows for its shift from the domain of indeterminacy to the domain of a structured form. When it is transformed into a set of grammatical rules, its chance of being successfully decoded increases. Herbert's tendency to endow a hidden truth—be it enclosed in works of art, ancient scripts, or biographical accounts—with properties of a *text* deserves stronger emphasis. His method implies the existence of a language, which may greatly facilitate expression and communication, and even though the message may remain undecoded, its newly recognized linguistic form opposes formlessness and shapes the obscure.

Despite the determination with which Herbert makes use of emblematic interpretation based on a hidden verbal meaning, the poet's reading does not always render such meaning transparent. In fact, it rarely does, and he is quick to acknowledge the negative outcome of his explorations with a sure sense of defeat: "I did not manage to break the code" (106). It leaves us with the impression that the most intriguing part of his pursuit lies in the narrative's meandering cognitive journey, in the process through which the answer to this enticing enigma is painstakingly sought, yet never achieved. Still, there is more to be learned, and I will elaborate on Torrentius's canvas later in this study.

The Initiation

Herbert as an art critic tends to be an iconoclast to create his own canon of pictorial masterpieces. This desire to reevaluate or even to reject such widely acclaimed masters as Jacob van Ruisdael is informed by his personal taste and a sense of mission. As we know from his poetry, he has no problem with rejecting the aesthetic centrality of Leonardo da Vinci's *Mona Lisa*.[21]

At the core of this evaluative task lies Herbert's understanding and acceptance of epiphany as the defining moment in embracing a work of art. The instant he first encounters Torrentius's painting serves as a classic example of this illuminating discovery; at once he experiences an epiphany and recognizes the still life as a masterpiece. Because of this and similar encounters, epiphany for Herbert becomes one of the most crucial factors in judging a work of art. Moreover, it is a versatile tool which can evoke, as we shall see, a glimpse of magic.

In the 1960s, for example, Herbert visited the famous paleolithic frescoes in the Lascaux Cave. There, he was introduced both to one of humanity's oldest artistic achievements and to the element of magic which it contains. There are several passages in his essay on Lascaux that are crucial to the development of his discourse on epiphanic art. At the very threshold to the entrance of the cave, Herbert's narrator mentions a heavy, locked door. It is before this door that he, in the company of other tourists, was forced to stand "in darkness awaiting initiation."[22] Once inside, the first image he sees on a wall in a long procession of painted bestiary is that of a bicorn, a two-horned beast that is clearly the fruit of the prehistoric artist's imagination: "Its small head resembles a rhinoceros, yet it is unlike any living or fossil animal. Its mysterious presence forewarns that we shall not view an atlas of natural history but a region of ritual and magic" (8). Herbert first expresses his anxiety over his anticipated initiation into a magic ritual and then comments on the bicorn. Both moments are meaningfully interconnected. They inform the reader about something that the tourists in the caves—poorly served by the local guide's "stammering explanations" (8)—may not be entirely aware of. The prehistoric paintings of Lascaux should not be judged on a purely mimetic or formal basis, Herbert believes, but as an expression of sacred formulas and rites.[23] Although, at a certain point, the narrator also appreciates the masterful technique and mimetic virtuosity of the cave painters, his initial impression of the bicorn as an enigmatic creature sets the tone of the whole unfolding experience.

The Lascaux frescoes show more of their impenetrable side as colorful geometric signs appear on the walls covered with pictures of animals. These scattered dots, dashes, squares, and circles create an indecipherable text. What are they? A metaphysical treatise of the prehistoric people? Or, sheer ornaments? Once again, the script cannot communicate anything specific and functions more as a decorative abstraction which nevertheless only increases the sense of mystery pervading the cave.

As the procession of frescoes unfolds, the visitor enters an apse leading to a shaft in the rock. Here he encounters "the ultimate mystery" (11), or, in the literal and decidedly more emphatic translation—"the mystery of mysteries."[24] The scene painted inside the shaft (otherwise known as the Well) is significant from an iconographic point of view, for it contains the first-known representation of a man. Though the scene depicting the man is both simple and dramatic, its meaning remains in dispute. In it, the man is pictured lying on the ground with a group of animals nearby: a bison pierced by a spear, a bird, and a rhinoceros seemingly fleeing. How is one to make sense of this scene? Herbert, intrigued by its iconographic enigma, reviews existing theories. According to one, this so-called Well Scene represents either a hunting trip or a shaman in ecstasy. Because Herbert declines to offer a hypothesis of his own, the reader of his essay remains puzzled.

In Herbert's narrative, the experience of Lascaux has a clearly purposeful structure. Through a series of increasingly mysterious animal representations and geometric signs, we are led to the final Well Scene, whose iconographic enigma functions as the apex of the visitor's sojourn. Lascaux reveals itself to the beholder's eye as a gradual initiation directed toward a final mystery. And the last stage defies a total decoding. Only now can the mystery be fully experienced and celebrated.

The Poetics of Illumination

Der Augenblick ist Ewigkeit.
—Johann Wolfgang von Goethe

Finally, Herbert's cognitive journey takes a more specific course toward illumination as the highest and most desirable contact with art. This particular type of response is elicited by the author's encounters with buildings, whether it is the Notre Dame Cathedral in Paris, Binnenhof in the Hague, or the paintings by Piero della Francesca and Jan van Eyck. In all these moments, an illumination (as unmotivated, seemingly, as an act of grace) defines the power of art to transcend the beholder's state of mind and to elevate it to an aesthetically intriguing and rewarding meditation. During Herbert's trip to Crete, for example, an ecstatic illumination overcomes his initial disappointments caused by a famous group of frescoes. Those paintings—*Dolphin Fresco, La Parisienne, Cupbearer,* and *Toreador Fresco*—depict various aspects of life and nature on Crete, and are located in the Archaeological Museum in Herakleion. Excavated by Sir Arthur Evans at the turn of the century, they form a canonical group of paintings from the late Minoan period. For Herbert—the traveler so eager to encounter authentic works—they bring only disappointment and disbelief. The subversive energy that prompts Herbert to avert his gaze from other overly popular Western works of art (textbooks and guidebooks being the chief venues of this popularity), compels him to reject the frescoes. On this occasion, however, he does not target the typical tastes of the tourist but criticizes the destructive process of restoration which prevents him from experiencing the frescoes in a meaningful way. Unlike the immaculately preserved Lascaux wall paintings, the Minoan murals were heavily damaged during the volcanic eruption that destroyed the ancient civilization of Crete. Today, a tourist looking at the badly reconstructed wall paintings from Knossos studies not ancient art but the state of nineteenth-century archaeology. Its rather liberal methods of restoration only annoy Herbert, who sees the result of Evans's reconstruction as guesswork, oddly combined with the archaeologist's Victorian sensitivity. "Their women reminded me of ours, so beautifully painted by Whistler,"[25] he quotes Evans, indirectly mocking the mixed Minoan-Victorian efforts at restoration. Comparing the murals to sick patients that expect sympathy and understanding, Herbert can hardly hide his disillusion regarding what he sees in Crete.

When, finally, the desired moment of revelation occurs in the Herakleion museum, it comes unexpectedly. Yet, any chance of indulging his curiosity is thwarted by the bell that signals the closing of the museum for the day. This time the artwork that inspires his epiphanic moment is the Hagia Triada Sarcophagus, a limestone coffin painted in *fresco buono*. With the exception of one completely destroyed upper part, described by Herbert poetically as "a white cloud of non-existence" (15), the coffin is intact. No modern hand had retouched this artifact, and what was not taken away by time and the elements faithfully attests to its totality. The object represents the virtue of wholeness, rare in ancient artifacts, which stimulates the writer's epiphanic perception. "I experienced illumination" (14), he exclaims in utter joy.

The next day, he attempts to see this work of art as it really is, to study and to memorize it in its entirety, with all its painted scenes, lines, and colors. He describes the frescoes in detail. In this manner he hopes to preserve his epiphanic experience. Unlike photographic reproductions, he claims, the individual visual memory can record the images exactly and lend them a personal touch. But the sarcophagus defies a systematic approach of interpretation, and Herbert compares its description to a slaughter. Because the sarcophagus's scenes were revealed to him "in the bright and sudden light of a simultaneous presence" (15), the act of describing their content cannot give justice to their startling revelation. Despite that obstacle, Herbert undertakes a description of the series of scenes covering its walls. The essence of the sarcophagus is inexpressible, but the account, rendered with the utmost simplicity and precision, successfully evokes the iconographic content of the fresco with its many chromatic subtleties. Stripped of unnecessary adulation, his depiction is elegant, permeated by a desire to present adequately the work at hand. The poet's eye follows with rapture the scenes of the ancient sacred ritual represented on the walls of the sarcophagus. This involvement of the eye allows for a vigorous verbal reconstruction of the artwork, in particular its passage from reality to the other world.[26]

The painted panels relate the succession of the rites pertaining to the cult of the dead, from the offering of an animal through the libation to the appearance of the dead. That final act of resurrection, evidence of the ancient belief that life is invincible, produces the strongest impression on the visitor's mind. Thus, before describing the scene, he shifts from his down-to-earth report to an inspired invocation: "now we are touching the core of the scene, the ultimate mystery, the mystical *arche*" (16). Such elevated rhetoric prepares the reader for an enlightened experience and calls for an empathic and spontaneous reaction. Now comes the moment of envisioning the world of the dead, culminating in the singular image of a deceased man: "He has a shape of a statue, of a herma, tightly wrapped up in a light garb like a cocoon, mysterious as an apparition, concrete as a stone . . . indifferent and overbearing" (16). Struck by the effectiveness of the magic ritual that lured the dead to return to this world, Herbert calls the last stage of passage "the ultimate mystery" (in the original, "*tajemnica tajemnic*"). This is the exact repetition of the phrase he used to describe the core of the well scene in Lascaux and, as such, it interconnects both scenes; each scene in its apprehension of eschatological mystery defies rational explanation.

Clearly, the sense of detached objectivity and poetic enchantment is instilled in Herbert's ekphrastic word. To emphasize the link between the sarcophagus and the Egyptian Book of the Dead (and perhaps in reference to his own struggles with various mysterious scripts), Herbert renames the sarcophagus the Minoan Book of the Dead. For him it embraces the totality of ancient civilization by paradoxically capturing the "happy moment of illuminating knowledge and inspired sobriety" (15). The nearly contradictory combination of vision and erudition that Herbert ascribes to the anonymous Cretan artist corresponds again to the division between a scholar and an artist inherent in his discourse on art. He qualifies this fusion as a "happy" occurrence—indeed, the rarest adjective in his vocabulary. Does this mean that Herbert, carried away in his exhilaration, projects these two approaches onto the fresco painted on the ancient coffin? Not necessarily. Rather, we witness the moment of a perfect match between his critical apparatus and the Cretan painting; in turn, the immanent poetics of the fresco relates to Herbert's approach to it—thus the cycle is complete.

Comparing these experiences is an instructive lesson. The Lascaux and Minoan frescoes are divided at the very least by space, time, and the individual sensibilities of their makers. The first series of wall paintings is of monumental scale, whereas the Minoan is on a small coffin. But, as we have noticed, they stimulate the same response in the narrator, who is quite overwhelmed by the mystery of each.

What other aspects do these two examples have in common? Is it just the fact that they both belong to the genre of sacred art? Although that factor plays a certain role, the value and real meaning of those rites had been almost entirely lost and forgotten, a fact that Herbert never fails to mention. Despite the complexity of the matter, the progressive character of both the Lascaux and Hagia Triada Sarcophagus frescoes binds them. The naturally created system of corridors and halls in the Lascaux Cave and the cycle as the compositional principle of the coffin's panels form a passage leading from reality to the mystery of death. The paintings' progression, organized in a staccato rhythm, stimulates Herbert's ecstasy.

Other epiphanies recorded in Herbert's essays support my claim concerning the construction of a passage as an indispensable form for his epiphanies. Let us, then, return briefly to Torrentius's *Still Life with a Bridle* (see figure 2), a clearly delineated example of an epiphany produced by a secular work of art. Its effect merits nearly all of the writer's descriptive energy and attention. In a lyrical exultation, Herbert recollects what happened in the Royal Museum in Amsterdam:

> I understood immediately, though it is hard to explain rationally, something very important had happened; something far more important than an accidental encounter in a crowd of masterpieces. How to describe this inner state? A suddenly awakened intense curiosity, sharp concentration with the senses alarmed, hope for an adventure and consent to be dazzled. I experienced an almost physical sensation as if *someone called me, summoned me.* (78 [italics mine])

The ecstasy, immediacy, and irrationality of this experience have a lasting effect on his memory and state of mind. This moment is organized

Figure 2. Torrentius (Jan Simonsz van der Beek), *Still Life with a Bridle*, 1614, oil on canvas, 52 × 50.5 centimeters, Amsterdam, Royal Museum

as a parallel to the conversion of Saul, who—as reported in the Acts—on the road to Damascus had a powerful vision of God: he saw the heavenly light and heard His voice. As imagined by such masters as Caravaggio, who in his canvas included the horse as a player in the episode, the sheer power of the divine illumination struck Saul from his horse. Herbert is also on a journey, but unlike Saul, he has only the sensation of hearing a voice, which remains ambiguous and is deliberately preceded by the conditional "as if." This cautious gesture in exemplary fashion distinguishes his epiphany from any other religious form of revelation.

To reinforce his first confession regarding his revelatory response to Torrentius's painting, Herbert reiterates the ecstasy of the moment: "I myself do not know how to translate my stifled shout when I first stood face-to-face with the "Still Life' into comprehensible language, nor the joyous surprise, the gratitude that I was endowed beyond measure, the soaring act of rapture" (96). Then, in a skeptical frame of mind, the poet examines more closely the cause of his impression. With a sense of mission instilled in him during this memorable epiphany in Amsterdam's Royal Museum, he begins a different, hermeneutic journey focused on Torrentius's single still life. He, of course, has not experienced any conversion but feels as though he has been summoned to absorb and explicate to his readers the power of art.

The impassioned recollections of the epiphany compel the writer to probe the limits of language and of the rhetorical devices of the inexpressible. In both instances, Herbert makes an attempt to express the character (but neither the content nor essence) of his experience. He can describe only his immediate response, because in articulating the content of the epiphany, he is confronted with an insurmountable obstacle: insight granted by epiphany cannot be subsequently rationalized and articulated to the reader. At the end of his journey of the eye, Herbert encounters only silence and solitude. Though enlightened, he is deprived of communicating the substance of this experience to others, which, to use one of Brodsky's favorite phrases, in "his line of work," is not a trifle. The content of his illumination remains concealed—unexpressed because it is inexpressible.

When the ephemeral moment of revelation is gone, what remains is the shadow of memory and the tangible artifact that produced it. The lack of any other proof of what actually happened causes a nostalgic desire to recall and control it intellectually through description. Herbert makes an effort to separate his rapture from its cause and renders his depiction with detachment. He evokes Torrentius's only extant work in *Still Life with a Bridle* in the same ekphrastic manner as do the Lascaux Cave paintings in the volume *Barbarian in the Garden*. In both cases, the author provides first an inventory of the objects represented in the work and then a more elaborate and poetic description. Accordingly, Torrentius's painting is examined on two separate levels: first, as an assortment of common household utensils briefly illuminated as if by lightning and second, as a nonobjective void issuing from its background. The first of Herbert's descriptions represents the canvas's basic composition as consisting of two planes. In its opening ekphrastic unit, the objects, their placement on the canvas, their color, and their volume are described; in the other, the painting's background is depicted. The representation of the mundane utensils in Torrentius's still life is accomplished in the form of three ekphrastic sentences, each so condensed as to be almost without verbs. Such a description gives the reader an objectively precise idea of the still life's content and genre, its perfectly static ("dead" as Derrida emphatically writes) appearance, and its essence, which lies in its "thingness."

The quest for thorough knowledge of the artwork that has produced the epiphany is characteristic of Herbert's method. Shifting from an ecstatic response to description, Herbert separates his rapture from its cause, and in a quite detached manner renders this lucid depiction: "on the left side a potbellied pitcher of burnt clay in a warm, saturated brown; in the middle a massive goblet, called a *romer,* half-filled with liquid; and on the right side a silver-gray pewter pitcher with a lid and spout. In addition, two porcelain pipes, a piece of paper with music, and a text on the shelf where the utensils were standing. At the top, metal objects I could not at first identify" (79). The list of objects is modest. They exude austerity rather than the opulence one sees, for instance, in Willem Heda's still lifes. The objects themselves are commonplace. We can imagine them in the hands of coarse but jolly companions drinking and singing in a smoke-filled inn somewhere in seventeenth-century Holland—Adriaen Brouwer's paintings reenacted many such scenes. Deprived of human presence, however, the mundane utensils in Torrentius's canvas suggest the pleasure of living. Their incongruity with the lofty experience of epiphany seems to confirm the notion of irrelevance so frequently indicated in the theory of epiphany. Hence, we sense one of the painting's numerous dualities. Here we have both its evocation of "low-plane reality and its participation in the 'higher' discourses of culture" such as studies of the epiphany.[27]

Torrentius's still life does not represent the best argument for the validity of the genre, generally considered one of the "lowest" in the arts.[28] The utensils are suggestive of more than the simple life. Through rigidly symmetrical arrangement, alluding to a higher order and harmony, the objects participate in this canvas's complex format, its transcendence of everyday life. Moreover, the painting's unusual quality lies in juxtaposing (mainly through the use light and color) the utensils against the black void of the background and, as an extension, the mimetic aesthetics against the sublime.

The second portrayal of the painting is longer, more detailed and elaborate, though not overly so. It mentions again the painting's colors, the light, and certain physical attributes of the objects. Our attention is focused on the objects' thickness and weight, or on the manner in which they are positioned next to each other on the canvas:

> On the left side, then, a clay jug with a warm, brown glaze on which a small circle of light has settled. In the middle a tumbler, called a *romer*, made of thick glass and half-filled with wine. Finally a pewter pitcher with an energetically protruding beak. These three vessels, lined up facing the spectator in a position of attention, stand on a barely outlined shelf near two pipes with their stems turned down, and the lightest detail of the painting, a white-hot piece of paper with a musical score and text. At the top is the object I could not decipher at first, which seemed to be a piece of old armor hanging on the wall; at closer observation, it appeared to be a chain bridle used to tame exceptionally skittish horses. (98–99)

This description also includes the enigmatic object only half-visible in the background. What we see is, indeed, hardly recognizable. More imaginatively, we could say that the bridle resembles the face of a ghost emerging from the depths. In fact, Herbert compares it to a "threatening, hieratic, somber . . . specter of the great Commander" (99). Envisioned as an emissary of death, the bridle echoes the apparition of the deceased painted on the wall of the Hagia Triada Sarcophagus, which mesmerized Herbert during his trip to Crete in the 1970s. At this point, Herbert's observation is limited to the seemingly imprecise way in which the painter represented the ominous bridle. Only the highlights of the bridle can be detected, in deliberate contrast to the other objects in the painting, which are represented with such compact precision that they "assume an intensified and swollen reality" (98).

Herbert plays for a while with the notion of Torrentius's still life as an allegory of restraint or Temperantia, only to reject this iconological solution in the end. However, a powerful restraining and governing force can be felt in the painting's perfectly symmetrical arrangement of all the objects (including the bridle, which in itself symbolizes control) as well as their rounded fullness, which corresponds to the shape of the canvas itself. Indeed, they are painted so clearly that Herbert has no trouble in persuading us that Torrentius captured their very essence as things. One could declare that Torrentius also captured the essence of the still-life genre, which Schopenhauer considered the highest form of objective painting.

In a painting created with such a rigid sense of order and economy of artistic means as *Still Life with a Bridle,* each nuance, each chromatic or compositional accent has significance. Therefore, it must be of special importance that the painter conceived the bridle with less painterly definition and volume. Painted as if from a far distance, it emerges half-real, half-ghostly—as Herbert wants it—and as light and immaterial as a spider web. Behind the painting's other objects, endowed with a solid and tangible appearance which catches "the essence of the species" (98), the barely recognizable bridle attains an especially ambiguous status. In effect, Herbert sees on the canvas seven clearly delineated objects and one so vaguely defined that he perceives it as an apparition veiling the background.

Why would Torrentius, the "master of illusory realism," avoid a clear definition of this metal implement? A technical fault on his part is out of the question. Torrentius's mimetic craft, for which he was known among his contemporaries,[29] suggests a deliberate purpose in contrasting the bridle with the other objects in the painting. This is especially relevant historically, given that the cost of Dutch paintings was calculated according to a fine and well-detailed finish. As Svetlana Alpers observes, "time was devoted to execution, not to invention."[30] Let us then assume for a moment that Torrentius, in organizing the symmetrical character of his composition, chose an uneven number of objects (seven) and radically transformed the eighth object so it would lose some of its thingness, or substance. Such a gesture might be viewed as a response to a rather formalistic challenge to arrange the given quantity of items on the canvas to bring balance to the whole composition. But Torrentius cherished—as Herbert reminds us—such technical difficulties, and managing the group on this painterly surface should not have constituted any problem for him. Judging by the results, it did not.

Let us instead suppose that by playing with seven objects on the canvas the painter wanted to capitalize on the symbolic meaning of the number *seven,* which stands for the totality of God's creation. This numerological perspective offers one serious advantage: the painting's progressive structure becomes more noticeable. Herbert, however, skeptically rejects interpretations that derive from esoteric sources. Justly praised by a critic as a gifted iconologist, he is a cautious spectator who prefers to protect the mystery of the canvas rather than accept any ready solution.[31]

So far, I have indicated certain compositional and spatial principles of the artifacts that inspire epiphany. Yet one may note in this context that Torrentius's still life seems oddly placed between the Lascaux cave paintings and the frescoes of the Hagia Triada Sarcophagus. If so, there exists a possibility for bridging—with some historical background—this apparent inconsistency. Briefly, the genre of still life did not originate, as has often been assumed, in early-sixteenth-century Flemish art but earlier, in fourteenth-century Italy. The characteristic representation of inanimate objects in Italian painting of the time derives from ancient Roman painting. Charles Sterling argues that the beginning of the modern still life goes back to the specific Roman artistic form called xenia, that is, the representation of inanimate objects on murals.[32] In xenia, objects such as fruit, vessels, and vegetables were conceived within certain schemes that are also present in sixteenth-century Flemish still-life painting. This crucial fact provides the missing link between the art of antiquity and the late Middle Ages in the north of Europe. Sterling's argument offers substantial historical evidence which validates the connection between the seemingly different works of art prompting Herbert's epiphanies.

The scheme that connects them, as Sterling sees it, is further corroborated in a structural analysis offered by Bryson (17). In discussing antique Roman murals and their progression—marked by stages and degrees—toward epiphany, Bryson uses Villa of the Mysteries as the best-known example of Roman figurative murals representing all stages of initiation. On the walls of Villa of the Mysteries, painted men and women conduct their enigmatic service, which is perhaps a part of the Dionysiac cult. Bryson describes these stages in terms of a passage "from the preparation for the rite, still taking place in the real world, across the attendants as they approach the mystery, to the break-through moment at which consciousness, modified by the ritual, opens on to other dimensions, and the divinities . . . make their appearance" (46). At this point, Bryson finds common ground between xenia and the murals at

Villa of the Mysteries in their inner motion by establishing that the same structural progression delineates them. To quote Bryson, "their structure of movement from the real to the unreal, across a series of precisely designated thresholds, is exactly the principle of their construction" (46). The progressive structure of Torrentius's canvas also becomes quite apparent in this interpretation. It consists of three clearly defined stages: the ordinary vessels in the foreground, the "threatening, hieratic" ("Still Life with a Bridle," 99) bridle in the middleground, and, finally, the black background opening to the "perspectives of infinity" (79). The eye of the beholder proceeds from one stage to the next, thereby reconstructing the inner dynamics of this still life. In sum, xenia, the prototype of the modern still-life painting, transcend material reality in the same manner as Villa of the Mysteries, the Hagia Triada Sarcophagus, and Torrentius's *Still Life with a Bridle*. All these pictorial texts are interrelated by inner movement from the visible to the invisible.[33]

During his travels, Herbert came across only a few paintings which stimulated his epiphanic experience. These works are informed by inner movement to which the traveler's mind is particularly conducive, for his world—as every traveler's world tends to be, at least on the surface—is in flux. When epiphany occasioned by these parallel movements occurs, it heightens his sense of identity and allows him to focus on the everlasting richness of art. The traveler's passage to rapture is indeed an open road, lined with coded markers that tell more than the miles he endured.

5

Images of Darkness

Delineating the Void

The Void is truth.
—Stéphane Mallarmé

In his exploration of Dutch culture and art, Herbert employs a particular way of looking at objects which is characterized by focusing on the background. This stratagem allows him to decentralize the main motif and underscore the marginalized aspects of vision. Stanislaw Baranczak associates this perspective, which Herbert employs in his poetry for slightly different purposes than in his essays, with an apocryphal, non-canonical view: "The canonical version of a myth or a stereotyped image of an object usually isolates the character or object to a certain extent, focusing on the central figure in the plot or on the object's schematic features. It is sometimes enough just to take the background or surrounding context into consideration to perform another unmasking, another discovery."[1] This approach is best illustrated in Herbert's encounter with Torrentius's *Still Life with a Bridle*. Scrutinizing the somber canvas, Herbert brings to the reader's attention its peripheral black background. Here, Herbert allows his apocryphal spirit to work on a scale hitherto unknown in his writing. By revising the status of Torrentius's modestly sized, circular painting from an unknown canvas to an unjustly forgotten masterpiece, he questions the workings of the canon of western European painting. In analyzing the black depths of Torrentius's canvas, he reveals the existential and metaphysical anxieties hidden therein.[2] In this sense, the black background is emblematic of all Herbert's images of darkness represented in the volume *Still Life with a Bridle,* and its reading prompts the farthest-reaching journey of his eye.

In fact, Herbert's investigation of this and similar images of darkness characterize the last stage of his travel writing, which had begun with his study of the phenomenal aspects of the new reality, discovered through travel. In her groundbreaking study of the poet's approach to the visual arts, Bogdana Carpenter comments on his "extraordinary sensitivity to color, light, and texture" and other sensual details present in his descriptions.[3] This deserves emphasis, precisely because without his heightened receptivity to the physical aspects of art and reality, the illuminating moments of epiphany and the sublime would never occur.

The stark images that create those moments conceived in similarly dark chromatic tonalities and determined by negative aesthetics, suggest noumenal reality. Their almost minimalist purity and simplicity is complicated by a polarized meaning. These images may signify either the manifestations of the abyss or the intimations of eternity. In this sense, they correspond to the two centers that humans, according to Schelling, confront during a metaphysical experience: negative abyss and harmonious infinity. Herbert does not readily adopt the link between the depths of the human soul and the abyss, and neither does he achieve a balance between the two centers. Instead, Herbert's metaphysical instinct prompts him to seek the images of the threatening abyss outside the boundaries of the self while allowing the distinction between a positive and a negative metaphysical experience to fluctuate over time. Significantly, in Herbert's last essays, the threatening image of the abyss prevails entirely over the bliss of eternity.[4] What unifies this bilateral metaphysical perspective is art, be it architecture or various pictorial genres.

In one of the *Apocryphas* (the fictionalized counterpart of Herbert's essays on Dutch culture in *Still Life with a Bridle*), we come across another geometrically shaped image of murky blackness. Entitled "Home," the apocryph tells the story of a failed Dutch expedition team that has to spend a winter in the darkness of a "polar hell" (135). There, the members of the party build a small shelter, and, because their new shelter has neither ornaments nor openings other than the door, they paint (in black) a portal and two windows on the front wall. Upon their departure for Europe, they abandon the house. When one member of the team turns his head, he sees behind him "two false windows where pitchy darkness lurked" (143). This Magritte-like painterly device demonstrates that some Herbertian images of darkness, whether created by human beings or not, evoke the power of ontological formlessness whose uninhibited energy penetrates even into architecture. Although this most orderly of the visual arts frames chaos and delineates it geometrically, it cannot entirely control the presence of the void. Somewhere in the background chaos lurks.

So far, Herbert employs simple means to bridle formlessness. Geometry and rhythm, even if present only through the regular striking of a clock in "Home," bring consolation "that time is not an abyss or black mask of nothingness" (141). To a varying degree, every human activity and effort, performed intentionally or not, confronts and opposes the dark void. Controlled by the human tendency to impose form on substance, the black windows of the abandoned house resemble the canvases of Kazimir Malevich as if they were moved from some white museum wall to a white polar landscape. Though not construed as abstract paintings, they defy easy classification, and their rhetoric of visualization becomes apparent only within the chain of similar images in Herbert's essays, the chain connecting his earlier and more recent essays, in which Torrentius's black background is a critical link.

Herbert quite carefully prepares the initial appearance of Torrentius's black background as an independent image, as if separated from the main body of the painting but equal in significance to the foreground. The initial appearance of Torrentius's *Still Life with a Bridle* is preceded by and interwoven into a complex system of dark backgrounds mirroring each other. It reflects in particular the many dark settings in canvases executed by Gerard Terborch, who specialized in portrayals of Dutch burghers. Herbert notices that the black backdrops against which Terborch placed his affluent Dutch men and women appear in chromatic juxtaposition to the bright colors of his foregrounds. He characterizes them in two paintings as a "heavy, dark background";[5] as a "dark wall" suggestive only of the canvas's background (69); and as "*noir d'ivoire"* marked by "irregular stripes of deep juicy brown" (69). His apocryphal point of view facilitates the process by means of which a painting's background "becomes differentiated and sonorous" (69) only to appear ultimately in the role of a threatening force of death. Herbert evokes this force in his essay "Gerard Terborch: The Discreet Charm of the Bourgeoisie," which includes an imaginary monologue by Terborch. While looking at Terborch's self-portrait in the Mauritshius, Herbert fancies the Dutch painter saying:

> Yes I knew well the world of poverty and ugliness, but I painted the skin, the glittering surface, the appearance of things: the silky ladies, and gentlemen in irreproachable black. I admired how fiercely they fought for a life slightly longer than the one for which they were destined. They protected themselves with fashion, tailor's accessories, a fancy ruffle, ingenious cuffs, a fold, a pleat, any detail that would allow them to last a little longer before they—and we as well—are engulfed by the black background. (77)

Terborch's imagined monologue clarifies the background's revelatory function. Its dark abyss, devoid of objects, represents the final destiny of all human matter. Moreover, it introduces an interpretation of eschatological premonitions in the form of the *horror vacui* complex. The greater the Dutch burghers' fear of death, the more it was denied by their acquisition of things; the more acutely they sensed the final void, the more eagerly they filled it with objects. Amidst his mixed feelings of sympathy and irony toward the Dutch, Terborch articulates the terror of our own finality, which, Herbert believes, his painting powerfully expresses. Somewhere in the background of the painter's canvases, Herbert sees more than we are prepared to see on their surfaces.

However, for the seventeenth-century Dutch artists, the black background did not symbolize eschatological foreboding but represented an entirely different issue. Especially for still-life painters who were preoccupied with the question of better visibility of objects, the use of a dark background (and their reason for favoring it) was a solution to a technical problem. Like the Dutch scientist Anton van Leeuwenhoek, who discovered that sand grains stand out against a piece of black taffeta, they realized that a strong contrast between the foreground and the dark background gave their canvases a much desired precision in rendering objects, a clarity and precision close to the three-dimensional effect of a relief.[6]

The understanding of the dark ground in terms of a purely pictorial method stems from the Dutch orientation toward mimetic aspects of representation, which in Herbert's reading is balanced with other, not necessarily pictorial, values. In his treatment of the images of darkness, be it the representation of night or black geometric forms taken from the visual arts, Herbert fully develops their figurative and nonfigurative inner opposition on a truly Manichaean scale. When their manifestations in the visual arts enter the fray, the dynamics of the confrontation between form and formlessness grow ever more complex. In particular, as I have mentioned already, it involves Herbert's scrutiny of Torrentius's canvas, for which the author employs an argument derived from two distant spheres: negative and mimetic aesthetics.

Upon his arrival at the Royal Museum in Amsterdam, Herbert has no premonition of what would become his long and nearly obsessive fascination with a single Dutch painting. Even before its title is disclosed—a calculated procrastination on his part—another mystery is born on the pages of his essay: that of its creator's life. It is as though the elusive secrets of the painting reflect those of its creator. And this mysteriousness in itself provokes an authorial complaint. Words seem not to serve Herbert accurately. Aware that it is impossible to resolve the conundrum of the painter's life (so little of it is known), the writer engages all his descriptive skill in commenting as aptly as he can on the painting.

No adherent of any feasible moralistic or emblematic reading, Herbert focuses his attention in "Still Life with a Bridle" on what would quite naturally escape our eyes: the dark, murky, and empty space beyond the bridle. Hence, after his initial inventory, he commences with his task of describing the part of the still life that fascinates him the most: "black, deep as a precipice and at the same time flat as a mirror, palpable and disappearing in perspectives of infinity. A transparent cover over the abyss" (79). But can anything be flat and still signify depth, tangible yet brimming with invisible waves of nothingness?

Herbert conceives the antinomic ekphrasis of the background differently from the description of the objects that fill the foreground. He focuses on the background's haunting quality. He is able to emphasize the whole structure of *Still Life with a Bridle* as a threshold between the world of things (form) and nothingness (formlessness), between the phenomenal world and noumenal reality. As a master conjurer of words, he subjects his descriptive style to paradoxicality, typical as well of his

poetic imagery. The absence of verbs, which creates a condensed stillness and tranquility enhanced by his choice of nouns such as "precipice," "infinity," "abyss," indicates the metaphysical quality inscribed
into the painting's background. Thus the painting plays a liminal and
transitional role. It exists as a passage between thingness and nothingness. As a result of this descriptive stratagem, Torrentius's sole opus
becomes one with its creator's own mysterious existence.

Furthermore, the nouns appear according to a certain alternating
pattern. While "a precipice," "an infinity," and "an abyss" suggest an
unlimited space purged of any allusion to reality that invokes yet another world, the alternating "mirror" and "cover" indicate the presence
of a material obstacle. The fact that the cover veiling the precipice and
its threatening truth—commonplace in esoteric philosophy[7]—is actually described as transparent builds up the description's paradoxicality,
which conjoins what is visible and what is invisible. The dichotomy of
transparency and material obstacle also defines the relationship between
Herbert's two descriptions of the painting. In his first portrayal, the
background serves as a "transparent cover over the abyss," but in the
second, it exists as a sort of impermeable wall of basalt. Furthermore,
Herbert clearly states that the background, whether it connotes the
immaterial or the material void, is conceived as a tondo, a circular
canvas, and thus endowed with a form.

Herbert understands the image of the void in the visual arts in terms
of indefiniteness and formlessness, as pure nonexistence, which he treats
solely as an ontological concept divorced radically from any moralistic
bent. In this respect, his approach toward history as a destructive abyss
differs remarkably from his view on art, which opens up into a metaphysical abyss.

The Pupil of Death

Herbert's double description of Torrentius's *Still Life with a Bridle* reinforces the effect of textual mirroring so crucial to the volume's poetics.
One ekphrasis reflects and complements the other. Both descriptions
also mirror the original still life, thus further multiplying the series of
reflections. However, the fact that the author repeats his description
implies his awareness of a serious limitation in his quest for truth.
Mistrusting the results of his pursuit, he reiterates his verbal reflection.

The rebounding role of this doubled description becomes dazzlingly complicated. It is, after all, a reflection on the reflection of a mirrorlike painting reflecting reality. In deference to this multiplicity, the second description's opening sentence reinforces the painting's resemblance to a mirror: " 'The Still Life with a Bridle' is in the shape of a circle somewhat flattened 'on the opposite poles,' and creates the impression of a slightly concave mirror" (98). Thus its circular shape is reminiscent of the mirror in the painting by Jan van Eyck in his *Giovanni Arnolfini and His Bride.* Even though such canvases, which preceded Torrentius's still life, were not themselves circular but only depicted interiors with round mirrors, Herbert's interpretation of Torrentius's still life as a mirror allows me to connect the painting with the old Flemish iconographic tradition. It should be repeated, however, that still lifes on circular canvases were a rarity at the time.

Still Life with a Bridle belongs to those unique paintings that are open to both historical and anachronistic interpretations. In fact, the strongest appeal of Torrentius's painting lies precisely in its oscillation between two opposite—mimetic and negative—visual modes. The reading of its genre as a mimetic representation of the objects therein is historically correct. However, its sublime (nonobjective, negative) vision, which encompasses the background, cannot be corroborated by historical data. Support for this perspective can be found, rather, within the labyrinth of modernist art and aesthetics, a phenomenon Herbert otherwise tends to reject.

Undoubtedly, the visual legacy of modernism and its search for the nonrepresentational informs Herbert's reading of Torrentius's canvas. Piet Mondrian's painterly studies of a single tree documented the stages of his successful search for a completely objectless vision. It was Wassily Kandinsky who was the first to reject objects entirely, followed by Kazimir Malevich, who replaced negated phenomenal reality with black geometric figures. In his highly conceptual canvases, the artist sought to establish a totally new relationship between the visible and invisible worlds. Initially, he considered his nonrepresentational art an evocation of the fourth dimension. Only later did he describe it in such metaphysical terms as the "cosmic infinite," the "void," and the "eternal sensation."[8] After *Black Square,* Malevich repeated the same ideas in his *Black Circle,* another suprematist canvas totally devoid of the representation of earthly things. While *Black Square* inspires Herbert's perusal of several black backgrounds in Dutch paintings, it is the lesser known *Black Circle* (see figure 3) that returns like an echo in Herbert's interpretation of the black background in Torrentius's painting.[9] Formally, in its circular shape, the canvas' background forms a precise parallel to Malevich's black suprematist figure painted on a white background. Although the choice of geometric form may be more meaningful to a visual artist than to a writer, a square and a circle indeed embody different values. A circle represents perfect closure, whereas the square stands for symmetry and equality; more important for my further analysis, the circle's lack of corners implies organic shapes, be it the eye's pupil, the sun, or the full moon.

Both *Still Life with a Bridle* and *Black Circle* are fundamental to Herbert's formulation of negative aesthetics. The poet's interest in this complex problem dates to the 1960s, when he published the volume of poetry *Study of the Object*. There, he included two poems directly related to the type of negative imagery presently under discussion. One of them, entitled "Revelation," evokes death as a manifestation of the black void. Ironically, according to the poem's premonition, exactly at the end of one's life can things be ultimately revealed:

> I shall sit
> immobile
> my eyes fixed
>
> upon the heart of things
>
> a dead star
>
> a black drop of infinity[10]

Here, for the first time in Herbert's oeuvre, we encounter the striking image of a black drop: a small, round, black object employed as an eschatological symbol. This image anticipates a unique set of later images, especially the black backgrounds evoked in Herbert's essays.

Similar images of rigorously delineated blackness appear also in the poem entitled "Study of the Object." This poem depicts the genesis of an artistic object and refers to Malevich's *Black Square* twice in lines 26 and 39.[11] The motif of the black square serves as a nonobjective image placed between the world of objects and the chasm. Malevich's rejection

Figure 3. Kasimir Malevich, *Black Circle,* 1913 (1923–29), oil on canvas, 105.5 × 105.5 centimeters, Petersburg, State Russian Museum

of objects is reinforced here through the description of the square as "the simple dirge / for beautiful absence."[12] The genesis of the object (a simple chair) performed in Herbert's poem is complete only with the subsequent transformation of its mundane status and function:

> We ask reveal o chair
> the depths of the inner eye
> the iris of necessity
> the pupil of death. (135)

Like the black background in Torrentius's painting, the chair has the power to reveal death—the ultimate destiny of human life. It is endowed with the potential of disclosing what only the "pupil of death" can see. Aside from its haunting cognitive capacity, the pupil of death is associated in the poem with inner vision ("inner eye"; 138), which derives from the mystical tradition and was appropriated in the nineteenth century by Caspar David Friedrich for his deliberations on the visual arts. It also reminds us of the mirrors and backgrounds described or alluded to in Herbert's *Still Life with a Bridle.* Its semantic potential remains associated with the pupil of the physical eye and thus possesses the properties of roundness, blackness, and luster. As such, the pupil of death represents the smallest of all mirroring surfaces evoked in Herbert's essays and coincides, on the level of aesthetic negativity, with Malevich's *Black Circle* and Torrentius's black background in its representation of a circular black void. In an eschatological sense, they all reflect the impenetrable other world.

Revelations of the Night

The images of darkness recall Herbert's visit to Siena, the city whose painterly heritage and urban plan he glorified in the essay "Siena" included in *Barbarian in the Garden.* In this medieval city, at night, resting after a stroll through the winding, narrow streets, he experiences a revelation filled with luminous darkness. Concrete and devoid of "deadly abstractions," the town's airy scenery permeated by the light of a full moon creates for Herbert a moment of poetic and sensuous relief. In a gesture consistent with his understanding of beauty as stimulating the ecstatic, sudden moment of vision, he stresses the aesthetic appeal of the Piazza del Campo, which is "one of the world's most beautiful squares" (50–51). Then this passing moment of beauty turns unexpectedly into a dark revelation:

> Above the Piazza del Campo—luna plena. The shapes stiffen. A chord is strung between heaven and earth. Such a moment gives the feeling of crystallized eternity. The voices will die. The air will turn into glass. We shall remain here, petrified: I, raising a glass of wine to my lips, the girl in the window arranging her hair; the old man selling postcards under a streetlamp; the square with the Town Hall and Siena. The earth will turn with me, an unimportant item in a wax museum, visited by no one. (50–60)

In his desire to freeze this moment, Herbert translates it into a spatial category, into a cityscape. This single passage of time, snatched from earthly temporality, still exists in cosmic motion, never completely motionless. Entirely devoid of the fear of death or other ominous foreboding, this almost crystallized instant guarantees the continuity of individual bodily existence. In such a tender rendition of eternity (unusual in the context of his poetry), Herbert would be Herbert and the denizens of Siena would remain themselves along with the world of objects. Immobile, though circling through space, this image of night in still motion—conceived on the scale of a gigantic three-dimensional work of art—bears a certain mark of redemption through beauty. Could we therefore claim that what arrests this moment in all its splendor is its beauty? If so, only on a certain level, because treating the scene as a vestige of Dostoyevsky's and Nietzsche's aesthetic concepts would not give full justice to Herbert's practice of the metaphysical moment. This perceptive device, which injects poetry into his essays, points beyond aesthetic experience and transcends into a metaphysical experience.

Saint Augustine, the theological father of such metaphysical revelations, aptly described as an "intersection of eternity with time,"[13] recalls in his *Confessions* a moment when he and his mother "in a *flash of the mind* attained to touch the eternal Wisdom [italics mine]."[14] In Saint Augustine's archetypal experience, his sense of eternity momentarily approximates a positive transcendence. Notably, Herbert's Sienese vision is equally devoid of a negative tone.

I would like to illustrate this transition from the aesthetic to the metaphysical using the testimony of another poet, Jarosław Iwaszkiewicz.[15] Iwaszkiewicz, whose poem on Siena Herbert quotes in his essay "Siena," recalls that when he saw the array of frescoes in that city, as well as those in San Gimignano (works by Simone Martini, Lorenzetti, Ghirlandajo), he was inspired to write a series of poems: "Together they exhibited a great sensation of the unity of the world, this metaphysical exit beyond the 'monadic' enclosure, whether in connection with animals or stars, whether in the feeling of unity in nothingness or unity in eternity. Perhaps it does not matter."[16] For Iwaszkiewicz, too, art does not serve as a mere pretext for aesthetic pleasure. Whereas Iwaszkiewicz's agitated mind blurs all divisions known to mystics, theologians, and philosophers alike, Herbert's Sienese vision stresses silence, stillness, motion, and the ordinariness of a momentarily conjured eternity.[17] The sheer surplus of beauty in Siena causes a positive transcendence in which only sound is filtered out. Grasped without the terrifying rites of a passage through death, its purely visual quality remains unquestioned.

However, twenty years later, all vestiges of positive eternity have vanished in Herbert's eschatological deliberations. Though still closely connected with and prompted by the artistic and the beautiful, his images of the eternal acquire an intensely obscure quality. A meaningful correspondence with the Siena vision is effected through Herbert's encounter with a nocturnal cityscape and the sky as seen above Holland during a solitary walk. The night sky remains as opaque as the dark, impenetrable wall of an old building, but it is clear that it serves as the building's background; the darkness thickens and obliterates the facade's features. Thus metamorphosed, it reveals itself as "a sculpture of God without face. It emerges from the night similar to a rock growing from the ocean; not a single ray of light reaches this place. A dark mass of matter against the background of night's blackness" (6).[18] Herbert uses a double negative construction to articulate this dark revelation: not only is there no light shed on God's appearance, but it turns out that He, in fact, has no face. An intensely dark image placed against a black sky and liberated from the traditional representation of God as man, this unlikely likeness has its roots in the early-twentieth-century search for ultimate reality in the visual arts. Again, one may trace in this image an awareness of modernist abstract painting as practiced and articulated by Kazimir Malevich.

In the 1920s, Malevich began to recognize the value of sacrum in his *Black Square*. While contemplating the canvas, he saw in it the featureless face of God and believed that this sacred vision would be accessible to other viewers. In a letter to Pavel Ettinger, he argued that "If some gray-haired wise old man would penetrate this mysterious face of the black square, then he would probably see the same as I do."[19] According to Malevich, the traditional depiction of God's visage represented as a man's face, entirely devalued by centuries of use, had become "rubbed out as smooth as an old coin" (239). The need for a different form of representation was urgent, and the new image was radically revised by him and conceived in terms of negative aesthetics.

Concurring with Malevich's rejection of realistic and representational cult images, the Herbertian image repudiates God's incarnation in the human body, whether as God the Father or as Jesus. Yet Herbert, to whom the "blasphemous" attempts at reinventing the sacred in the arts come as an already established part of modernist tradition, does something remarkable with this heritage. By envisioning God's negated countenance, he restores in word the divinity's nonfigurative presence in art prior to avant-garde experimentation.

The passage from negative aesthetics to negative theology, which became a part of Malevich's experience, sheds light on Herbert's own spiritual development. Perceived by some critics as an agnostic, Herbert indeed seldom speaks directly to God in his poetry and expresses doubts concerning his ability to experience meaningful contact with Him.[20] But this state of affairs remains true only of his earlier poetry. As Justyna Szczęsna notes in her article, Herbert the agnostic has become a norm of critical perception. In contrast to this, she directs her attention to numerous instances in Herbert's poems which testify to the poet's attempts at "opening towards God, seeking Him."[21] Another indication that God exists as the metaphysical basis of Herbert's worldview is posited by Jan Sochoń, who concludes that God is a necessary "counterbalance to Nothing."[22] Certainly, Herbert does not speak of regular contacts with God, so when he does, their exceptional status is quite convincing.[23] Although not consumed by dilemmas of faith, Herbert shows that his nocturnal revelation gravitates to the unspeakable and unknowable God of negative theology, the ultimate mystery of the world. Rare as they are, this and similar moments call for a revised view of the poet's agnosticism.[24] In the case of the present survey, however, the trajectory of Herbert's images of darkness ranges from the aporia of consciousness to the renewed search for spiritual expression. The author illuminates their multidimensionality by juxtaposing form to formlessness, death and nothingness to eternity. Understood in terms of negative aesthetics, Herbert's images of darkness invite further investigation into their complexity, for they are also sublime.

The Hallowed Background

Ironically, because of its round shape, Torrentius's canvas was used as a lid to cover a barrel of raisins. Centuries later, the painting found its rightful place on a museum wall in Amsterdam, where later still it caught the attention of a radical connoisseur who preferred its murky beauty to hundreds of other Dutch works hung there. Herbert flouts the accepted canons of art criticism in his unorthodox and imaginative interpretation of Torrentius's canvas. In a most unusual fashion, he focuses as much attention on its nonobjective dark background as he does on its objective content, thereby going against the norm of perception by which dark backgrounds are usually considered a (rather meaningless) painterly convention.

As we have seen, the author describes the black background of Torrentius's still life twice. It is the second ekphrasis that introduces the interplay between foreground, background, and lighting: "The light of the painting is peculiar: cold, cruel, one would like to say clinical. Its source is beyond the painted scene. A narrow shaft of brightness defines the figures with geometric precision, but it does not penetrate the depths, it stops before the smooth, hard wall of the background, black as basalt."[25] Even if traditional critical interpretation would disregard what was as common to many paintings of that era as the black background, Herbert's approach in this respect differs. In his view, the void of the background stands for the dark netherworld, impenetrable even by sharp beams of light.

Evidently, Herbert's perception of the painting testifies to more than one inner contradiction. In his view, there seem to exist two perspectives in this canvas. The convex shapes of the kitchen utensils illustrate what Ortega y Gasset defines as a proximate vision, and the empty background and the spectral bridle represent a distant vision.[26] Torrentius, in a stroke of genius, combined these two incompatible visions into one canvas. As it is, Herbert's reading of the painted objects and their illusionistic representation follows the pre-Kantian mimetic aesthetics of beauty, and his focus on the objectless background follows Kant's (and other philosophers') idea of the sublime. This is not to suggest, however, a structural or semantic split of the painting. On the contrary, the power of Torrentius's still life stems precisely from his combination of this bifocal vision.[27]

The sublime does not apply only to this painting, because all Herbertian images of darkness are marked by its presence. In fact, both nocturnal visions in Herbert's essays encompass the aesthetic polarization of the Dutch canvas, though the degree and intensity of the sublime in them vary.

In referring to the sublime, I use only those elements from the history and theory of this aesthetic category that can be directly applied to Herbert's work. As Lyotard explains: "Certain 'objects' and certain 'sensations' are pregnant with a threat to our self-preservation, and Burke refers to that threat as terror: shadows, solitude, silence, and the approach of death may be 'terrible' in that they announce that the gaze, the other, language or life will soon be extinguished."[28] This sublime terror, which stimulates a frightening but lofty response, can be traced in Herbert's images of the dark sky, the black building, and a precipice of the background in *Still Life with a Bridle*. But Kant's conception of the sublime in painting is of greater importance for Herbert's art discourse because the philosopher introduces the notion that the infinite may be represented within the finite by means of a "negative presentation." Hence, Kant validates negative aesthetics in painting.[29] Herbert's synecdochal interpretation of infinity visible in his images of darkness coincides with this idea. Kant, however, limits the notion of negative presentation to Judaic law, which forbids graven images. One could argue that such sublimity is achieved through means of negative presentation in Herbert's nocturnal vision of a building perceived as God's face.

Lyotard makes sure the reader knows that Kant does not elaborate on this idea. Only then does the French philosopher take a decisive step further. In his writings on the modernist American abstract painter Barnett Newman, he completely divorces the sublime from its traditional link with figurative representation in painting and links it with the instant of vision. Herbert also takes this leap of imagination to endow his dark images with limitlessness, one of the oldest properties of the sublime.

Herbert bridges the extreme poles marked by Zagajewski and Brodsky. His dark epiphanies—informed by Malevich's painting and conceived within negative aesthetics—anticipate Brodsky's moment of a black vision.

PART **3**

JOSEPH BRODSKY

6

Strategies of Disappearance

I found here not my homeland, but the homeland of my soul.
—Nikolay Gogol on Rome

Echoes

From the first exhilarating moment that Joseph Brodsky observed Venice from a vaporetto[1] in the early 1970s to his final return, borne on a funeral barge to his burial site on the cemetery island of San Michele, the various enigmas of this historic city appeared to him in many guises.[2] After emigrating from the Soviet Union and acquiring a teaching post in the United States, Brodsky had made it his habit to visit Venice in the winter, at the beginning of the semester break. This tradition dated back to his first year in Ann Arbor. The salary he earned as a Russian literature instructor at the University of Michigan was just enough to allow him to escape from the rigors of academe and fly to the most popular of Italian cities in the season most unfriendly to tourists. Winter in Venice possesses a peculiar charm to those born in the north of Europe, and Brodsky, who spent his formative years in Petersburg, was no exception. His more or less regular visits to Venice constituted the basis of the poet's special relationship with the city.

In the eyes of the writer-traveler narrating *Watermark,* Brodsky's precarious existence on the world stage found a parallel in certain aspects of the sinking city. In several prescient passages in his book-length essay, such recurring premonitions came true in 1996, when Brodsky—who for years had suffered from a heart condition—died in New York City.[3] It would be difficult, however, to reduce Brodsky's response toward Venice in *Watermark* to his unsettling *Wunderlust* or to parallels with Gustav Aschenbach's fascination with death.

Watermark is as much a travelogue about Venice as it is a treatise about mirrors and their hidden, unpredictable meanings. Thus Brodsky's Venice may be viewed from two mutually exclusive perspectives, where the appearance of the antiworld that looms ominously from the other side of the mirror signifies the disappearance of reality. This anti-universe presents a great creative challenge: the daunting task of describing the ineffable, the purely nonrepresentational. Nonexistence, one of the most enduring obsessions of twentieth-century painting, seems to be a concept more aptly conducive to visual expression than to its manifestation in any other art form.[4] However, at least since Stéphane Mallarmé, the evocation of ontological or metaphysical negativity in literature has been a salient feature of the modern tradition, and Brodsky is a masterly exponent of this complex noumenon.

In *Watermark,* Brodsky conceives his creative task as a chain of strategies which, linked together, effect the gradual vanishing of various aspects of reality. As such, this gradation of visibility contributes to the metaphysical perspective with which he endows his winter travelogue. In Venice, a metaphysical void envelops the world in the same intense manner as it does in Brodsky's poetry. Indeed, writes the critic Valentina Polukhina, the void permeates Brodsky's verse as if it were the fourth element of reality.[5] One may look no further than the Venice as represented in *Watermark* and the Venice of "Venetian Stanzas," for both indeed extend toward the state of nonexistence. In these works, the city of canals is represented in a thematically similar way, although the representation in "Venetian Stanzas" is more condensed. Brodsky's Venice in verse was written before *Watermark* and serves as a framework for the prose version. Does the genre of the latter necessarily make it a lesser work?

Clearly, Brodsky describes a poet's transformation into a prose writer in terms of loss: "A poet turning to prose . . . is like the shift from gallop to trot, a time-exposure photograph of a monument, or Apollo's one year's service as a shepherd for the flocks of King Admetus."[6] As such, it is a triple loss of momentum, of immediacy of account, and of artistic freedom. This loss is made even more profound by the use of language which otherwise serves the poet—by his own admission—as the ideal vehicle for the highest form of artistic expression. However, as Brodsky claims elsewhere, poetry and prose do not always have to be diametrically opposed, and there are a few poets who can successfully make the transition from poetry to prose without losing the fervor and immediacy of the latter. As he exemplifies this precept in his essay "A Poet and Prose," Osip Mandelstam and Marina Tsvetayeva leave their own poetic mark on the art of essay writing through "linguistic and metaphorical density,"[7] laconism, and retrospection.

"Sentenced" to work in the purgatory of prose, Brodsky nevertheless wrote excellent essays.[8] Varying in theme and method but written with the same searching intensity, his three volumes of prose explore a linguistic medium new for him, and they evoke a variety of new contexts and topographies. It is illuminating to see how Brodsky makes the shift from his poetry, which takes Venice as its muse, to prose, focused on the same subject. Written in 1982, his "Venetian Stanzas I" and "Venetian Stanzas II," each consisting of eight regular octaves, outline the same representational aspects of the city we see later in *Watermark*. The "Venetian Stanzas" serve as a succinct, almost cryptic blueprint that ultimately enriches his longer essay.

Brodsky's experimentation with the genre of prose is linked to his exile in the West. The poet's involuntary move from one continent to another was followed by a leap, perhaps even riskier in its far-reaching consequences, into another language. In America, Brodsky the Russian poet became the English-language essayist. In his new linguistic incarnation Brodsky also continued to write verse. For many familiar with Russian, this latter endeavor proved only partly successful; David Bethea comments that "the barrier to Brodsky's total bilingualism comes when he attempts to translate his 'rhythmic signature' into English" (231). This is undoubtedly true. However, the poet's change in language, when complicated by his change in genre, offers a quite different evaluation. Unrestricted by meter and rhyme, Brodsky's English prose is allowed freer reign, and this venue constitutes a veritable gold mine for his creative invention. In this respect, the poet "pupates," to borrow Bethea's term, as an English essay writer with astonishing ease. Yet never one to accept easy explanations, Brodsky's own commentary on this shift to English prose is contradictory. In one instance, he acknowledges a sense of entertainment (*razvlechenie*);[9] in another, he achieves a "therapeutic comfort";[10] and in a third, gains the vantage point of a "distanced observer."[11]

Whatever the case, it is particularly instructive to observe how the poet in Brodsky speaks through certain rhythmic patterns in his prose writing. Here I will engage in what Jean-Pierre Richard calls a *microlecture*[12] to illustrate this aspect by means of a single anaphoric sentence: "Hence many a broken marriage, hence many a lengthy poem, hence poetry's metaphysical affinities, for every word wants to return to where it came from, if only as an echo, which is the mother of rhyme."[13] The artistic effect of this sentence develops not only from its rhythmic and musical flow, which possesses the metronomic quality of recurrent waves, but also out of an imperceptible metamorphosis from the thematic to metatextual level. Simultaneously, the writer postulates and utilizes the device of repetition within a single sentence. In this sense, this passage is entirely in keeping with Brodsky's aesthetics.

In Brodsky's *Watermark,* rhythm, freed from the rigorous metric pattern that was indispensable for his verse, is engendered not only by the regular recurrence of a word and a phrase but also by an object, a character, or a myth. In this respect, *Watermark* is a remarkable work. A slim volume of 135 pages, which its author thought to be of lesser value because of the stigma he attached to it as a commissioned work,[14] it is, nonetheless, one of his most architectonically conceived and elegantly executed essays. Its rhythm, in its peculiar reverberating variation, constitutes *Watermark*'s most striking feature and explains the essay's particular appeal.[15] Brodsky places the echo at the core of his volume's poetics and uses it to connect his metaphysics, which he evokes through various modes of dissipation. Manifested thus as an echo, repetition possesses the quality of diminishing recurrence. The gradual appearance of a subject—whether it be a woman, an object, or a concept—and the equally slow recession of that subject, followed again by its return, then fading away completely, constitute what I call *Watermark*'s echoism. It also figures largely as the driving force to the volume's negative aesthetics. In fact, this ebb and flow becomes paramount when Brodsky formulates the conception of Venice's "excessive redundancy, of the mirror absorbing the body absorbing the city" (22), which is resolved by its eventual dissolution (25). This assertion can be buttressed by several of *Watermark*'s leitmotivs, which serve as Brodsky's compositional, descriptive, and philosophical devices.

Before I discuss at length these strategies, I would posit *Watermark*'s repetitive organization against Brodsky's near-programmatic essay "In Praise of Boredom" from the volume *On Grief and Reason: Essays*. Although written as both celebration of and admonition against boredom, this commencement address describes the languorous state as resulting from the repetitive nature of time. As such, boredom results from the acceptance of the emptiness of infinity and for this reason alone one should not resist it. Brodsky's recommendation, however, carries with it a caveat. Boredom experienced in a vacuum is wasteful. A more constructive version of the state lies in the realm of art.

Brodsky, the master of regular verse, knows how the recurring elements of rhythm and syntax support the unique semantics of his art. Though recognizing the value repetition plays in his art, he does not faithfully adhere to the Platonic opposition that exists between the copy and the original. His notion of repetition of the original in its copy is based on their differences and the lack of exact mimicking.[16] Echoism, with values of the original fading away, illustrates this best.

From the moment Brodsky arrives in Venice, reiteration in various guises informs the city's imagery. In the harbor, at the very outset of the book, the scent of seaweed, reminiscent of the air of Petersburg, Venice's twin, reminds the traveler who he is.[17] Again, the teeth of his Italian hostess repeat the sparkle in her eyes, which in turn, corresponds to the pleonasm of the silver dust of the stars above. Almost astonishingly, Brodsky brings this iterative concept one step further when the hostess, whom he characterizes as a "sight," redoubles her person, in effect, and takes the form of a woman who is introduced to the author as her sister, only for the sister to disappear completely from the essay.

This repetition, or doubling, carries over into the larger population. Brodsky moves throughout the city as if he were but a seeing eye. This eye, in keeping with his environs, has developed by way of evolution, he fancies, from that of a fish. The citizens of Venice transmogrify into fish as if to multiply the number of fish that swim in the polluted and congested canals. Similarly, the writer-traveler finds in the regular rhythm of the wavelets of Venice's waters a duplicate patterning of the four hundred windows of the buildings on the Piazza di San Marco (*Watermark*, 132). Moreover, the waves, which embody in their ebb and flow a sense of time, return to the narrative in the form of music (96). By the same token, Venice's mazelike canals echo the labyrinth in Knossos. There are numerous mirrors everywhere, including the surface of the water, which "reflects and refracts everything" (83). As though mimicking what the writer's eye beholds, an eerie complexity enters into the narrative which acts as a kind of overlay or counterpart to Venice's confusion of streets, causeways, bridges, and isles. Even the Almighty is involved in this scheme of multiple repetition: because He created us according to His own image (61), we are naturally a duplicate of Himself.

And thus begins a narrative of dazzling wordplay, an inventive and cunning catalogue of doublings, resonances, parallels, and rhythmic recurrences. Brodsky uses his art to shape ingeniously the spirit of Venice, the city of his soul; yet it is a city, he informs us, whose spirit belongs to the world of dying echoes and fading reflections.

At this point, Brodsky, through the piling on of like images—of echoism—advances a concept of representation based on the multidimensional reciprocity of its elements. In other words, all things, animate and inanimate, that make up the universe of Venice participate in a sort of kinship. Their mutual complicity by means of reflection allows one to speak of this phenomenon in terms of a universal empathy which originates in the writer's imagination and his apparent love for the city. To suggest that reflection is the binding element between the phenomenal and noumenal worlds is not to limit our discussion to the spiritual and material unity of this relationship, for it is an intensely intimate and emotional form of correspondence. Intimism, which best exemplifies this, is the practice among painters of selecting as subject matter familiar scenes in cozy interiors. In Brodsky's reversal of this concept, however, intimism is transferred outdoors. There, the sun touches the surfaces of objects with affection, infinity is "twenty meters away" (7), the mist shrouds the city as tightly as a garment; the closeness of things and noumenal reality creates the deceptive impression that everything near is also available or otherwise possible on the "other side." The proximity of the visible world eventually evolves into the chilling vision of an infinite void. That unexpected shift, which illustrates well Brodsky's avoidance of ready-made formulas, takes place at the culminating point of his travelogue: the flight into another dimension occurs within the domestic enclosure of one of Venice's old palaces.

Given that repetition also assumes the form of metatextual observation, according to which "interpretation is tautology" (82), we should turn our attention to the traveler as the interpreting subject in *Watermark*. It is that traveler's gaze that enables the pattern of diminishing repetitions and guarantees the ongoing process of reflection. His eye equals his I's very existence. This equation becomes Brodsky's signature piece in *Watermark*, his exertion of authorial control over the proliferation of reflected images.[18]

Mirrors, natural and manufactured, are Venice's trademark. They enhance the seen-seeing relationship because they turn the narrator's "I" and eye into an object that is seen and made visible. The self is objectified by the reflection in a mirror or on the surface of water, by either someone else's gaze or by one's own eye.[19] The act of seeing oneself does not involve sketching the narrator's facial features, for what he employs in this respect is his use of ellipsis. He willfully omits all the physical (and, supposedly, superfluous) features that combine to create an identifiable portrait of himself. The effect of this erasure on his person is tantamount to the ravages that time will claim later. Only once does the narrator allude to his most striking feature—his red hair—and only because this singular characteristic echoes one of Venice's most esteemed citizens: Antonio Vivaldi.

Sight, a synecdoche for the body, mediates between the environment and the mind. In contrast to thinking or doing, as Maurice Merleau-Ponty describes it in his studies on the phenomenology of perception, the act of seeing for the creative individual precedes all other activities, including the most important, the process of writing. It also coordinates all functions of the body; the eye "stays open when the body is stricken with paralysis or dead" (106). The author's more "practical" eye engenders the seeing/seen relationship through its reflection in the mirror, where the eye is seeing and being seen, a reflection in which the eye is objectifying and is objectified. This reverse action obliterates the subject-object split but still remains open to other processes. The predominantly visual perception sharpens the writer-traveler's awareness of his physicality, of the existence of his body. His is not a disembodied mind meditating on beauty and metaphysics while surrounded by Venetian mirrors. To be sure, as the subject of the seeing/seen relationship, the narrator is also subordinated to the laws of diminishing reflection. The diminution of his presence is a part of his moment of vision.

In a Venetian Guise

Listen closely to the foreigner's footsteps along the deserted, sun-warmed embankment of the Great Venetian Canal.
—Osip Mandelstam on Goethe

In one of Brodsky's better-known essays, "In a Room and a Half," the poet depicts his parents' dwelling in Petersburg. In it, Brodsky, then a young poet, isolates himself from the rest of the small cramped apartment by building a partition of bookshelves and suitcases. These valises prefigure, if only symbolically, the mobility of his life-style after his expulsion from the Soviet Union. Brodsky, who perceived his experience of exile not only in terms of displacement, strives to unravel the meaning behind his temporal existence, which, he hopes, would help him to overcome his sense of otherness. Susan Sontag aptly notes that Brodsky's mental journeys possess a "characteristic premium on speedy assimilation of what there was to know and feel, determination never to be duped, rueful avowals of vulnerability."[20] His numerous travels bespeak this observation in various ways. Whereas his trip to Istanbul can be understood in terms of a (failed) search for the Byzantine roots of Russian Orthodox culture, his visits to other countries—Sweden, Poland, and England, for example—had ceremonial objectives: receiving the Nobel Prize, being granted other prestigious awards and honorary doctorates, or giving lectures and attending conferences. Brodsky's sojourns in Venice, however, took quite a different turn.

Venice is his city of choice, and he intricately links it to Petersburg, where he was born. But Petersburg, in comparison, is not subjected to the rules of negative aesthetics, although it too is a metropolis of canals, waterways, and bridges. Yet, for all its distance, this Baltic city makes its powerful presence felt in *Watermark:* its spirit pervades Venice and determines Brodsky's outlook on almost everything he sees. Though seldom mentioned by name, Petersburg's presence is undeniable, echoing Venice like a twin city, and Venice in turn mirrors certain aspects of

Petersburg. This is not without consequence. Because of the Russian city's legendary power to produce myths, its mythic dimension that emerges in *Watermark* doubles the travelogue's potential. *Watermark* is, indeed, a tale of two cities. The writer-traveler, through a series of associations, recalls the image of Petersburg from the moment of his first arrival to the "sinking city" on the shore of the Adriatic Sea. What further impressions he harbors have their counterpart in the city in the north of Europe. Everything connected with the element of water—the canals, the murky surface of the water, or the characteristic scent of seaweed—awakens his deepest childhood memories.[21] Petersburg reverberates wherever his eye settles. In the two decades that the poet visited Venice, he was also returning to another, more familiar city, a city that he thought he'd abandoned but never really had.

It would seem, then, to be a mere trifle for Brodsky to adapt to a place so close, if not in spirit, then at least in topography, to his native home. But, strangely, he cannot. The garb of a Venetian he wishes to wear fits but poorly because the process of adaptation has an inherent danger, one eloquently presented in Apollinaire's short story "The Disappearance of Honoré Subrac." Subrac, who must adjust in a manner similar to camouflage in nature, loses his distinctive features and becomes wholly assimilated with his environs. The gist of the story, of course, is that Subrac eventually disappears. This we should bear in mind while we peruse the narrator's wishful play at mimicry.

An outsider, "a nameless lodger, a nobody"[22] dressed in a raincoat, visits Venice, his favorite city. His ability to absorb the local culture and tradition greatly varies. One could assimilate to a new country simply by acquiring its language, but for various reasons our traveler never becomes fluent in Italian. His desire for complete acclimatization is wistful and passive. It is a desire for an adaptation which occurs only on the surface and prevents any meaningful influence from seeping in. Inevitably, this process leads to a kind of simulacrum that avoids any actual entrance into Venetian life.

The mechanism of camouflage in nature gives safety to creatures in hostile environments. Likewise, mimicry is "high on the list of every traveller" (4), for it offers a tourist the comfort of anonymity in alien or even hostile surroundings.[23] In Brodsky's Venice, it mainly serves to protect and hide the individual acutely aware of his otherness. Though the concept of mimicry derives from nature, its content in *Watermark* is taken from the realm of culture. And within the realm of culture, mimicry is synonymous with artifice, repetition, and parody. As an example, let us again return to the harbor scene. When for the first time he steps off the overcrowded vaporetto onto the Venetian equivalent of terra firma, his dress becomes a matter of great importance, or at least noteworthy enough that he should remark on it. What he wears is rather outdated, the narrator tells us, consisting of a dark brown, broad-brimmed Borsalino hat and a white London Fog overcoat. In this apparel he hopes to look anonymous, but, in effect, he has outfitted himself with either clothes that he imagines the inhabitants to wear or clothes so extraordinary that they serve as a means of escaping his own persona. The results are unintentionally humorous, and Brodsky shares the joke with us: the fog, prevalent at that time of year, and the color of the environs, reduced to a film noirish shade of gray make him (he fancies) a protagonist of a melodrama. This mimicry, played out through eclectic elements, represents the traveler's rite of passage into the city with which, over the years, he has never ceased to be fascinated.

There also exist imaginary scenes in which the narrator playfully impersonates either a solid Venetian bachelor or a potbellied, married gentleman. It is as though the season, with its wan winter light, welcomes such reveries. Alone, his thoughts turn inward, and once more he conjures his image as if in a plotless movie: "I should be wearing a cloth cap, dark serge jacket, and a white shirt with an open collar" (66), the narrator muses as he strolls alone the Fondamenta Nouva against the extemporaneous "greatest watercolor in the world" (65)—the waterways of Venice. In his fantasies of mimicry, he also employs other details, typical of Italian commonplace aesthetics: the oleograph of the Madonna that decorates his rented room or the chintz curtains on his window. They enhance the verisimilitude of his parodistic arrangements and simultaneously belong to his repertory of mental assimilation. Expressing his desire to connect, to break through the wall of otherness, they reveal the traveler's solitude, which in the insular reality of Venice he feels keenly. As he claims, "no tribe likes strangers and Venetians are very tribal" (61).

Thus Brodsky treats his narrator as the alienated self, whose presence he organizes through a variety of literary devices, such as the double, simulacrum, simile, repetition, allusion, and numerous other forms of reflection. He allows, however, for the self to exist on yet another bodily plane, likening it to a fish that takes the waters of Venice for its natural element. In Brodsky's view, water is the "democratic" leveler that brings the citizens of Venice and tourists together.

The city's domination over the narrator continues, as does his game of mimicry. The impulse to hide oneself in a place shrouded with its own mysteries concurs and competes with an urge to be well dressed. Yet, there is no disparity here, for elegant clothes are indeed a remarkably easy medium of transformation. Why, the narrator wonders, does everybody have to "go ape about shopping and dressing up in Venice" (25)?[24] Elegance, an Italian national trait, in Venice becomes a form of compulsory art, a part of the cityscape and heritage.[25] This penchant to promenade in finery, in effect to masquerade, seems natural for the people of a city with such a long history of carnivals and masked balls, and is not so far removed from his own proclivities—whatever motives he might claim. It is Venice's past glory that draws his attention, and what he does not observe on the shoulders and heads of the casual passersby, he is willing to see on the piazzas themselves: "these streets are like wardrobe racks: all the clothes are of dark, peeling fabric, but the lining is ruby and shimmering gold" (104). Clothes make the man, make the city, he seems to be telling us. An aesthetic imperative abides. In Venice, particularly, there is a natural inclination to parallel the dreamlike beauty around him. Parallel, but not compete. An effort must be made to curb that instinct, for the inferiority of human anatomy in comparison to Venice's visual superiority has to be concealed: "No matter how well endowed, in this city one's body, in my view, should be obscured by cloth, if only because it moves" (24). The simple attempt at shopping for clothes turns into a succession of trials and tribulations in which the shopper-narrator makes wrong decisions and forgets his size, taste, and actual needs. Compulsively stimulated, the need for camouflage entraps an individual in more "precarious" situations than shopping. This lightly treated mimicry is an entrapment in which, by blending entirely with the environs, one should be aware of one's total disappearance, of which the fate of Honoré Subrac—its literary precursor—warns.

Ultimately, all such attempts are ridiculed and short lived, because the skeptical narrator, in search of his reinvented image as a Venetian denizen, simply accepts his old skin. Yet Brodsky's use of these parodic mechanisms is unthinkable without the aesthetic context of negativity.

The type of parody which causes disappearance implies a mechanism of reflection that does not multiply or double an image but progressively negates it. For example, the waters of Venice reflect exteriors, and one surface mirrors another surface, which, in a sequence of maddening multiplications, implies yet more surfaces. Mirrors are endowed with the unlimited potential of creating new reflections, but this unlimitedness is only one of two directions that Brodsky explores. According to the order of negativity which Brodsky creates in this travel essay, infinity is usually engendered by lessening, decreasing, and negating images. But we shall dwell on this mechanism in greater detail in the following chapter.

Luster and Dust

> *Around me are the stars and waters*
> *Worlds mirror'd in the ocean, godlier sight*
> *Then torches glared back by a goudy glass;*
> *And the great element, which is to space*
> *What ocean is to earth, spreads its blue depth.*
> —Lord Byron

The Venice of Brodsky's *Watermark* is an intertextual creation in which the suggestive power of language implies "more than reality can provide" (75). In this sense, the city is an inexact textual echo. Among its many literary predecessors we find Henri de Régnier, Marcel Proust, Thomas Mann, and William Hazlitt. Brodsky is also familiar with the Russian tradition of cultural journeys in Italy as codified by Aleksandr Herzen, Osip Mandelstam, Anna Akhmatova, and others. The visual tradition of Venice itself, which I focus on here, is shaped by the combined efforts of its native sons—the painters Vittore Carpaccio, Giorgione, Titian, Giovanni Antonio Canal—and by those who were not born there and lived for most of their lives outside Venice, the most obvious being J. M. W. Turner.

The luminous colors and sensuous light which soften the city's architectural forms epitomize what is known, at least since Bellini's famous paintings and in its many ensuing reincarnations, as the quintessential Venetian style.[26] But Brodsky's visual evocation of Venice absorbs and synthesizes that centuries-old visual perception of the city in a limited way. This is not to say that Brodsky shapes his vision of the city in a neotraditional manner by slightly reaccentuating the vast icono-graphic repository of Venice. Aware of this more or less fixed heritage, he reacts to it as emphatically as he does to the city itself. But to sustain his own vision he transforms the city's more obvious aspects into a sublime vision. It is a particular creative faculty, as defined by Coleridge that allows him to interpret the phenomenal aspects of Venice as an original noumenal vision.

In terms of the visual tradition that preceded him, the key to Brod-sky's reinvention of the city's representation exists not only in the artists whom he mentions in his narrative but also in those names which he does not invoke. In other words, I propose to discuss Brodsky's mode of visual awareness and its roots in two different, though complementary, perspectives. Of equal importance are what the author allows to surface in the text and what he decides merely to suggest or imply. I would like to illustrate the first method by explicating briefly one of his charac-teristically erudite digressions. In it, he defines the nature of the winter light in the city as "the light of Giorgione and Bellini, not the light of Tiepolo and Tintoretto" (81).[27] The method of invoking painters' names, even if selective, is not always an effective way of indicating the tradition. However, it works in this narrative because Brodsky puts them in the specific context of each of those four artists' styles. Because in Venice, at this particular time of year, the rays of light touch the objects tenderly, the intimacy of the whole phenomenon, as rightly he observes, is closer to Giovanni Bellini's and his student Giorgione's use of light than to the more dramatic and theatrical light used by the later masters, Tiepolo and Tintoretto.

How does Brodsky imply the efforts of other visual artists not di-rectly mentioned in his essay to underscore his own representation of Venice? The Venice stereotyped by visual artists is a city of colors, light, and canals enlivened by the water's luster. The popular image of the Queen of the Adriatic, as it is sometimes pompously called, also includes the carved stones of its architectural monuments and other features of the city, including gondolas and carnival scenes. We owe one of the oldest schematized representations of the Venetian *vedute* to Giovanni Antonio Canal's copious paintings, etchings, and drawings. In fact, we all, sooner or later, are introduced to this popular version of Venice. Brodsky becomes familiar with the city through equally diverse sources. Whether they are cheap memorabilia or high-brow artifacts,[28] they prompt him to see the original, to compare the perceptual canon to reality. With the exception of his first visit there, during which the need to acclimatize himself to his surroundings briefly prevails over his own sensitivity, the writer forges—under the city's spell—his own vision of Venice.

To discuss this, let us first look at the work of another visual artist, who does not necessarily exploit the existing repertory of images and clichés which have immortalized Venice in our cultural memory. I have in mind John Ruskin's *The Stones of Venice,* a collection of essays that made its author's international reputation. Richly illustrated by Ruskin himself, the book documents the city's many architectural monuments. Brodsky shares with him the same fascination for the city's stones but limits himself to a few selected architectural masterpieces. Ruskin's Venice is a tangible and solid architectonic construct. Finely rendered and exquisitely colored, his drawings evoke the Venice of older architectural styles. Ruskin, obsessed with the surfaces of the city's buildings, scrupulously records their details and types of ornamentation, whether conceived in sculpture, mosaics, or frescoes. To contrast the gray walls of northern European architecture with the penchant for color demonstrated in Venice—the gesture which sets him even farther apart from Brodsky—he glorifies the rich hues of green, porphyry, azure, and gold decorating its palaces and churches.[29] This color-oriented aesthetics subordinates the buildings' inner structure to the chromatic principles of their surfaces.[30]

The styles which Ruskin considers the purest samples of Venetian architecture are Byzantine and Gothic. Everything built afterward, with a few exceptions in the early Renaissance buildings, demonstrates a growing decay of taste. He ascribes the rise and fall of Venetian architecture to spiritual forces rather than to the decline of the republic's political and economic might. *The Stones of Venice* is the fruit of a learned person who engages all his intellectual energy and artistic skills in documenting and describing, measuring and drawing the city's landmarks. The moral flavor of his book on Venetian monuments is due, partly, to his application of the ideas he had previously elaborated on in *The Seven Lamps of Architecture.* As such, Ruskin's *The Stones of Venice* was an enormously influential book which turned the Venice of his era into an international center for artists and travelers.

During Ruskin's stay in Venice, the city's look was closer to that of the Republic of Venice.[31] Yet Ruskin the purist avoided everything that was built after the sixteenth century. Since then, the eclectic buildings of the late nineteenth century and, in particular, the modernist designs of the twentieth century have changed the city's panorama. Critical of their negative effect on the city's skyline, Brodsky, in a spirit similar to Ruskin's, has his own theory of the rise and fall of the Venetian splendor. He enthusiastically favors the oldest buildings, constructed in the fifteenth and sixteenth centuries, even those not built by famous architects.[32] In fact, Brodsky, quite unimpressed by the most influential figures in Western architecture, mentions work by the architects Mauro Coducci and Pietro Lombardo of Toscany but does not include in his canon the exquisite High Renaissance churches San Giorgio Maggiore and Il Redentore, built later in Venice by Palladio. In the same manner, another High Renaissance masterpiece, Sansovino's Zecca (Mint), appears on the pages of *Watermark* only indirectly.[33]

With the same disdain expressed by Prince Charles in his well-advertised war on architectural modernism, Brodsky attacks the contemporary architects and their modernist designs.[34] One notable exception is the Stazione Termini (Venice's railroad station), with its "rectangular splendor of neon and urbanity" (*Watermark,* 8)—though this tolerance may have more to do with his traveler's instinct than with any less dogmatic and exclusive approach toward modernist buildings.[35] For the Russian writer, the simplicity of modernist architecture, exemplified by "the concrete crate of the Bauer Grunwald Hotel" (130), belongs to the same category as the overly ornate older structures, such as the Church of Saint Moise. Both represent bad taste, and their heavy facades, whether complicated by ornament or not, do not comply to the local tradition of building light and delicate structures, probably best exemplified by the Doge's Palace and Ca' d'Oro.[36]

Venice's skyline, composed of brick and stone churches, palaces, and hospitals, represents only one, but certainly the most tangible and concrete, of the visual elements that contribute to Brodsky's representation. The reader is usually made privy to this treasured substance of the city in quick dynamic flashes. Brodsky's dedicated *flâneur* does not favor any steady point of view, say, a window in his hotel room, for his contemplation. Instead, the city reveals itself in instantaneous images while he is walking, occasionally, getting lost in its winding streets and *piazzette*. Steering himself away from the main passages of the city and its glamorous and popular monuments, his eye discovers its less-traveled nooks and crannies.

In Brodsky's Venice, the city's texture of crumbling stones is also subservient to forces besides pollution and floods. He employs light along with a limited range of colors to render the negating effect of the fog on the look of the city as well as to emphasize its ephemerality. The mysterious and transitory effect with which the mist envelops the city was successfully depicted by J. M. W. Turner and James McNeill Whistler. Despite the stylistic differences between the two painters, both men emphasize the city's rich palette and soft light in a manner reminiscent of the tradition established in the early-Renaissance Venetian school of painting. But it is the groundbreaking representation of the city's transitory modes as captured by Whistler in his monochromatic etchings that justifies a comparison with Brodsky's vision.

In 1879, Whistler arrived in Venice and stayed there for over a year.[37] He went with the specific objective of executing twelve etchings commissioned by the Fine Art Society in London. While in Venice, he rarely worked in oils; instead he made copious pastels and etchings. By avoiding a contour in those etchings, he developed a suggestive line in which he eloquently hinted (rather than depicted) the nocturnal aura enveloping distant buildings. Intimately evoked bridges and passageways, mysterious lagoons and palaces emerge as specters in the city caught between the seemingly infinite sky and sea. A nuanced gradation of black-and-white tones, accentuated with brown, adds to Whistler's captivating *Nocturnes* and *Nocturne: Palaces*. His experimentation with the impressionistic effect of his technique further contributes to the success of his two sets of Venetian etchings.[38] On the basis of what William Sickert defines as "a feast of frail and dainty sketches on copper,"[39] a poetic testimony to Venice's hidden life was founded.

How can we now find common ground between Brodsky's and Whistler's respective visions? Not only separated by time and informed by different cultures but also working in different media, these artists seem to be unlikely subjects for comparisons.[40] On the surface, only the fact of their belonging to the colony of expatriate artists who worked in

Venice and thematized this city in their works justifies such an endeavor. Yet their perception of Venice and the thoughtful manner in which they gradually eschew its reality make their work closer in spirit than one might assume. Whistler opens his finite etchings of Venice toward infinity, and Brodsky goes a step further and opens his creation of Venice to both infinity and the void. Thus, it is the metaphysical affinity, an affinity of the essence of their respective visions, that warrants the comparison.

One could point out further similarities. They both share with Ruskin a sensitivity to the oldest stones of Venice and with Turner a fascination with the air of Venice. Both glorify its waters. Both work in a limited palette of black and white with little exception. Whistler changes the murky air of his Venice by inserting an unexpected source of light.[41] Likewise, Brodsky illuminates the atmosphere by describing the varying degrees of the city's light in his travelogue.

This gentle working of the light proves indispensable for Brodsky's metaphysical vision of Venice. The winter light is without warmth. Although it does not soften the buildings' rigid contours, it activates the city's outward appearance. In winter, the light puts the city in motion, awakens its frozen appearance, and energizes its inhabitants. Its main purpose is simple but fundamental: to bring objects—engulfed by darkness—back to the realm of the visible, to shape them in a more pronounced way, to make them entirely present to one's sight. As such, the winter light of Venice has yet another duty, as it makes the boundary between the visible and invisible fluid.

The reduction of light causes a decrease in the colors' intensity. This is partly due to the season, for "winter is low in colors" (23), and partly due to Petersburg's looming presence. However, on sunny days the sky is pure blue. And there is another source of chromatic diversion in Brodsky's image of the city, brought to Venice by its buildings' red brick facades. Yet all these touches of color do not include such bright hues as yellow, green, and orange. Through this rather consistent chromatic elimination, Venice takes on the appearance of a northern European city.

Sometimes the water in the canals fluctuates between blue, gray, and brown, though usually it reveals its pitch-black depth. Black, in fact, is one of the predominant colors of the city in Brodsky's essay, where "pitch black water at night rivals the firmament" (97). This blackness, fused with the whiteness of ice and snow, produces various shades of gray. In its tricolor composition, Venice as pictorial representation belongs to the print-making branch of artistry. Or, to find a medium in sync with Brodsky's line of work, to the art of writing with black ink on white paper, to literature (40).

The departure from an established painterly tradition reveals a different image of the city, pervaded by the aura of extremes. Simplifying its external side, the author directs our attention to the city's other, less-visible existence. The schematization of its phenomenal aspects, as represented by its chromatic arrangement, prepares space for the anti-universe of Venice. Acknowledging the spiritual and material unity of the universe, Brodsky depicts this anti-city as an infinite space where all forms are negated, as a creation close to an abstract painting. One further step toward this vision is through such transitory aspects of the city as its famous *nebbia*. If the light makes things visible, the fog conceals them, and, in the case of this particularly dense Venetian fog called *nebbia*, the concealment is perfect. This variety of fog obliterates "not only reflections but everything that has a shape: buildings, people, colonnades, bridges, statues. . . . The fog is thick, blinding, and immobile" (59). Fog, a formless matter, engulfs every form. As Brodsky's essay makes clear, *nebbia* does not affect the city in the same manner as snow does, for snow does not obliterate forms entirely: snow is not an active formlessness but an intervention of nature that reshapes objects and transforms the visible world into an overall white picture.

In the struggle between light and fog, Brodsky demonstrates how the elements determine the visual appearance of the city. The opposition between thingness (*veshchnost'*), sanctioned by the clarity of light, and eternity (*vechnost'*) as envisioned in Brodsky's poetry develops in this narrative into a tension between thingness and nothingness, quite analogous to Herbert's metaphysics. Time, however, does not necessarily oppose eternity, but its endless duration finds its continuity in eternity. Dust, the tangible and visible expression of time, bridges both these dimensions. And there is plenty of dust in Venice. The luster of her encrusted architecture and the sheen of her mirrors disappear under a dusty patina. Dust's patient work—as envisioned in the description in one of the Venetian interiors—discolors objects and makes them so brittle and weak that they eventually disintegrate. As if in an art nouveau painting, Venice exists on the surface of reflections, luster, and dust. Underneath, however, exists a Venice of hidden depth.

Una Lacrima

What makes Brodsky's strategies of disappearance complete is his use of the image of a tear, for a teardrop is instantaneous and short lived. With this image, Brodsky elegiacally speaks to the reader about the sorrows of parting with Venice. Shedding tears—a quintessentially Romantic aesthetic response—makes a brief comeback in this melancholy book.

The Romantics in general were fond of showing their intense emotions and tears were the favorite means to exteriorize them. Both men and women of the first half of the nineteenth century threw flowers, cried, and frequently fainted. This whole repertory expressed not just grief but also elation. As a standard aesthetic response it was performed in public; art galleries, the theater, and the opera were eminently appropriate spaces for weeping, crying, and passing out. The public eye of the twentieth century, in comparison, remains exceptionally dry. Now, accepted behavioral patterns reflect a wariness of exultation and, even more so, skepticism about the theatricality associated with such emotional outbursts.[42] Publicly shed tears are restricted to events of tragic proportions, such as funerals, and if they are stimulated at all by the artistic, it is usually through the devotional figurines of weeping Madonnas.

Tears as an aesthetic response have no better chance on the contemporary literary stage. In *Watermark,* their indiscriminate streams having run dry since Romanticism, are replaced by a single tear. Here, the sovereign pearllike drop symbolizes Brodsky's premonition of parting with Venice. This single tear, as salty as the Adriatic sea, represents the sad element of water.[43] That is how the theme of his arrival in Venice, as he construed it, is balanced by the theme of departure. And yet it does not stand only for a projection of grief but is an objective visualization of the invaluable worth of Venice in the narrator's eyes: it is "an acknowledgment of the retina's, as well as the tear's, failure to retain beauty" (109). The departure from Venice has, as the narrator phrases it, an optical character.

Very few books venerate cities of note in the absolute sense that is expressed in *Watermark.* In the elegiac tone so distinctive in Brodsky's poetry, the city, likened to a loved one, is wept over and bidden good-bye: "a disappearance of the beloved, especially a gradual one, causes grief no matter who, and for what peripatetic reason, is actually in motion" (110). Thus, the strategies of disappearance play a prominent role in Brodsky's representation of the city. In fact, in *Watermark* dissipation equals representation.

7

Empty Mirror

I am going to seek a great Perhaps.
—François Rabelais's attributed last words

If one is not fearful of the unfolded abyss into which one can irrevocably fall—
fall into oneself and fly forever in the black precipice—the hole becomes a cor-
ridor. The corridor of the spirit—our inner path.
—Andrey Bely

Joseph Brodsky, described by David Bethea as the first truly metaphysical poet of Russia,[1] undertakes in *Watermark* to address a number of
most complex metaphysical notions, not least of which is the issue of
God. Brodsky finds the proof of God's existence in the simple fact that
we do not know when we will die; therefore it follows that we do not
entirely control our life and, in particular, the way we leave it. This
incontrovertible moment, according to Brodsky, is decided by a higher
force, by an intervening God. Equally absorbed by another pivotal, and
vigorously discussed, issue of metaphysics, Brodsky's imagination explores what Rabelais skeptically called a "great Perhaps," that is, the

question of the afterlife and what possible form it takes. In an era when the relationship between body and mind is most relevant to philosophical inquiries, the narrator's investigation into the nature of death and the hereafter seems all the more pertinent. But it is Brodsky's own confrontation with this "great Perhaps" as it appears to him in Venice that makes the investigation truly poignant. In it, he gives an account of his tour of an old Venetian palace, an account which he organizes according to a clear representational scheme. In this narrative, which is manipulated through a series of skillfully punctuated shifts, the author changes the nature of the tour from its initial design as a "house tour" to a peregrination into the underworld, and finally, to a journey before the beginning of time.

The representation of the afterlife in *Watermark* is related to Brodsky's repeated poetic gesture of confronting death. Beginning with his early elegy "Stikhi na smert' T. S. Eliota" ("Verses on T. S. Eliot's Death"), death resonates throughout Brodsky's writing with particular force. The extent to which Brodsky contemplates his losses can only be compared to Rainer Maria Rilke's intense preoccupation with the condition of humans as mortal beings. Brodsky is concerned with this subject in his analytical writing as well. He chooses in his essay "Footnote to a Poem" to examine Marina Tsvetayeva's poem "Novogodnee" ("New Year's Greetings"), which she wrote immediately after receiving news of Rilke's death. Even more telling from the perspective of *Watermark* is the fact that Brodsky interprets "Orpheus. Eurydice. Hermes"— Rilke's daring poetic attempt at evoking the perspective of one who has died—in his essay "Ninety Years Later." Here, Eurydice, purified by her complete obliviousness to all earthly matters, represents the individual afterlife in terms of estrangement of the soul. The reasons for the evocation of death in Tsvetayeva's and Rilke's poems vary: Tsvetayeva's intense cry evokes death only in her poem's circumstantial aspects, although it is the death of a friend and one of this century's greatest poets, whereas Rilke, on the other hand, targets the realm of the dead as if in an attempt to unveil its hidden mystery. His preoccupation is thematic. What connects these two poets in their inquiry into the nature of death is an underlying belief in the invincibility of the soul.

For Brodsky, the finality of our existence represents both the circumstantial and the thematic aspects of his obituaries-reminiscences dedicated to his late friends. Why does Brodsky engage in a dialogue with their spirits? To recall their presence and reenact the past? To resist oblivion? Written to "please the shadow," as he puts it on one occasion,[2] of his late poet-friends, they demonstrate his austere grief and his lasting feelings of gratitude and admiration toward such members of his "extended family" as W. H. Auden and Stephen Spender.[3] Reflected in the poet's memory, these lasting shades of memory resist death because the brotherhood of the dead and the living, as Gabriel Marcel believes, counterbalances death.

But how long is a poet remembered? Horace believes that eternity is guaranteed by his work, or, to use modern rhetoric, his word. In *Watermark*, Brodsky follows Horace in his belief that the metaphor (77), hence the poetic Word, provides continuity. Yet he qualifies this continuity because the Word, once uttered, becomes independent and even alienated from its creator. We can assume, moreover, that the death of a poet represents a special case for Brodsky as a Russian poet. It stems from the Russian poetic practice initiated by V. A. Ozerov, and mastered by M. Y. Lermontov in his "Death of a Poet," written shortly after Pushkin's death. Within this tradition, verses on the death of another poet continue to bind the past with the present and strengthen the bond between the dead and the living poets. Much in the same spirit, Gerald Janacek considers Brodsky's "Stikhi na smert' T. S. Eliota" not just an expression of admiration for Eliot but also part of a "paradigm of admiration for all the poets."[4] Yet in *Watermark*, Brodsky goes beyond his mourning for the late poets. In the essay's revelatory moment his narrator both confronts and is confronted by the dehumanized antiworld.

An attempt to overcome the fundamental cognitive limitation which death presents to human knowledge is best expressed in the subversive desire of those who peregrinate to the realm of the dead. Orpheus, Homer, Virgil, and Dante—poets who evoked imaginary journeys to the underworld—make a special case where the literal meaning of their excursions and their literary craft stand apart. Life after death, whether it is divided on an ethical basis into the Inferno, Purgatory, and Paradise, or is unified in the form of Hades, challenges Brodsky's—the metaphysical poet's—imagination and his visionary potential. How to make a compelling description or, at least, an approximation of the "other shore" that is not otherwise available to our direct experience?

In *Watermark*, Brodsky's treatment of the archetypal theme of *katabasis*, the journey to the underworld, is a logical continuation of his representation of Venice, of the vanishing of the city's image. This Venetian version of afterlife harks back to his earlier travel essay "Flight from Byzantium." In his reading of this essay, Tomas Venclova, who contextualizes the text within the Russian tradition of travel writing, describes how Brodsky creates the vision of eternity as interwoven with the image of contemporary Istanbul.[5] The afterlife envisioned in *Watermark* gains a similar effect of unreal reality: the tour Brodsky takes through an old Venetian palace and the unfolding of his vision are tightly fused to create one unified image. This evolving image, as we shall later see, is a part of his probing of the modernist concept of negativity.

The archetypal tendency to see the netherworld as an organized space, with a rigid order that distinctly opposes chaos, is shared by cultures, religions, and mystical insights throughout the ages. Dante envisions the space of the netherworld in *The Divine Comedy,* accessible to him as a guided journey, in terms of a system of regular circles. On the other hand, Emanuel Swedenborg conceives it as a city very much like other cities in this world, and one of his followers, Oscar de Lubicz Milosz, believes that the space of the afterlife is shaped entirely in accordance with reality, with all the implications that follow. In his vision of the afterlife, Brodsky combines reality with the mythological and literary heritage, evoking an orderly spatial arrangement of the netherworld. Characteristically, Brodsky finds the afterlife in one of Venice's historical buildings, conceived within a system of "infinite halls and chambers" (76). This notion of eternity confined to a limited space has precedents in Russian literary tradition, of which the most persuasive is the bathhouse full of spiders that Dostoyevsky envisioned in *Crime and Punishment.*[6]

Brodsky ties his notion of the afterlife to other traditions as well. Like Dante, who wanders in the underworld,[7] Brodsky positions his revelatory experience within a passage, which I understand as both the physical act of moving through space and the mental meanderings his pace inspires. His pathway functions also as an intertextual passage from one literary allusion to another, all of which implement a transfiguring shift from reality to a metaphysical postulate. At the end of his passageway through the palace, he registers a moment of bleak revelation. It is this singular instance of insight that I will examine within the dynamics of the passageway.

In the case of Herbert's and Zagajewski's essays, I interconnect their epiphanies with the multilayered aesthetics of movement. This methodology of motion defines, too, the numerous winter pilgrimages which Brodsky faithfully had taken to Venice, his habit of strolling the city, crowned by the dark illumination which occurred to him during the palace tour. Thus I couple Brodsky's expansive vision with the dynamic rhythm of his pace. As demonstrated by Bidney, patterns of epiphanic instances are not only richly individualized,[8] but also can be understood as rhythmic and energy-projecting entities. In other words, what Brodsky the epiphanist presents in *Watermark* is an elemental revelation intricately linked with a progressive structure.

A Study in Porphyry

Towards what abyss is it in progress?
—William Wordsworth

The manner in which Brodsky enhances the metaphysical portrayal of the city of Venice prepares the ground for his revelatory experience. This revelation develops logically from the encroachments of the anti-world and from the diminishing echo-based parallelisms which are his main methods of evoking Venice's ontological negativity. To this end, Brodsky also employs the image of the city as a labyrinth. He compounds its complexity by the depiction of another, smaller labyrinthine system— the old palazzo's interior.

In the social sense, the familiar Venice the traveler visits is mostly the "outer" city inhabited by American expatriates: intellectuals and artists. The city's heart, with its old local families and their historical dwellings, remains, with one exception, inaccessible to him. Access into the "Venetian inner sanctum" (48) is not easy to gain, and Brodsky's account of the house tour (given by its owner) and what transpires from it derives, at least partly, from his expectations as an outsider.[9]

First, the narrator evokes the spatial passage through a splendid old palace which has been largely uninhabited for generations—more exactly, for three centuries—due to prolonged legal claims and suits made by "several branches of a family that had given the world a couple of Venetian admirals" (48). When the fate of this dark labyrinthine structure is finally decided, a reception is given to celebrate the momentous occasion. At this point, the narrator, in a party of three, is given a tour.

Its account begins as an excursion to the palace's oldest parts, first to its eighteenth-century rooms and later to its sixteenth-century chambers. From the start, the unfamiliar, eerie territory causes a vague sense of doubt and uncertainty that dominates the visitor's mind. The group, guided by the new owner, first enters a long gallery. The dim light makes visible frescoes swarming with putti on the convex ceiling,[10] while on the walls are discernible monumental oil canvases alternating with marble sculptures, which are smaller in scale, hardly even visible. The color of the paintings, crucial for the representation of the interior, vacillates from dark brown to wine red, but porphyry is the hue that prevails. Brodsky limits his ekphrasis to the color and size of the works of art. The paintings' subject matter and the names of their creators remain uncertain to the visitors, who do not venture to ask questions. In such confusing circumstances, voice and sound seem inappropriate, for the stillness reigning here is far from the variety associated with hushed voices in museums. The members of the group, rather, are as mute as fish, capacity for speech having been left behind in the palace's twentieth-century quarters.

Envisioned as a transitory path, what originates as a regular house tour gains traits of a quintessentially aporetic journey, if we bear in mind that the word *a-poros,* means both a passage and doubt. It is indeed an aporetic path through unknown territory which clarifies only the role of the owner as an initiating guide.[11] The strange aura of this empty place, with its dim light and stillness, enhanced by its dusky canvases and an elongated passage, contribute only partly to its qualification as "a mine of heavy porphyry in a state of abandonment, in a state of perpetual evening, with oils obscuring its ores; the silence here was truly geological" (51). The very nature of this airless space—as evoking the underworld—would remain enigmatic, if it were not for its pretext.

To enter the intertextual meanderings of this passage, I shall quote first the opening strophe from Rilke's "Orpheus. Eurydice. Hermes," a poem which begins with the following description of the underworld:

> That was the strange unfathomed mine of souls.
> And they, like silent veins of silver ore,
> were winding through its darkness. Between roots
> welled up the blood that flows on to mankind,
> like blocks of heavy porphyry in the darkness.[12]

Brodsky's admiration for the poem notwithstanding, the textual parallels existing between his and Rilke's descriptions clarify the Russian poet's strategy in representing the palace's hidden character. Without explicitly disclosing to the reader the function of this strange place, Brodsky subtly suggests its eschatological nature by building a textual similarity to one of Rilke's better-known poems. What this gesture suggests exactly is the gallery's function: perceived as a subterranean passageway, it is an entrance leading to another realm. It now becomes necessary to point out the essentially nonhomogeneous nature of the surroundings: despite the figures of putti, at this stage of the tour, there are no allusions to Christian symbolism, the fact reinforced by hints of Rilke's Greek underworld. Contrary to the widespread notion that Brodsky's metaphysics is Christian, the other universe unfolding before his eyes is everything—Rilkean, Greek, pagan, pre-Christian— but solely Christian. The function of the palace as representing the netherworld, qualified as neither a *Paradiso* nor an *Inferno,* thereby is given also an ancient lineage, which combined with its Russian counterpart of the afterlife as a confined space, makes for a heterogeneous whole.

As Brodsky's description evolves from the visible aspects of the palace's reality and its literary tradition, another element of its representation comes into play: the polysemous quality of the paintings, engendered by the lack of light. The walls in the subwaylike space are decorated with long-forgotten paintings of obscure origin and subject matter (hence the direct allusion to Rilke's pretext: "oils obscuring ores"). As an introductory phase to the journey, the dark red hue of porphyry on the canvases—the color of wine and blood—still symbolizes some form of life. It is significant that the visitor's tortuous and torturous passage leading toward his moment of revelation is facilitated by works of art. Thus Brodsky's peregrination through the underworld is also ekphrastic.

The unquestionable appeal of Rilke's poem attracts Brodsky's attention on two different occasions: he first retextualizes its imagery in *Watermark* and again later, in the analysis offered in his essay "Ninety Years Later." In the latter essay, Brodsky compares Rilke's image of the netherworld as an underground system of halls and passageways specifically to the ancient Cappadocian caves. Out of this textual geology Brodsky creates the genealogy of his vision in *Watermark.*

A Study in Yellow

*The cradle rocks above an abyss, and common sense tells us that
our existence is but a brief crack of light between two eternities
of darkness.*
—Vladimir Nabokov

Negating any hint of life, the next phase of the haunting passageway
brings an unexpected shift into another dimension. The passage changes
from evoking the posthumous eternity into another form of eternity
which precedes life, into what Nabokov calls the "prenatal abyss."[13]
Brodsky characterizes this stage of the palace tour as yet another set of
chambers, of a dusty yellow color. This portion of the passageway stands
for lifelessness; essentially, it represents a still life. Painted by Brodsky in a
pale yellow hue that defines a seemingly infinite panorama of abandoned
chambers, it symbolizes the effect of negativity. The dearth of bright
color and the reduction of light, the absence of sound and human
presence, and, finally, the lack of exit suggested by the infinite perspective through the enfilade—all these elements transform the yellow and
dusty passage into an unreal interior. Along the way, the visitor observes
a rather curious negation of objects: he perceives the shape of furniture
and other paraphernalia in terms of their "dissipation back into time"
(54). At this juncture, the passage which leads to the end of time is
transformed into a passage to the beginning of time.

   The dust that covers this interior, modeled after a still life, is a
projection of time onto a visible sustenance—its "flesh," as Brodsky,
quoting himself, says. In a self-parodic gesture, he inserts here a phrase
from his poem "Nature Morte," and thus refers to a pictorial genre that
underscores his eye's journey. Dust, so close to ash, suggests the inevitable decay of matter, as foretold in the well-known biblical phrase "ashes
to ashes, dust to dust." In general, its presence affects an object's surface by giving it a deceptively unified appearance, causing its discoloration. Brodsky depicts the dusty interior's quiet and secluded existence in terms of its disintegrating retreat from life whose direction
moves backward in time to the origin of the matter: "They were shedding, those curtains, and some of their folds exposed broad, bald,
threadbare patches, as though the fabric felt it had come full circle and

was now reverting to its pre-loom state" (53–54). The withdrawal of all forms and objects in this interior into a time existing before humanity's creative effort and labor prepares the effect of a void. The peculiarity of this interior lies in the vacillation between its half-natural and half-cultural status and results from the absence of human beings. Striving to achieve the point of view of the object, an approach which would question the traditional Cartesian subject-object split,[14] Brodsky takes this daring representational task to its extreme. His design is to evoke the glimpse of the objects' preexistence, of the dark moment of their prenatal abyss.

The discoloration of the interior brings to mind an earlier intriguing detail—the pale yellow color of the palace owner's "parchment" skin, which signals his illness.[15] His yellowish pallor matches his surroundings and thus gives him the appearance of someone partly claimed by the afterlife. In this respect, the Italian owner-guide, though not yet a ghostly inhabitant of the underworld, is framed by death and shares an ontological ambiguity with his inherited abode.[16]

Let us now recall that the pale yellow and dark porphyry combined with occasional accents of marble white in the passage correspond to more than Brodsky's subdued palette as a governing visual principle of Venice. Again, the textual passage leads to his analysis of "Orpheus. Eurydice. Hermes" in "Ninety Years Later," where he comments on the same palette as employed by Rilke. He connects the German poet's painterly ideas directly to the art of his time to the vaguely defined artistic trends at the turn of the century. Brodsky's attribution of Rilke's sense of color to the "Worpswede-soft bed of Northern expressionism . . . wrinkled by the pre-Raphaelite-cum-Art-Nouveau aesthetic idiom of the turn of the century"[17] is modified elsewhere in his essay by mention of the influence of Odilon Redon and Edvard Munch. Though he considers Rilke's emphasis on color "substantial" and quite original ("Rilke's own"), at the same time he reduces the colors themselves to inspirations derived from Clare Westhof's circle or from other artistic movements of the time. Whether he rightly ascribes Rilke's "dated aesthetic idiom" (389) to his wife's friends at Worpswede or to other influences is not relevant here (though the association with Redon is not without substance). The accuracy of Brodsky's painterly notions concerning Rilke's visual awareness is overshadowed by another aspect of his critique.[18] One can trace here a certain nonchalance toward what was fashionable art in Rilke's time as well as toward the composite painterly effect the German poet creates in this poem.

Why then does the same author first retextualize the spatial and coloristic vision of Rilke's version of the underworld in his travelogue and minimize its value a few years later, in his essay? These contradictory gestures of acceptance and disapproval might have been a result of two different approaches undertaken by him. The point of view assumed in *Watermark* is that of the creative persona of the writer, whereas the other view is that of a critic and expert. This clear division of roles is analogous to Pieter Bruegel the Elder's drawing *The Artist and the Connoisseur* (Vienna, Albertina), which represents an artist intensely focused on his project while the ironically smiling connoisseur looks from behind the painter's shoulder at the canvas. The artist has disheveled hair, while the connoisseur wears eyeglasses, which symbolize here both *scientia* and a rationalized distance. Bruegel captured the two perspectives, which we similarly find in Brodsky's changing evaluation of Rilke's palette.

Yet another possible explanation lies in Brodsky's manipulation of the temporal context which surrounds Rilke's poem. Brodsky demonstrates that the visual evocation of the underworld was an inherent part of Rilke's Zeitgeist, and therefore, it happened to be an act of passive absorption of ideas that circulated in his milieu. Rilke's position hence reflects neither critical distance nor an intellectual effort to select his own tone from the visual currency of the fin-de-siècle. When Brodsky almost ninety years later reworks this image in his travelogue, he creates a different situation. By selecting and retextualizing this particular "dated" imagery, he claims it as his own visual legacy. Artistic tradition thus cannot be employed passively. To activate such a legacy, Clare Cavanagh observes, one employs the dialectics of "creative appropriation and inventive disruption."[19] Applying this rhythm to Brodsky's stage design of the netherworld, we find this appropriation in the mine-like scenery and in the synthetic coloration of the passageway. His disruptive shift to a completely different line of modernist tradition, however, occurs later.

Though the initial doubt regarding the palace's unreal aspect is removed, a certain degree of the representational ambiguity remains. Brodsky redefines the palace's interior by following the principle of a "sensory unreality." This term, fashioned by Hugo Friedrich in his influential study of modernist lyrics,[20] signifies a creative mechanism according to which the tangible (skin, fabric, dust) and sensuous, even obviously real aspects of imagery participate in creating the opposite effect of nonreality. All these aspects, which Brodsky combines with many other intertextual and visual sources, form a composition which transforms reality in order to negate it.

A few lines later, Brodsky shifts to another line of modernist visual tradition, to the rejection of objects by abstract painters. At this final stage of his journey, he returns to his initial concept of the netherworld as "infinite halls and chambers" and unites this concept with quite diverse, if not contradictory, Christian and pre-Christian sources. Thereby the palace in its function as the netherworld is given a further heterogeneous lineage. Any doubt regarding the figurative role of the palace ceases to exist: the continuity of spiritual existence in the imagined afterlife, in the afterlife that crosses a domestic space, is enhanced.

A Study in Black

> For instance, an open window at night; a room with no one inside; a night made of absence and inquiry; no furniture; at most a hint of indefinite sideboards, with a dying mirror in the background.
> —Stéphane Mallarmé to Henri Cazalis

> For now we see through a glass, darkly, but then face to face.
> —1 Corinthians 13:12

We know now that Brodsky's vision of Venice is not simply limited to Thomas Mann's notion of the city as one permeated by death. Rather, the manner in which the writer extends the horizons of his travelogue beyond this tradition is most visible in the final stage of his passageway through a series of chambers. Here, the narrator-visitor is eventually granted his single revelatory experience. This last part of the tunnellike succession of rooms, decorated with "mostly rectangular" mirrors (54), causes an increasing sensation of disappearance. The narrator describes a strange self-discovery unfolding in front of his eyes: "I saw myself in those frames less and less, getting back more

and more darkness" (55). His vanishing, a part of Brodsky's wider strategy of echoism, is complete at the point when he takes a step toward "a
largish, three-by-four-foot gilded rectangle," and instead of himself sees
"pitch-black nothing" (55).[21] The combination of vision and movement, of the revelatory instant and motion, constitute the core of his
dark illumination.

Brodsky as an epiphanist does not elaborate on the content of this
revelation but paints it in a few broad strokes. The mirror, the vehicle of
the epiphany, endowed with nearly magic properties, absorbs the reflection and causes a complete erasure of the speaker's portrait. The positive side of the mirror and its reflection lessen, and their negative side
thereby increases. Perfectly synchronized with the final negation of the
self and his surroundings, the revelation of nothingness in the mirror
speaks of human fear. What it implies is a deletion of the speaker in
terms of his future death.[22]

Before the initiate's voyage is over, he reaches the edge of the black
abysmal mirror but refuses to be seduced by its alluring emptiness.
Apparently, the impulse to merge into the eerie void is not a part of his
mental makeup, and he is neither subjected to Empedocles's complex,
which urges one to jump into the black chasm, nor inclined to follow
Henri de Régnier's epic foray into the other side of the mirror. The fact
that the visitor resists crossing the boundary drawn precisely along the
line of the amalgam, despite the intensity of the experience and the
mirror's hunting allure, may also speak of the triumphant life forces in
him.[23] He withdraws from further penetration of the black abyss because he cannot forsake his identification with the side on which things
exist. Life for him must go on.

Although it takes only one step toward the black rectangle of a
mirror for the narrator's vision to occur, anticipation and suspension
built up to this moment through the aporia as the passage and the aporia
of the mind's doubt and fear. The negation of the narrator's reflection—
his portrait by subtraction embodied in the mirror—stands for a crucial
moment in the journey of his eye. With the realization of his own
potential nonexistence, the narrator's journey exceeds the status of an
eschatological pilgrimage. This is for him the truth of the void perceived
in a split second in the black mirror, which nullifies the much gentler
notion of the netherworld as a progressive system of corridors and
chambers—the netherworld as architectural continuity.

There are further dissimilarities to the other literary forays into the hereafter. "In Virgil and Homer the motive for the underworld journey is to learn the future, the kind of knowledge ordinarily closed to mankind," writes Northrop Frye.[24] As we know, this motive is not part of the visitor's design. Rather, he is illuminated unexpectedly, satisfied with the epiphanic vision of nothingness which he does not even wish to explore at length. The sublime void, glimpsed in the mirror, can be an eschatological alternative to dread, since it does not promise the soul's survival in the afterlife. And what if indeed the void awaits him? Such a supposition brings to mind certain ontologically negative aspects of the experience which transcend this revelation as illuminating the future of the single individual. Indeed, the vision in the looking glass acquires the all-encompassing totality, because, on the one hand, it informs the visitor of both the prenatal and the posthumous abysses, and on the other, it divines a separate concept of the absolute nothingness prior to the creation of the universe.

Herein lies the reason for the complex composition of Brodsky's metaphysics. A traditional Christian framework would not allow the writer to speculate about the nothingness of the abyss and similarly exult matters of pure nonexistence. To allow for such potential nothingness, he retreats to the time preceding the biblical genesis. His journey toward the origin of time gives him greater creative freedom as a metaphysical writer. The black abyss he sees symbolizes the enigmatic era of which very little is said in the Old Testament; it represents the dark emptiness before God's creation of the universe ex nihilo. Before the beginning of time and space, only the void and dark waters of the *materia prima* reigned. Of all Brodsky's images of darkness, be it the sky or water at night, the vacuous mirror is the most radical and elementary. It withdraws to the ontological status that equals zero, to the primordial void and darkness which reason cannot approach. This is what Brodsky rediscovers at the end of his passage—the purest nonbeing, which would be undone through God's gradual labor.

At the same time, his vision is unthinkable without the vehicle of the mirror, which Polukhina calls "one of the most persistent" in Brodsky's poetry (202). It introduces the context of the limited mortal knowledge received "through a glass darkly." The mirror as the vehicle of the illumination thus brings to mind Saint Paul's promise to the Corinthians, in which he speaks of the absolute and direct ("face-to-face") insight gained after the rites of passage through death. In this context, the content of the illumination can be defined in terms of an empty eternity.

The "vicious, viscous" (52) vacuity which precedes the revelation of "pitch-black nothing" (55) takes the shape, as we have seen, of a tunnel (at this point, Brodsky writes of a subwaylike space) with a gradual diminution of light. Light as the key factor in organizing spatial depth is characteristic of Claude Lorrain's paintings. In fact, Lorrain belongs to the small contingent of painters who enjoy a moment of recognition in Brodsky's essay. His tunnels of increasing paradisiacal light fading upward to the heavens are traversed from an opposite end in Brodsky's passage. However, whereas Lorrain evokes the harmonious infinity of the skies, Brodsky's negative abyss opens into darkness and chthonic waters. The negative quality of his black mirror is best understood by what it does *not* represent. It is neither the "divine dark" of Meister Eckhart's vision nor any mystic's conception of night.[25] Its blackness and nothingness conjure no nihilistic temptations but rather the discovery of an empty ideality, to use Hugo Friedrich's phrase, unconditioned by ethical norms and open to a new, previously inaccessible sphere of imagination.

Perhaps a useful vantage point for a further investigation of Brodsky's conception of the black mirror is, once again, a comparison with Ruskin, who undertook a description of the blackened mirror of the Venetian waters only to conclude that its darkness was caused by a dense crowd of boats and people. Thus, Ruskin's black mirror of water reflects life and motion, and is a realistic observation. In counterpoint to this image, *Watermark*'s pivotal scene takes place when the narrator gazes at the rectangle of the black mirror. Its pure black surface is, at best, representative of chthonic waters. Such a transformation of reality stands in opposition to the three-dimensional world of living creatures and objects. In fact, the black mirror represents their end. It negates all the attributes that are inherent to or constitute objects.

With this final vision of pure nothingness, the passage through the palazzo enacts the transition from thingness (the antiques in the palazzo's yard depicted as precious objects) to radical nothingness, with all the intervening stages of gradual negation enumerated. By contrast, the fundamental metaphysical tension in Brodsky's poetry evolves from thingness to eternity, from *veshchnost'* to *vechnost'*. In Brodsky's poem "Torso," for instance, a black mirror is a sublime entrance to transcendence: "This is the end of things. This is, at the road's end, a mirror by which to enter."[26] Similarly, the mirror appears in "Venetian Stanzas II" in terms of an "exit for objects."[27] However, the author uses *Watermark* to probe a more radical metaphysical concept. What he formulates here is the possibility of the imagination to envision *primordial* nothingness. As part of Brodsky's negative poetics, the entire passage in the palace, along with the persistent transformation of reality, reach an absolute point where ontological naught is achieved. The black mirror, a synec-doche of the void, reveals itself in its purest, eternity-defying presence.

The whole experience in the palace has a clearly punctuated rhythm. It envisions the afterlife fashioned according to diverse ideas; then, the return of things to *materia prima;* and, further, nonbeing prior to gen-esis. Its framework consists of contemporary settings: it begins at the party and concludes when the visitor steps into a room with a television set. Brodsky, who belongs to those few poets for whom the inner connec-tion between poetic vocation and vision has never lost significance, restores in *Watermark* the capacity for visionary imagery. In this respect, his conception of the afterlife opposes T. S. Eliot's belief that contempo-rary poets have lost this creative power.[28] Brodsky conceives this in the spirit of his own time: his vision is tantamount to a short circuit of two incompatible realms, a brief opening onto dark and empty transcen-dence, which addresses itself to our sight more than any other sense.

Let us, then, take a look at the black and empty mirror as if it were a picture. Its description is kept to a minimum. All that we learn from the ekphrasis is that this object-erasing looking glass is rectangular and framed; moreover, the frame is gilded. It is a picture indeed. Defined as an abstract image, conceived within modernist aesthetics, it derives from a specific approach and a peculiar type of seeing which imposes a schematized form on vision. To be sure, Brodsky's way of seeing does not derive from the sort of geometrization of reality which is best formu-lated by Cézanne's painterly ideas. His black rectangle representing nothing stems directly from avant-garde aesthetics, especially and most obviously from Kazimir Malevich's experimental painting. Specific ref-erences to Malevich's suprematist canvases occur with intense, irregular frequency in Brodsky's poems; the poet usually does not obliterate his sources but exposes them by mentioning in the familiar manner of friendly speech Malevich's first name or playing with the memorable titles of his works.[29] The direction in which the allusion to Malevich's suprematist canvases (see figure 4) evolves in *Watermark* differs from that in Brodsky's verse; this time, the author declines to attach the black rectangular looking glass to Malevich's name.[30] But all the properties of the painter's art are present: a certain coldness conjoined with the absence of light, time, motion, things, and colors. Even the black rectangle's sole positive feature, its inviting depth derives from Malevich's painterly vision of ontological negativity. Yet, its geometric outlines stand for the curbed formlessness for which the specific shapes of a square, rectangle, or circle are of secondary importance. Brodsky's appropriation of Malevich's suprematist canvases bears characteristics of postgeometric thinking.

Like Herbert, Brodsky employs Malevich's radical images of nonthingness to evoke the idea of pure nothingness. And again, like Herbert, he is aware of the power that geometry has for framing and capturing formlessness. Black is the medium of the mind, as Odilon Redon once suggests, and a black square or a rectangle of nothingness is different from the blackness of the night sky. Such forms visualize ontological emptiness by offering a creative freedom from natural images of endlessness as the ocean and sky.

Brodsky's passionate, albeit selective, rejection of the avant-garde and contemporary art in general is a well-known fact which I have already indicated in my discussion of his opinions regarding architecture. With all due respect to his preferences, however, even the most biased viewer may find surprising treasures in this art, which the greatly disappointed Russian writer considers "accretions." I have in mind the visual territory of the void explored by Ad Reinhardt in his series of black paintings. His huge rectangular canvases, of similar size but varied texture, repeatedly reveal their creator's fascination with nonexistence. Minimalist and precise, their shiny black surfaces look like mirrors. The artist, who aspired in his work to evoke nothingness, considered black "the dark of absolute freedom"[31] and was reluctant to perceive in his negativism an expression of existential anxieties. In my mind, the black empty mirror—the sign purified from traditional meaning—is shared by Brodsky and Reinhardt in their expressions of the void; they both are capable of generating the emptiness of the black reflective surface.

Brodsky's negative revelation indicates the degree to which his Venetian vision is conceived as liminal phenomenon open to the nothingness that pervades the city's thingness. He strives to maintain the perfect balance between reality and his vision by assimilating certain elements

Figure 4. Kasimir Malevich, *Black Square,* 1913 (1923–29), oil on canvas, 106.2 × 106.5 centimeters, Petersburg, State Russian Museum

of the domestic interior in a manner reminiscent of those paintings that are half abstract and half representational. In their pattern of abstraction one can still recognize some aspects of reality, and, vice versa, their representation of reality is so eerie and fragmentary that it reveals its other, nonobjective side. From this real unreality, Brodsky traverses a passage to be initiated into the other reality in order to emerge from this experience bearing a mark of the metaphysical initiate.

The netherworld, in every imaginable form, expresses the human need for continuity; its imagined realm resists the aporia of consciousness, which questions the existence of the afterlife as an unjustified supposition. Deprived of the option of continuity, one is doomed to meditate over the infinite nothingness of the abyss. Brodsky's Venetian travelogue tests both alternatives.

Afterword

We are as much as we see.
—Henry David Thoreau

The hope for adventure and the anticipation of seeing new things precede travel like the mapping of the route. Expectation and preparation bracket the peculiar state of mind of someone planning a trip. It is the intent that matters. The future is a horizon that the eye of the traveler-to-be scans, for a journey promises the experience of the new and the unpredictable. More than a mere adventure or any cognitive-sensory experience, epiphany as a heightened perceptive moment extends the limits of travel and signals the inner experience, not confined to one's mind but open to the visual arts.

During their separate visits abroad (Brodsky in Venice, Herbert in Amsterdam, Zagajewski in New York), the poets' metaphysical anxieties are given concrete visual form, structured as a passage from a visible reality to an invisible one or as a transformation of reality into a sublime vision. They articulate the phenomena of their metaphysical anxiety and fear of formlessness by transforming these unsettling feelings into a coherent artistic vision whose very fabric is taken from the visual arts. Here the invisible appears through the visible and thus enhances the idea of the material and spiritual unity of the universe.

The enigma of vision is usually relegated to the sphere of visual thinking. In this study, however, the vision is paired with the kinetic act of travel and passage; thus it is a vision conceived during an action of moving and as an integral part of that movement. The creative capacity of vision is quintessentially Romantic in nature. As M. H. Abrams observes, "Of all Romantic innovations, none has so preempted the attention of poets, novelists, and painters (and the critics of poetry, novels, and painting) as the concern with the eye and the object and the need for a revolution in seeing which will make the object anew."[1] Hence Zagajewski's, Brodsky's, and Herbert's poetic styles significantly influence their visual sensitivities because as poets, *voyants,* seers, their cognition assumes a predominantly visual character. Consequently, my reading is based on the post-Romantic elements of their work, in particular, on their primary vehicle of reinventing the Romantic paradigm: the contemplative and metaphysical perception of the visual arts. This problem cannot be properly articulated without these writers' attempts at interpreting painting and incorporating these attempts at the center of their vision.

These three writers speak for voiceless pictures. In this respect, the results of their preoccupation with works of art may not be different from art criticism. However, as I have shown, their use of the descriptive tool known as ekphrasis bears a poetic staple. The oldest known account of ekphrasis is Homer's description of Achilles' shield in the *Iliad.* Significantly, Homer generates the representation of the shield through a process of its making, framing the work of art in a tale. The fusion of such descriptive elements with a narrative is a persistent thread in the travel prose written by Brodsky, Herbert, and Zagajewski, as their ekphrasis springs from their highly individualized poetic preoccupation with images. Within this constellation, only Herbert does not subordinate the appearance of Torrentius's canvas to his narrative. Rather, the opposite development takes place: it is his acquaintance with the painting that generates a story. The impulse for the further narrative—his seeking the hidden meaning of this still life—is linked to his reading of the painter's life and the historical period during which he lived. Like

Vasari, Herbert brings the story of his own research—in fact, years of research—into his account.

In this respect, it is Brodsky who makes a more radical attempt at a complete incorporation of Malevich's suprematist icon into his story. In a sense, he fictionalizes the black mirror, by turning its perception into a meaningful episode, into a culminating point of the house tour. Furthermore, if Alberti was right in his assumption that Narcissus was "the inventor of painting,"[2] Brodsky demonstrates through inserting into his story the object-erasing mirror that the objectless vision introduced by the twentieth-century avant-garde closed the history of painting, brought it to the final conclusion. At least for Brodsky, the history of European painting seems indeed to end with the experiments of the first wave of the European avant-garde. Thus Brodsky's black mirror functions as a meta-picture through which he discusses larger painterly and conceptual issues.

Zagajewski certainly is the most affirmative beholder of art in this group. As far as his story is concerned, he writes a narrative in which the episode of his epiphanic encounter with Vermeer's painting plays the role of the final cause. All the initial elements of "Flamenco," whether his discussion of Saura's movie or Huxley's experimentation with mescaline, lead to the culminating moment at the Frick Collection. And yet such a strategy explains more about his own aesthetics than it does about Vermeer's actual historical and artistic values, because it is Zagajewski who speaks through Vermeer in "Flamenco" and who acts as a ventriloquist in other epiphanic events related in his essays.

The fact that the institutional setting of the museums frames Zagajewski's and Herbert's responses to art is a part of an evolution which has turned a museum into a testing ground of art. Only Brodsky chooses a different spatial frame for his vision, for he believes that Venice is not itself a museum but a living artwork. Yet all three writers are extraordinary beholders: they bridge their personalized perception of the visual arts not only with the institution of a museum but with the universe of texts, with their own poetry, and with the reading public.

Notes

Introduction

1. Joseph Brodsky, *Watermark* (New York: Farrar, Straus and Giroux, 1992), 116.

2. Samuel Taylor Coleridge, "Biographia Literaria," in *The Critical Tradition: Classic Texts and Contemporary Trends,* ed. David H. Richter (New York: St. Martin's Press, 1989), 306.

3. Could these poets respond to art with the same ardor as in a museum in their own native countries? Most likely yes, but curiously they did not leave any account of epiphanic occurrences happening in their homeland. The only possible exception one can find is in Zagajewski's "minor epiphanies," which—barely mentioned in his most recent book of essays, *Another Beauty*—occurred to him in Cracow and which revealed new aspects of reality without the component of travel.

4. Stanislaw Baranczak, *A Fugitive from Utopia: The Poetry of Zbigniew Herbert* (Cambridge: Harvard University Press, 1992), especially 12–18.

5. Hence Herbert's down-to-earth description of *Painter in His Atelier* by Adriaen van Ostade in *Still Life with a Bridle: Essays and Apocryphas.*

6. Morris Beja, *Epiphany in the Modern Novel* (Seattle: University of Washington Press, 1971). For further reading on epiphany, see Ashton Nichols, *The Poetics of Epiphany: Nineteenth-Century Origins of the Modern Literary Movement* (Tuscaloosa and London: University of Alabama Press, 1987), and Martin Bidney, *Patterns of Epiphany: From Wordsworth to Tolstoy, Pater, and Barrett Browning* (Carbondale and Edwardsville: Southern Illinois University Press, 1997). Epiphanies in Polish literature are discussed by Ryszard Nycz, "'A closed sliver of the world': On the Writing of Gustaw Herling-Grudziński," trans. Jolanta Dutkiewicz, *Sacrum in Polish Literature,* ed. Halina Filipowicz, special issue of *Renascence: Essays on Values in Literature* 47 (1995): 221–29. Nycz defines the poetics of epiphany in modern Polish poetry as "records of intense, disjointed, sudden *vestiges of presence* that testify to the unusual value of individual things in their everyday existence"; Ryszard Nycz, "Poetyka epifanii a modernizm (od Norwida do Leśmiana)," ("Poetics of Epiphany and Modernism: From Norwid to Leśmian,") *Teksty Drugie* 40 (1996): 21–22. All translations, unless indicated otherwise, are mine.

7. I refer here to Mary Ann Caws's definition of the passage as textual; Mary Ann Caws, *A Metapoetics of the Passage: Architextures in Surrealism and After* (Hanover and London: University of Press of New England, 1981), 11.

8. In fact, Abraham, Isaac, Jacob, Israel, and Moses experience theophanies while on the road; their divine illuminations indicate the extent to which the biblical visions and conversions were interconnected with the experience of wandering.

9. Bidney's study—based on the Bachelardian employment of four elements, according to which Bidney classifies epiphany—defines epiphany in terms of a moment of "imaginative or poetic intensity" (1). This notion I apply to my reading of Brodsky's *Watermark.*

10. Brodsky and Herbert occasionally produced witty and charming doodles.

11. Interestingly, all three poets knew each other; in fact, Zagajewski was a close friend of both Brodsky and Herbert. The Russian Nobel laureate translated Herbert's poetry while still living in the Soviet Union and later wrote two occasional pieces on his work; he met Herbert only in 1990, at Zagajewski's wedding with Maria Wodecka in Courbevoie, France.

12. Brodsky made this notion quite explicit in his essay "A Writer Is a Lonely Traveler," *New York Times Magazine,* October 1, 1972, 84.

Chapter 1

1. Mickiewicz makes for a spectacular example of someone caught between
    these two approaches and who along the course of life accepts one against
    another: on the one hand, he did not join the November Uprising of
    1830; on the other, in 1855 went to Turkey to support the anti-Russian
    forces there. Before he left Paris, he burnt his archives, which included his
    unpublished poetic works.

2. The New Wave was a movement of the young generation of Polish artists
    which originated in the 1960s; among its leading artists were Ryszard
    Krynicki, Adam Zagajewski, Stanislaw Baranczak, and Julian Kornhauser.
    In the mid-1970s, their rejection of the speech controlled by Communist
    censorship, combined with their political involvement, brought them
    together with political dissidents. Because the New Wave supported the
    student protests in March 1968, the group is often referred to as "Gen-
    eration 68." Zagajewski's essay in *The Unrepresented World* was considered
    one of the group's manifestos. For a detailed analysis of the New Wave's
    approach to Herbert, see Marian Stala, "Contemporaneity and Reality:
    Toward a Reading of Zbigniew Herbert by the Artists of Generation 68,"
    trans. Katarzyna Owczarek, *The Other Herbert,* ed. Bożena Shallcross,
    special issue of *Indiana Slavic Studies* 9 (1998): 121–35.

3. "But once Zagajewski has made his choice for privacy, for the inner life,
    he is faced with the a more difficult problem, and one which is less spe-
    cific to Poland. To write against the public and historical life, and in favor
    of the private and individual life, is still to be conditioned by the public,
    even if one's response to it is a negative one. In *Solidarity, Solitude,* Zaga-
    jewski turns his back on one definition of life and of its purpose, but it is
    not yet clear what he has turned toward"; Adam Kirsch, "The Lucid
    Moment," *New Republic* (March 1998): 38.

4. Kirsch writes that "When Zagajewski begins to write about things not
    conditioned by history—and, in his books, this is clearly the role set aside
    for poetry, as opposed to prose—we find him strangely inexplicit" (38).
    Taking the opposite stand, Jaroslaw Anders describes in the poetic terms
    what are Zagajewski's specific preoccupations once he abandoned the
    sphere of history: "He prefers to listen to the world, contemplate his
    double-headed doubt and bask in the light of small things, occasionally
    even mocking his dreams"; Jaroslaw Anders, "Between Fire and Sleep,"
    Los Angeles Times, February 1998, 6.

5. Cavanagh discusses the question of whether the poet's divorce from history is total and what new directions it ensues. Her case is, of course, Zagajewski's lyric poetry. Clare Cavanagh, "Lyrical Ethics: The Poetry of Adam Zagajewski," *Slavic Review* (Spring 2000): 1–15.

6. As Zagajewski said to me, *Another Beauty* is filled with minor and major transcendences (phone interview, January 16, 1999).

7. In the literal translation, *In the Other Beauty.*

8. "He is not disinherited, for he has found his home in the common heritage ever present in the very art and architecture that surrounded him in his youth"; Czeslaw Milosz, preface to *Tremor,* by Adam Zagajewski, trans. Renata Gorczynski (London: Collins Harvill, 1987), 12.

9. Czeslaw Milosz, "Opinie: O *w cudzym pięknie* Adama Zagajewskiego," ("Opinions: On *Another Beauty* by Adam Zagajewski,") *Zeszyty Literackie* 64 (1998): 165. This issue consists of several critical commentaries by various authors.

10. In it, Zagajewski confesses that the only source of consolation is for him the art created by others; see Adam Zagajewski, "W cudzym pięknie," *List. Oda do wielości* (*Letter. Ode to Plurality*), (Paris: Instytut Literacki, 1983), 25.

11. As March and Anders, the translators of Herbert's *Barbarian in the Garden,* aptly rendered it.

12. On the methodology of Herbert's movement see Giorgio DiMauro, "Setting Maps into Motion: The Aesthetics of Wandering in Zbigniew Herbert's Essays" (1999): 29–41.

13. Adam Zagajewski, *Another Beauty,* trans. Clare Cavanagh (New York: Farrar, Straus and Giroux, 2000), 33.

14. On these two types of vision see José Ortega y Gasset, "On Point of View in Art," *Partisan Review* (August 1949): 822–36.

15. Elizabeth Bishop, "The Map," *The Complete Poems 1927–1979* (New York: Noonday Press, Farrar, Straus and Giroux, 1991), 3.

16. Zagajewski, "A View of Cracow," 78.

17. Ekphrasis—a poem describing a work of art—is considered in modern criticism a separate genre. Webb offers a historical survey of the term which is central to the interart discourse; Ruth Webb, "Ekphrasis Ancient and Modern: The Invention of the Genre," *Word & Image: The Journal of Verbal/Visual Inquiry* 15, no. 1 (1999): 7–18.

18. Elżbieta Kiślak, "Podróż i doświadczenie historii" ("Travel and the Experience of History"), *Zdziwienia Kraszewskim,* ed. Marta Zielińska (Wrocław: Ossolineum, 1990), 121–30.

19. Adam Zagajewski, "Spring Thunderstorm," *Two Cities: On Exile, History, and the Imagination,* trans. Lillian Vallee (New York: Farrar, Straus and Giroux, 1995), 124. The Polish original was published in 1991.

20. José Rabasa, *Inventing America: Spanish Historiography and the Formation of Eurocentrism* (Norman: University of Oklahoma Press, 1993), 186.

21. Zagajewski, "Essentialist in Paris," 178.

22. Zagajewski, "Two Cities," 61.

23. Charles Baudelaire, *The Parisian Prowler: Le Spleen de Paris. Petits Poèmes en prose,* trans. Edward K. Kaplan (Athens and London: University of Georgia Press, 1989), 21. On the notion of the *flâneur* in Baudelaire's writing, see Jacques Derrida, *Given Time. Counterfeit Money,* trans. Peggy Kamuff (Chicago: University of Chicago Press, 1992), 155.

24. Let us keep in mind a fact of particular contextual importance. Zagajewski wrote these lines in the late 1990s, well into a new political era, when Poland had regained its independence from Soviet domination. Thus the post-totalitarian mindset frames his approach to reality. Now, we must overlook the temptation to criticize the blatant consumerism and other excesses of free-market societies. Instead, one should engage, as he exhorts, the dialogue with what is everlasting in our cultural legacy.

Chapter 2

1. Adam Zagajewski, "The Moment," *Mysticism for Beginners,* trans. Clare Cavanagh (New York: Farrar, Straus and Giroux, 1997), 40.

2. My notion of the *mouvement* derives mainly from French criticism, where it is employed in a manner close to the eighteenth-century idea of the emotional passage. For an elaboration of this concept, see also Paul de Man, "The Literary Self as Origin: The Work of Georges Poulet," *Blindness and Insight: Essays in Rhetoric in Contemporary Criticism,* introduction by Godzich Wlad (Minneapolis: University of Minnesota Press, 1983), 79–101, and Georges Poulet, *Mesure de l'instant* (Paris: Plon, 1968).

3. I refer here to the "small" epiphanies prompted by Velázquez's and Rembrandt's portraits (both are displayed in Munich's Alte Pinakotheke) as those that received less of Zagajewski's ekphrastic attention; the term *small epiphanies* is Zagajewski's (*Another Beauty,* 70).

4. Camus in his "The Rains of New York" makes two concurrent observations: first, that "New York rain is a rain of exile," and second, that the city's overwhelming spirit puts him "out of (his) depth." Albert Camus, "The Rains of New York," *Lyrical and Critical Essays,* ed. Philip Toddy, trans. Ellen Conroy Kennedy (New York: Vintage Books, 1970), 182, 184.

5. For an elaboration of this mode of perception, see Karl Heinz Bohrer, *Suddenness: On the Moment of Aesthetic Appearance,* trans. Ruth Crowley (New York: Columbia University Press, 1994).

6. As Seamus Heaney, another adherent of the illuminating moment, claims, "Description is revelation!" Heaney made this observation in his letter to Nichols, 208.

7. Adam Zagajewski, "Flamenco," *Solidarity, Solitude: Essays by Adam Zagajewski,* trans. Lillian Vallee (New York: Ecco Press, 1990), 162.

8. The painting was retouched and the birdcage next to the window is probably a later addition. The picture on the background wall is attributed to Caesar van Everdingen; Vitale Bloch, *All the Paintings of Jan Vermeer,* trans. Michael Kitson (New York: Hawthorn Books, 1963), 31.

9. Albeit fascinating, Zagajewski's discussion with Gombrowicz goes beyond the scope of this book, especially in light of the fact that Gombrowicz could be qualified as one of the most anti-epiphanic writers.

10. William Blake, "The Marriage of Heaven and Hell," *Complete Poetry and Prose of William Blake,* ed. David V. Erdman, commentary by Harold Bloom (Berkeley and Los Angeles: University of California Press, 1982), 39.

11. Aldous Huxley, *The Doors of Perception and Heaven and Hell* (New York: Harpers and Row, 1990), 38.

12. Marcel Proust, *The Captive,* trans. C. K. Scott Moncrieff (New York: Albert and Charles Boni, 1929), 515.

13. Bernard Berenson, *Aesthetics and History* (Garden City: Doubleday, 1948), 89.

14. William Gass, *On Being Blue: A Philosophical Inquiry* (Boston: David R. Godine, 1976), 76.

15. Although Vermeer's *The Music Lesson* is among the holdings of the Buckingham Palace in London.

16. In a matter-of-fact style, Pops writes that "Her affair is none of our business"; Martin Pops, *Vermeer: Consciousness and the Chamber of Being* (Ann Arbor: University of Michigan Research Papers, 1984), 42.

17. Zagajewski, "The City Where I Want to Live," 55.

18. Martin Scammell, "Loyal toward Reality," *New York Review of Books* 14 (1998): 39.

19. Ryszard Nycz, " 'Every one of us is a stranger': Patterns of Identity in Polish Literature in the 20th Century," forthcoming in the collection of essays *Framing the Polish Home: Postwar Cultural Constructions of Hearth, Nation, and Self,* ed. Bożena Shallcross (Athens: Ohio University Press, 2002).

20. Zagajewski, "Changes in the East," 221.

21. Zagajewski, "Two Cities," 12.

22. I paraphrase here Heller's title; see Erich Heller, *The Artist's Journey into the Interior and Other Essays* (New York: Random House, 1965).

23. For instance, Barthes observes that the representation of objects solely in terms of their attributes excludes the representation of their thingness; Roland Barthes, "The World as Object," *Critical Essays,* trans. Richard Howard (Evanston: Northwestern University Press, 1972), 6.

24. Adam Zagajewski, "Morandi," *Canvas,* trans. Renata Gorczynski, Benjamin Ivry, and C. K. Williams (New York: Farrar, Straus and Giroux, 1991), 19.

25. Sven Spieker posits this question in his article "Still Life as Fetish," 68.

26. Zagajewski, "Fruit," 80.

27. Quoted in Rudolf Hirsch, "Edmund Husserl und Hugo von Hofmannsthal. Eine Begegnung und ein Brief," *Sprache und Politik: Festgaabe für Dolf Sternberger,* ed. Carl-Joachim Friedrich and Benno Reifenberg (Heidelberg: L. Schneider, 1968), 113.

28. Zagajewski, "Covenant," 21.

29. Zagajewski, "A View of Delft," 39.

30. Incidentally, in Zagajewski's work, Vermeer is the most often mentioned painter.

31. Adam Zagajewski, "Bezdomny Nowy Jork," *Jechać do Lwowa* (London: Aneks, 1985), 22.

32. Cichy discusses whether Zagajewski's poetry represents a religious phenomenon; Michał Cichy, "Opinie," especially 160–61.

Chapter 3

1. They are "Próba opisania krajobrazu greckiego" ("An Attempt at Describing the Greek Landscape"), "Labirynt nad morzem" ("The Labyrinth by the Sea"), "Akropol i duszyczka" ("The Acropolis and the Little Soul"), and "Akropol" ("The Acropolis").

2. On the relationship between Herbert and other Polish essayists, see the study by Piotr Siemaszko, *Zmienność i trwanie. O eseistyce Zbigniewa Herberta* (Bydgoszcz: Instytut Wydawniczy "Świadectwo," 1996). For my purposes, the most significant is the relationship between Herbert and Gustaw Herling-Grudziński, which Siemaszko interprets in terms of Herbert's influence. He also finds similarities in both authors' strong moral imperatives, their critical opinions of contemporary art and art history in general, and in their fascination with Piero della Francesca. Unlike Siemaszko, I see insurmountable differences in Herling-Grudziński's use of mystery as devoid of textual character and in his experience of epiphany as separate from travel.

3. It should be noted that Herbert seldom expresses interest in contemporary art, except in a few early reviews and obituaries on great modernists such as Fernand Léger and Maurice Utrillo.

4. Andrzej Kijowski, "Pielgrzym," *Twórczość* 5 (1963): 59.

5. These virtues resonate with strength in his poem "The Prayer of Mr. Cogito—Traveler." Ed Hirsch extends the cognitive perspective of a pilgrim also to the narrator in *Still Life with a Bridle;* see Ed Hirsch, "Fidelity of Things," *The New Yorker,* December 23, 1991, 100.

6. The etymology of the Polish word *pielgrzym,* like its English equivalent, preserves the meaning of someone who journeys through a foreign country (in Latin *peregrinus* or *pelegrinus* connotes a foreigner, someone who is abroad, and is rooted in the words *per-agros,* through field, land). For the historical survey of pilgrimage and its Polish tradition, see Antoni Jackowski, *Pielgrzymowanie (Pilgrimage)* (Wrocław: Wydawnictwo Dolnośląskie, 1998), 6.

7. See also Wiegandt's comments on this particular problem in her article "Eseje poety" ("The Poet's Essays") in *Czytanie Herberta (Reading Herberta),* ed. Przemysław Czapliński, Piotr Sliwiński, and Ewa Wiegandt (Poznań: Wydawnictwo WiS, 1995), 213.

8. Zbigniew Herbert, "Akropol i duszyczka," *Znak* 4 (1981): 7.

9. James Clifford, *Routes, Travel, and Translation in the Late Twentieth Century* (Cambridge: Harvard University Press, 1997), 3.

10. In 1958, using a small award, Herbert went on his first journey to the West; for two years he traveled in France, England, and Italy. In 1965, he left for another extensive stay abroad, again in France; he also visited West Germany, Greece, and the United States. In 1969 to 1970, he was a visiting professor at the University of California in Los Angeles. After a few years spent in Poland, he left his country in 1975 for Austria, West Germany, and Italy, only to return in 1981 to engage in the Solidarity movement. The period between 1986 and 1992 marks his last extended visit in Paris, from which he returned to Warsaw. He died there on July 28, 1998.

11. Obviously, many readers (not only theorists or champions of popular culture) would disagree with Herbert.

12. Zbigniew Herbert, "Siena," *Barbarian in the Garden,* trans. Michael March and Jaroslaw Anders (Manchester: Carcanet, 1985), 69.

13. Herbert, "Among the Dorians," 22.

14. Coincidentally, *Struna światla* (*A String of Light*), the volume of poetry with which Herbert made his debut, includes the poem entitled "Ołtarz" ("Altar"), an ekphrasis of an imaginary bas-relief representing a sacrificial offering; see Zbigniew Herbert, *Wybór poezji. Dramaty* (Warsaw: Czytelnik,1973), 39.

15. Herbert generally avoids footnotes, and this lack of information led his translators to translate into English the Polish translation of the passage from the *Odyssey* instead of using one of the existing English versions.

16. See, for instance, Ferdinand Protzman, "Justice Delayed?" *ArtsNews,* December 1998, 13–138.

17. Herbert, "Memories of Valois," 175. Also, he says, "Loud guides drive herds of tourists" (68). In another characteristic instance, he describes a typical tourist scene in Ermenonville: "The park is now the property of a Touring Club. Excursions are herded along described paths. Rousseau's tomb—*et voilà*. The cascade—*tiens, tiens, tiens*. The Altar of Dreams—*c'est à droit*" (179). Ironically, the spirit of Jean-Jacques Rousseau has also disappeared from Ermenonville, where he lived and meditated during his solitary walks.

18. It is still little known to the public that Herbert was a remarkable draftsman who often sketched while visiting historical sites. Recently one of his

drawings appeared on the cover design of a selection of poems; see Zbigniew Herbert, *89 wierszy* (*89 Poems*) (Cracow: Wydawnictwo a5, 1998). As evidenced by this single piece, his style has a certain neoclassical flavor reminiscent of the better publicized works of another talented draftsman, Joseph Brodsky.

19. Herbert's *Apocryphas* continue the tradition of imaginary biographies, the genre established by Walter Pater and later continued by Marcel Schwob and Marguerite Yourcenar.

20. Zbigniew Herbert, "Delta," *Still Life with a Bridle: Essays and Apocryphas,* trans. John and Bogdana Carpenter (New York: Ecco Press, 1991), 7. The Polish original appeared after the Carpenters' English translation.

21. Mikhail Bakhtin, "Response to a Question from Novyi Mir," *Speech Genres and Other Essays,* trans. Vern McGee (Austin: University of Texas Press, 1986), 7.

22. Herbert, "The Price of Art," 21.

23. Quoted in Svetlana Alpers, *The Art of Describing: Dutch Art in the Seventeenth Century* (Chicago: University of Chicago Press, 1984), xviii.

24. Quoted in Alpers, xvii–xviii.

25. Herbert, "Still Life with a Bridle," 98.

26. Bogdana Carpenter, "Zbigniew Herbert's Lesson of Art," *CrossCurrents: A Yearbook of Central European Culture* 11 (1992): 127.

27. "I call on you Old Masters . . . / make the serpent's scale of pride / fall from me. Let me be deaf / to the temptation of fame." Zbigniew Herbert, "Old Masters," *Report from the Besieged City and Other Poems,* translated, with an introduction and notes by John and Bogdana Carpenter (New York: Ecco Press, 1985), 10.

28. "When you are looking at the originals, you seem to be looking at the copies; and when you are looking at the copies, you seem to be looking at the originals. Is it a canal-side in Harlem, or is it a Van der Heyden?" See Henry James, "In Holland," *Transatlantic Sketches* (Boston: Houghton, Mifflin and Company, 1868), 382–83.

29. Compare Alpers, 27.

30. I cannot resist quoting the title and subtitle of Boehme's book in the English translation by John Sparrow (Castle in Cornhil: L. Lloyd, 1665) for it conveys the essence of Boehme's thought: *Forty Questions of the Souls concerning its Original, Essence, Substance, Nature or Quality, and Property,*

what it is, from Eternity to Eternity. Framed by the Lover of Mysteries Doctor Balthasar Walther, and Answered in the Year 1620 by Jakob Böhme called Teutonicus Philosophus. The book contains "an Explanation of the Philosphick Globe, or Wonder-Eye of eternity, or Looking-Glass of Wisdom, being One half Light or Dark Globe or half Eye with a Rainbow about it, parted, with Halves reversed, A Cross, and Heart, appearing in the Centre, with the Abyss everywhere, within it, and without it, in Infinity, being all Looking-Glass." Quoted in Christopher Geissmar, *Das Auge Gottes. Bilder zu Jakob Böhme* (Wiessbaden: Harrassowitz Verlag, 1993), 105.

Dutch translations of Boehme's work appeared as early as the 1630s. The popularity of Boehme's thoughts can be measured by the fact that his books, published in both the Lowlands and in England, were often richly illustrated with engravings. Many of these hermetic engravings depict God's eye; see *Das Auge Gottes.*

31. Baranczak, *A Fugitive From Utopia,* 8–62.

32. Herbert, "The Bitter Smell of Tulips," 60.

33. Herbert never mentions the book by title. In spite of his skeptical attitude toward scholarly authorities, they figure into both of Herbert's volumes; whereas for *Still Life with a Bridle* it is Eugène Fromentin, for *Barbarian in the Garden* it is the prominent American art historian Bernard Berenson.

Chapter 4

1. This approach is best epitomized in Herbert's interpretation of Dutch art as anticipating, mediating, and commenting on the events of tulipomania in his essay "The Bitter Smell of Tulips," included in *Still Life with a Bridle.* For a discussion of this essay, see Bożena Shallcross, "The Barbarian's Garden: Zbigniew Herbert and the Folly of History," *East European Politics and Societies* 1 (2000): 47–63.

2. Beja writes that what prevents epiphanists from seeing the Absolute Being, "makes them susceptible . . . to the material world." This tension is resolved in a different manner by Herbert, who, though endowed with a sensual perceptiveness, transcends its limitations (125). Herbert's notion of epiphany can be put in the context of Heidegger's philosophical ideas, especially those articulated in "The Origin of the Work of Art." Heidegger's expression that "self-concealing being is illuminated" (in Vincent van Gogh's *Old Shoes*) and, especially, his concept that truth occurs as unconcealedness through beauty are close not just to Herbert's concept of

the metaphysical moment in art but also to a degree to the whole modernist aesthetics of epiphany. Quotation from Martin Heidegger, "The Origin of the Work of Art," *Poetry, Language, Thought,* trans. and introduction Hofstadter Albert (New York: Harper and Row, 1971), 36.

3. Thomas Wolfe, *Of Time and River: A Legend of Man's Hunger in His Youth* (Garden City: Sun Dial, 1944), 55.

4. For example, Nycz discusses the triviality and irrelevance of the object which evokes epiphany as its primary criteria ("A Closed Sliver of the World," 219–27).

5. One could consider Johann Winckelmann the father of ecstatic art criticism as established in his *Geschichte der Kunst des Altertums* (1764), in which he describes with great passion the ancient statue of Apollo Belvedere.

6. The Romantic roots of epiphany are explored by Bidney. Another important predecessor of Herbert's method in the domain of art is the Victorian Walter Pater, who employed the "aesthetic moment" in both his art criticism and his novel *Marius the Epicurean;* see also Walter Iser, *Walter Pater: The Aesthetic Moment,* trans. David Henry Wilson (Cambridge: Cambridge University Press, 1987).

7. Nietzsche uses this term to refer to a split-second perception.

8. Herbert, "The Acropolis," 32.

9. Beja, *Epiphany in Modern Novel,* 42.

10. Herbert, "Piero della Francesca," 160.

11. Herbert, "A Stone from the Cathedral," 81.

12. Baranczak, *A Fugitive from Utopia,* especially 8–62.

13. Herbert, "Letter," 150.

14. "An incredible blindness caused him to introduce an element of violence to the thinking process. How could he overlook the fact that solving knots and problems is not an athletic show, but an intellectual operation, and this presupposes the acceptance of erring, helplessness before the tangled matter of the world, wonderful human uncertainty, and humble patience." Zbigniew Herbert, "Węzeł gordyjski" ("The Gordian Knot"), *Węzeł* 6 (1981): 45.

15. Herbert does not seek a surrealist type of mystery associated with the bizarre, for he seldom expresses interest in modernist art.

16. For more information, see *Ancient Scripts from Crete and Cyprus,* eds. Jan Best and Fred Woudhuizen (Leiden, N.Y.: E. J. Brill, 1988).

17. Patryk, "Altichiero," *Zeszyty Literackie* 32 (1990): 143.

18. Although, according to Mario Praz, Altichiero was not a painter of exceptional distinction; see Mario Praz, *Mnemosyne: The Parallel between Literature and the Visual Arts* (Princeton: Princeton University Press, 1970), 72.

19. I also found a few references to Torrentius in *Still-Life in the Age of Rembrandt* by de Jongh, the eminent expert on the subject of Dutch still-life painting. One of them is particularly telling: "Still-lifes in the form of what is usually referred to by the Italian name *tondo* were not very frequent in seventeenth century Holland. The *great* exception is the painting of 1614 by Torrentius in the Rijksmuseum in Amsterdam. A *less well-known* exception is the painting by Jan Olis [italics mine]." Eddy de Jongh with the assistance of Titia van Leeuwen, Andrea Gasten, and Hilary Sayles, *Still-Life in the Age of Rembrandt* (Auckland: Auckland City Art Gallery, 1982), 101. Although it is only a referential remark, it clearly indicates that Torrentius is not a completely *unknown* artist as Herbert would like him to be.

20. Alpers, *The Art of Describing,* 230.

21. In Jacek Łukasiewicz's reading, Leonardo da Vinci's *Mona Lisa* represents for Herbert only a "mechanical idol"; Jacek Łukasiewicz, *Poezja Zbigniewa Herberta* (Warsaw: Wydawnictwa Szkolne i Pedagogiczne, 1995), 50.

22. Herbert, "Lascaux," 8.

23. For an illuminating study of images invested with special magic power, see David Freedberg, *The Power of Images: Studies in the History and Theory of Response* (Chicago and London: University of Chicago Press, 1989).

24. In the original—"tajemnica tajemnic" (Zbigniew Herbert, "Lascaux," *Barbarzyńca w ogrodzie* [Warsaw: Czytelnik, 1964], 12).

25. Herbert, "Labyrinth by the Sea," *Twórczość* 2 (1973), 15.

26. Caws emphasizes the involvement of the eye in the process of reconstructing the threshold; *A Metamorphosis of the Passage* (1981).

27. Norman Bryson, *Looking at the Overlooked: Four Essays on Still Life Painting* (Cambridge: Harvard University Press, 1990), 14.

28. Bryson comments on the still-life genre as "still marginalized in today's professional art history" (*Looking at the Overlooked,* 10).

29. Constantijn Huygens, one of his peers, praised Torrentius as "a magician in representing still objects" (*Still Life with a Bridle,* 80).

30. "The high finish and detailed rendering associated with the growing distinction between the *kladschilder* (rough painter) and the *fijnschilder* is a common feature of mid-century painting in Holland" (*The Art of Describing,* 114).

31. For Wiegandt, Herbert's reading of Torrentius's still life indicates the painting's perfect impermeability. ("The Poet's Essays," 220).

32. According to Sterling, much of the evidence that links ancient Roman murals with the late Middle Ages was destroyed due to pillaging; see Charles Sterling, *Still Life Painting: From Antiquity to the Twentieth Century* (New York: Harper and Row, 1981).

33. A similar realization of the journey from the visible to the invisible was executed by Hieronymus Bosch. In his *Ascent to Heavenly Paradise* (Venice, Doge Palace), the deceased soar in ecstasy through a spiraling tunnel toward a paradisiacal light. Whether Bosch's painting caused anybody's epiphany remains an open question.

Chapter 5

1. Baranczak, *A Fugitive from Utopia,* 80.

2. On existential feelings in Herbert's poetry see Andrzej Franaszek, *Ciemne źródło. O twórczości Zbigniewa Herberta* (*Dark Well: On the Poetry by Zbigniew Herbert*) (London: Puls, 1998).

3. Carpenter, "Zbigniew Herbert's Lesson on Art," 130.

4. For instance, Torrentius's painting epitomizes both threat and ecstasy, fear and epiphany. This tension is present as a transition in the Eleusian and Egyptian mysteries.

5. Herbert, "Gerard Terborch: The Discreet Charm of Bourgeoisie," 67.

6. Alpers, *The Art of Describing,* 83.

7. Laura Goering, "Belyj's Symbolist Abyss," *Slavic and East European Journal* 4 (1995): 568.

8. Charlotte Douglas, *Kazimir Malevich* (New York: Harry N. Abrams, 1994), 24.

9. For a different approach to the interrelationship between Malevich and Herbert see Sven Spieker, "Still Life as Fetish," especially 70–78.

10. Zbigniew Herbert, "Revelation," trans. Bogdana and John Carpenter, in Czeslaw Milosz, ed., *Postwar Polish Poetry* (Berkeley, Los Angeles, and London: University of California Press, 1983), 132.

11. A metaphysical interpretation of Herbert's "Study of the Object," rare in the 1970s among Herbert scholars, is offered by Rymkiewicz, who was also first to indicate the parallel between Malevich's *Black Square* and Herbert's black square; see Jarosław Marek Rymkiewicz, "Krzesło" ("Chair"), *Twórczość* 1 (1970): 56.

12. Herbert, "Study of the Object," 135.

13. M. H. Abrams, *Natural Supernaturalism: Tradition and Revolution in Romantic Literature* (New York: W. W. Norton, 1971), 385.

14. Saint Augustine, *Confessions,* trans. E. J. Sheed (London: 1944), ix.

15. Jarosław Iwaszkiewicz (1894–1980), a poet of neotraditional bent and a member of the group Skamander, was an editor in chief (1950–80) of the monthly *Twórczość,* where Herbert contributed his works.

16. Jarosław Iwaszkiewicz, *Podróże do Wloch* (*Travels to Italy*) (Warsaw: Państwowy Instytut Wydawniczy, 1977).

17. Also in the essay on Piero della Francesca, Herbert summarizes his *The Baptism of Christ* as the moment which becomes eternity: "Over the battle of shadows, convulsions and tumult, Piero has erected *lucidus ordo*—an eternal order of light and balance" ("Piero della Francesca," 153).

18. Herbert, "Delta," 6.

19. Quoted in Sherwin K. Simmons, "Kasimir Malevich's *Black Square* and the Genesis of Suprematism 1907–1915" (Ph.D. diss., John Hopkins University, 1979), 231.

20. In particular in the earlier poem "Kłopoty małego stwórcy" ("The Minor Creator's Problems"). Critics are indeed divided in regards to the question of Herbert's agnosticism. For example, Baranczak comments in his *Fugitive from Utopia* that Herbert is disinherited from the biblical and religious sphere; for a similar approach see Janina Abramowska, "Wiersze z aniołami" ("Poems with Angels"), 74. On the other hand, Dedecius authored a serious attempt at defining God in Herbert's poetry as Cartesian God; see Karl Dedecius, "Uprawa filozofii. Zbigniew Herbert w poszukiwaniu tożsamości" ("Cultivating Philosophy: Zbigniew Herbert's Quest for Identity"), trans. Elżbieta Feliksiak, *Poznawanie Herberta*

(*Understanding Herbert*), ed. and introduction Andrzej Franaszek (Cracow: Wydawnictwo Literackie, 1998), 128–68.

21. Justyna Szczęsna, "Uwiedziony przez Boga" ("Seduced by God"), 80.

22. Jan Sochoń, "Szare numinozum" ("Grey Numinosum"), *Zeszyty Literackie* 33 (1991): 129.

23. Significantly, in one of four poems entitled "Brewiarz," ("Breviary") included in his last volume of poetry *Epilog burzy* (*The Epilogue of the Storm*), Herbert addresses God with the single prayerlike utterance "*Panie*" ("Lord"). One cannot dismiss the poet's "call from darkness" as mere rhetoricity; the grandeur of this apostrophe, outlined as a separate verse, brings sincerity to the confession that follows; Zbigniew Herbert, *Epilog burzy* (Wrocław: Wydawnictwo Dolnośląskie, 1988), 11.

24. One must be careful, however, in approaching this subject. The Polish critic Andrzej Tyszczyk finds God masked even in the clearly defined mythological image of Moira; see Andrzej Tyszczyk, "Herbert, Kant i Bóg" ("Herbert, Kant, and God"), *Na Przykład* 4 (1988): 33.

25. Herbert, "Still Life with a Bridle," 98.

26. Ortega y Gasset, "On Point of View in Art," 830.

27. In the 1960s, the renowned Polish painter Jerzy Nowosielski painted a still life that encompasses a similar bifocal vision. This small but fascinating work, painted on a wooden panel, represents three vessels on a table, one of which is knocked down, and two black squares suspended in the background as if they were the hovering spirits of abstraction.

28. Jean-Francois Lyotard, "Newman: The Instant," *The Lyotard Reader,* ed. Andrew Benjamin (Oxford: Blackwell, 1989), 245.

29. Lyotard calls it "a representation which represents nothing" ("Newman: The Instant," 246).

Chapter 6

1. A small ferry.

2. *Watermark*—a summary of his many trips to Venice—was commissioned by the Consorzio Venezia Nuova, a foundation sponsored by the Italian government. As a Fellow of the Consorzio, Brodsky was asked to write an essay inspired by Venice, as were other Fellows before and after him, to mention only Andre Chastel, Giuseppe Sinopoli, and Harold Brodkey.

3. Polukhina writes that the premonitions of early death appeared in Brodsky's poetry after his expulsion from the Soviet Union; see Valentina Polukhina, *Joseph Brodsky: A Poet for Our Time* (Cambridge: Cambridge University Press, 1989), 95.

4. For example, Georges Braque confessed that his early realization of non-existent space was a significant factor in his development; see *G. Braque,* introduction and ed. John Richardson (New York: New York Graphic Society, 1961), 24.

5. While discussing Brodsky's poem "Butterfly," Polukhina observes that it "can be viewed as an embodiment of Brodsky's four-dimensional perception of the world, which includes an embodiment of nothingness itself"; see *Joseph Brodsky: A Poet of Our Time,* 181.

6. Joseph Brodsky, preface to *Modern Russian Poets on Poetry,* ed. and with an introduction by Carl R. Proffer, selected and with a preface by Joseph Brodsky, trans. Alexander Golubov et al. (Ann Arbor: Ardis, 1976), 8–9.

7. Joseph Brodsky, "A Poet and Prose," *Less Than One: Selected Essays* (New York: Farrar, Straus and Giroux, 1986), 185.

8. Besides a number of essays which he never published in book form, Brodsky also penned introductions and forewords to other authors' works. Among them is his introduction to the Italian translation of Zbigniew Herbert's volume *Rapporto dalla Citta Assedita,* and a blurb for Herbert's *Selected Poems.* A concise description of the role both Milosz and Herbert played in Brodsky's poetry can be found in David Bethea, *Joseph Brodsky and the Creation of Exile* (Princeton: Princeton University Press, 1994), 258–59. The effect the translations from Polish poetry had on Brodsky's writing is discussed by I. E. Adel'geim, "'Rasshirenie rechi' (Iosif Brodskii i Pol'sha)" ("Expanding Speech [Josif Brodski and Poland]"), *Poliaki i russkie v glazakh drug druga* (*Poles and Russians in Each Other's Eyes*), ed. Y. E. Adel'geim, B. V. Nosov, and V. A. Khorev (Moskva: "Indrik": 2000), 144–53.

9. See Marianna Volkova and Solomon Volkov, *Iosif Brodskii v N'iu-Iorke* (New York: Cultural Center for Soviet Refugees, Inc., 1990), 22.

10. Galya Diment, "English as Sanctuary: Nabokov's and Brodsky's Auto-biographical Writings," *Slavic and East European Journal* 3 (1993): 354, 357. Diment's thesis regarding the function of English as a sanctuary is based on the fact that Brodsky's first English essay was devoted to his late parents, thus English helped to sublimate the pain.

11. *Joseph Brodsky: A Maddening Space. A Transcript* (New York: Joseph Brodsky, Lawrence Pitkethly, Jason Robards, Inner Dimension, Mystic Fire Video, 1989).

12. Jean-Pierre Richard, *Microlectures* (Paris: Éditions du Seuil, 1979), 2 vols. Richard's book consists of his interpretations of single phrases and short passages, which he reads as their authors' signature pieces.

13. Joseph Brodsky, "Altra Ego," *On Grief and Reason: Essays* (New York: Farrar, Straus and Giroux, 1995), 84–85.

14. His objection was based on a standard he maintained that any work produced normally outside the artist's interest is thus compromised; see Bożena Shallcross, "Morton Street 44," *Reszty nie trzeba. Rozmowy z Josifem Brodskim* (*More Than One Needs: Conversations with Josif Brodsky*) ed. Jerzy Illg, (Katowice: Książnica, 1993), 177. What is interesting in this respect is his admiration for Claude Lorrain, a painter who makes his appearance in *Watermark,* and who painted mostly commissioned works.

15. From this perspective, *Watermark* is close to *Images of Italy,* by Pavel Muratov. As Elena Davydova notes, Muratov's book is based on the principle of *nalozhenie, reverberatsiia, otrazhenie* (superimposition, reverberation, reflection); see Elena Davydova, "Venetsia–Peterburg: Kniga Pavla Muratova v kulture serebrannogo veka" ("Venice–Petersburg: Pavel Muratov's Book in the Culture of the Silver Age"), *Graduate Essays on Slavic Languages and Literatures* 8 (1996): 4.

16. An insightful commentary on the question of repetition is offered by Marek Zaleski, who relates Brodsky's understanding of mimesis to Nietzsche; see Marek Zaleski, "Nuda powtórzeń?" ("The Boredom of Repetitions?"), *Res Publica* 5 (1998): 37–43.

17. It should be emphasized that Antsiferov considers *zapakhi goroda* (the city's smells) to be one of its defining factors; see Nikolai Antsiferov, *Dusha Peterburga* (*The Soul of Petersburg*), (Paris: YMCA Press, 1978), 20.

18. This version of the artist as a mimetic creator is reminiscent of Pushkin's attempts to conjure the same effect in his poem "Ekho." To respond to the world of sounds by doubling its *vsiakii zvuk* (every sound) is a formidable undertaking, one that requires consummate mastery of his craft. And, of course, there are limitations, for not all voices and sounds can be reflected by his chosen medium.

19. A similar process can be observed in Brodsky's verse, where the poetic self is objectified by someone else's gaze and by God's eye; see also Bethea's interpretation of "The Butterfly" (248).

20. Susan Sontag, with an afterword by Mikhail Lemkhin, *Joseph Brodsky: Leningrad: Fragments,* (New York: Farrar, Straus and Giroux, 1998), 203.

21. Travel through foreign countries is of no interest to Brodsky if a given place does not generate historical or personal memories. For this reason he repudiates Rio de Janeiro: "This said, I can only add that Rio is a most abstract place. This is a city , which no matter how many years you spend there, won't generate many memories. For a native of Europe, Rio is biological neutrality incarnate" ("After a Journey, or Homage to Vertebrae," 66).

22. Joseph Brodsky, "Lagoon," trans. Anthony Hecht, *A Part of Speech* (New York: Noonday Press, Farrar, Straus and Giroux, 1980), 74. This poem was written during Brodsky's first visit to Venice.

23. In fact, the narrator claims that "the environment remains hostile no matter how well you have adjusted to it" (*Watermark,* 107).

24. I would like to point out Brodsky's choice of the verb, because to "go ape" cleverly implies a repetition. This detail demonstrates the consistency of Brodsky's echoism.

25. So much so that in 1562 a law had to be passed in Venice to suppress ostentation in civil dress and decoration.

26. "The Venetians' instrument is color; that of Florentines and Romans is sculpturesque form"; see Horst de la Croix, Diane Kirkpatrick, and Richard G. Tansey, *Gardner's Art through the Ages* (New York: Harcourt Brace Jovanovich, 1991), vol. 2, 682.

27. Nothing can better demonstrate Brodsky's erudition than the distinction of such subtleties. Milosz notes that Brodsky's essays prove that "in his youth he succeeded in educating himself better than in any school" (Foreword, 10).

28. Brodsky mentions in his essay all the Venetian memorabilia he came across in his youth in Leningrad. A part of the popular image of Venice were prints by A. P. Ostroumova-Lebedeva, a member of Mir Isskustva; however, Brodsky's vision of Venice radically differs from Ostroumova-Lebedeva's vision of the city. I would like to thank Nina Perlina for her invaluable suggestions regarding the iconography of Petersburg.

29. The opposite is true for Brodsky, who prefers grayness precisely because he is a Northerner (43).

30. Color preoccupies him to such a degree that he states, "of all God's gifts to the sight of man, colour is the holiest, the most divine, the most solemn," John Ruskin, *The Stones of Venice* (New York: Moyer Bell Limited, 1989), 114.

31. Although the railroad was already built; also the Florian Café (of which Brodsky was a patron) and the Danieli Hotel were in business.

32. Bohdan Paczowski writes with insight about Brodsky's passionate encounters with architecture in his essay "Oko Brodskiego" ("Brodsky's Eye"), *Zeszyty Literackie* 57 (1997): 127–36.

33. The building is merely implied as part of the wave of four hundred windows on the Piazza di San Marco.

34. It is enough to compare, for example, the following quotation describing contemporary architects as "that ghastly post-war persuasion that has done more harm to the European skyline than any Luftwaffe" (17) with the inflammatory rhetoric used by the British heir to the throne.

35. Brodsky's appraisal of Venetian architecture is not free of certain imprecisions regarding the data. In his essay, Paczowski points out these inaccuracies. *Watermark* also contains other minor errors: for instance, the pupil of the eye is not of black color.

36. Making a virtue of necessity, this stylistic feature was caused by the lack of a steady foundation. Because the city was built on piles, the preferred materials were brick and stucco. Much heavier marble, the financial consideration notwithstanding, was usually used as a surface coating.

37. At this point I should mention a rather amusing coincidence. Whistler's trip to Venice had artistic objectives but was also the result of a chain of misfortunes beginning with his bankruptcy and the sale of his house, the outcome of a libel suit (in which he prevailed) brought by him against John Ruskin.

38. For a more meticulous explanation of the artist's technical innovations in etchings see Katharine Jordan Lochnan's doctoral dissertation "Whistler's Etchings and the Sources of His Etching Style 1855–1880" (New York and London: Garland Publishing, 1988).

39. Quoted in Lochnan, "Whistler's Etchings and the Sources of His Etching Style, 1855–1880," 214.

40. Although Whistler spent some time as a boy in Petersburg, where his father worked as a civil engineer (and died there during the cholera epidemics), Whistler scholars pay very little attention to this period.

41. With the exception of his famous Venetian canvases, which are filled with a myriad of vibrating colors.

42. Brodsky, however, disregarded this behavioral taboo and wept, shedding tears during the doctorate *honoris causa* ceremony at the Silesian University in Katowice, Poland.

43. See Gaston Bachelard, *Water and Dreams: An Essay on the Imagination of Matter,* trans. Edith R. Farrell (Dallas: Pegasus Foundation, 1983), 11.

Chapter 7

1. Bethea qualifies Brodsky's metaphysical poetry as "Donnean." (*Joseph Brodsky and the Creation of Exile,* 83).

2. "To Please a Shadow" is the title of Brodsky's essay dedicated to the memory of W. H. Auden, included in *Less Than One.*

3. The commemorative essay "In Memory of Stephen Spender," written on August 10, 1995, subsequently published by *The New Yorker* and included in *On Grief and Reason,* turned out to be Brodsky's last prose piece—a coincidence that adds a further meaning to his text.

4. Gerald Janacek, "Brodskii chitaet "Stikhi na smert' T. S. Eliota,'" in *Poetika Brodskogo. Sbornik statei (Brodsky's Poetics: A Collection of Essays)*, ed. L. V. Losev (Tenafly, N.J.: Hermitage, 1986), 182.

5. Tomas Venclova, "A Journey from Petersburg to Istanbul," trans. Jane Miller, in *Brodsky's Poetics and Aesthetics,* eds. Lev Loseff and Valentina Polukhina (London: Macmillan Press, 1990), 142.

6. See Andrei Sinyavsky's comments on this theme in Abram Tertz (Andrei Sinyavsky), *A Voice from the Chorus,* trans. Kiryl Fitzloyn and Max Hayward. Introd. Max Hayward. (New York: Farrar, Straus and Giroux, 1976), 30–31.

7. Interestingly, Mandelstam emphasizes the kinetic aspects of Dante's sojourn: "both the *Inferno* and, in particular, the *Purgatorio* glorify the human gait, the measure and rhythm of walking, the footstep and its form"; Osip Mandelstam, "Conversations about Dante," *The Complete Critical Prose and Letters,* ed. Jane Gary Harries, trans. Jane Gary Harris and Constance Link (London: Collins Harvill, 1991), 400.

8. In particular, Bidney associates Tolstoy's epiphanies with a rhythmic movement; see chapter "Water, Movement, Roundness: Epiphanies and Histories in Tolstoy's *War and Peace*" (154–71).

9. I should mention here that it is also prompted by Henri de Regnier, whose *Provincial Entertainments* describes events on the other side of the mirror in an old Venetian palace and so had an influence on Brodsky's conception of Venice while he was living in Leningrad.

10. These putti may symbolize the otherwise skipped seventeenth century. An interesting reading of Brodsky's use of the baroque is offered by David Mac Fadyen, *Joseph Brodsky and the Baroque* (Montreal, Kingston: McGill's–Queen's University Press: 1998).

11. In the middle of the tour, the narrator is left to his own devices when his guide and the other visitors stay behind. Thus, as in Zagajewski's and Herbert's essays, his moment of revelation occurs in solitude.

12. Rainer Maria Rilke, "Orpheus. Eurydice. Hermes," *Selected Works,* trans. J. B. Leishman (New York: New Directions, 1967), vol. 2, 188.

13. Vladimir Nabokov, *Speak, Memory,* in *The Portable Nabokov,* selection and introduction Page Stegner (New York: Viking Press, 1971), 5.

14. Polukhina writes about a similar attempt undertaken by Brodsky in his lyrics (an attempt parallel to Zagajewski's inquiry into objecthood): "Objects . . . live their own lives, which are 'not ours to understand.' The poet, in turn, strives to understand this mode of existence. . . . Brodsky perceives objects from *their* point of view" (*Joseph Brodsky: A Poet of Our Time,* 149).

15. Brodsky develops the theme of illness in conjunction both with Susan Sontag's book *Illness as Metaphor* and with his autobiography.

16. The association of the color yellow with death was methodically explored by Dostoyevsky in *Crime and Punishment.* Implying once again the affinities between Petersburg and Venice, Brodsky allows the pale yellow colors that dominate Dostoyevsky's novel to be reflected in the chromatic spectrum of *Watermark.*

17. Brodsky, "Ninety Years Later," 389.

18. Brodsky does not think highly of Rilke's visual knowledge, despite the German poet's lifelong fascination for the visual arts and his books on Rodin and Cézanne.

19. Clare Cavanagh, *Osip Mandelstam and the Modernist Creation of Tradition* (Princeton: Princeton University Press, 1995), 16.

20. Hugo Friedrich, *The Structure of Modern Poetry: From the Mid-Nineteenth to the Mid-Twentieth Century,* trans. Joachim Neugroschel (Evanston: Northwestern University Press, 1974), 157.

21. In a striking coincidence, Adam Zagajewski recalls a photo representing Leonard Bernstein during his last public appearance, when the composer—dressed in a white tuxedo—left the stage toward the "black

rectangle of the wings" (*Another Beauty,* 27). The meaning of the whole image as the passage toward death is underscored by the interplay of the colors white and black, reminiscent of Malevich.

22. The visitor's death can be related to Roland Barthes's concept of the death of the author.

23. In his informative article, James W. Fernandez surveys various cultures prone to the belief that a mirror can offer a glimpse at the world of the dead: "The reversal of an otherwise identical representation—what is called the enantiomorphic effect . . .—has been suggestive as a metaphor for the condition of the dead, particularly in societies which emphasize their continuity and similarity with the living"; see James W. Fernandez, "Reflections on Looking into Mirrors," *Semiotica* 30 (1980): 32.

24. Northrop Frye, *T. S. Eliot* (New York: Capricorn Books, 1972), 68.

25. Though Robert Fludd, the seventeenth-century Rosicrucian mystic, envisioned a black square (five inches by five inches) in terms of the mystical insight; along each of the square's sides he wrote "*et sic infinitum.*"

26. Joseph Brodsky, "Torso," trans. Howard Moss. *A Part of Speech* (New York: Noonday Press; Farrar, Straus and Giroux, 1980), 73.

27. Joseph Brodsky, "Venetian Stanzas II," trans. Jane Ann Miller and the author. *To Urania* (New York: Farrar, Straus and Giroux, 1988), 93.

28. Speaking of Dante's vision of the afterlife, Eliot attributes it to the historical period during which the poet lived: "he lived in an age in which men still saw visions. It was a psychological habit, the trick of which we have forgotten that seeing visions—a practice now relegated to the aberrant and uneducated—was once a more significant, interesting, and disciplined kind of dreaming." Dante's sweeping panorama of the Christian version of the afterlife, well detailed and nearly epic in its length, seems to be unsurpassable by all standards. A case such as Brodsky, however, would complicate Eliot's claim. See T. S. Eliot, "Dante," *Selected Prose of T. S. Eliot,* ed. Frank Kermode (London: Faber, 1975), 209.

29. See Brodsky's references to Malevich's *White on White* in "Eclogue IV: Winter," (*To Urania,* 79).

30. Strictly speaking, Malevich's *Black Square,* with its dimensions of 106.2 centimeters by 106.5 centimeters, is not precisely a square but a rectangle.

31. Lucy R. Lippard, *Ad Reinhard* (New York: Harry N. Abrams, 1981), 146.

Afterword

1. Abrams, *Natural Supernaturalism,* 211.

2. Leon Battista Alberti, *On Painting,* trans. John R. Spencer (New Haven: Yale University Press), 64.

Works Cited

Abramowska, Janina. "Wiersze z aniołami." *Czytanie Herberta.* Eds. Przemysław Czapliński, Piotr Sliwiński, and Ewa Wiegandt. Poznań: Wydawnictwo WiS, 1995, 65–79.

Abrams, M. H. *Natural Supernaturalism: Tradition and Revolution in Romantic Literature.* New York: W. W. Norton, 1971.

Adel'geim, I. E. " 'Rasshirenie rechi' (Iosif Brodskii i Pol'sha)," *Poliaki i russkie v glazakh drug druga,* eds. I. E. Adel'geim, B. V. Nosov, and V. A. Khorev (Moscow: "Indrik": 2000), 144–53.

Alberti, Leon Battista. *On Painting.* Trans. John R. Spencer. New Haven: Yale University Press, 1966.

Alpers, Svetlana. *The Art of Describing: Dutch Art in the Seventeenth Century.* Chicago: University of Chicago Press, 1984.

Anders, Jarosław. "Between Fire and Sleep." *Los Angeles Times,* (February 1998), 6.

Antsiferov, Nikolai. *Dusha Peterburga.* Paris: YMCA Press, 1978.

Augustine, Saint. *Confessions.* Trans. E. J. Sheed (London, 1944), ix.

Bachelard, Gaston. *Water and Dreams: An Essay on the Imagination of Matter.* Trans. Edith R. Farrell. Dallas: Pegasus Foundation, 1983.

Bakhtin, Mikhail. *Speech Genres and Other Essays.* Trans. Vern W. McGee. Austin: University of Texas Press, 1986.

Baranczak, Stanislaw. *A Fugitive from Utopia: The Poetry of Zbigniew Herbert.* Cambridge: Harvard University Press, 1987.

Barthes, Roland. *Critical Essays.* Trans. Richard Howard. Evanston: Northwestern University Press, 1972.

Baudelaire, Charles. *The Parisian Prowler: Le Spleen de Paris. Petits Poèmes en prose.* Trans. Edward K. Kaplan. Athens and London: University of Georgia Press, 1989.

Beja, Morris. *Epiphany in the Modern Novel.* Seattle: University of Washington Press, 1971.

Berenson, Bernard. *Aesthetics and History.* Garden City: Doubleday, 1948.

Best, Jan, and Fred Woudhuizen, eds. *Ancient Scripts from Crete and Cyprus.* Leiden, New York: E. J. Brill, 1988.

Bethea, David. *Joseph Brodsky and the Creation of Exile.* Princeton: Princeton University Press, 1994.

Bidney, Martin. *Patterns of Epiphany: From Wordsworth to Tolstoy, Pater, and Barrett Browning.* Carbondale and Edwardsville: Southern Illinois University Press, 1997.

Bishop, Elizabeth. *The Complete Poems 1927–1979.* New York: Noonday Press, 1991.

Blake, William. "The Marriage of Heaven and Hell." *Complete Poetry and Prose of William Blake.* Ed. David V. Erdman. Commentary Harold Bloom. Berkeley and Los Angeles: University of California Press, 1982.

Bloch, Vitale. *All the Paintings of Jan Vermeer.* Trans. Michael Kitson. New York: Hawthorn Books, 1963.

Błoński, Jan. "Epifanie Miłosza." *Poznawanie Miłosza. Studia I szkice o twórczości poety.* Ed. Jerzy Kwiatkowski. Cracow-Wrocław: Wydawnictwo Literackie, 1985.

Bohrer, Karl Heinz. *Suddenness: On the Moment of Aesthetic Appearance.* Trans. Ruth Crowley. New York: Columbia University Press, 1994.

Brodsky, Joseph. "After a Journey, or Homage to Vertebrae," *On Grief and Reason: Essays.* New York: Farrar, Straus and Giroux, 1995, 62–80.

———. "Altra Ego." *On Grief and Reason: Essays.* New York: Farrar, Straus and Giroux, 1995, 81–95.

———. "Lagoon." Trans. Anthony Hecht. *A Part of Speech.* New York: Noonday Press, Farrar, Straus and Giroux, 1980, 74–76.

———. *Less Than One: Selected Essays.* New York: Farrar, Strauss and Giroux, 1986.

———. Preface. *Modern Russian Poets on Poetry.* Ed. and introd. Carl R. Proffer. Trans. Alexander Golubev et al. Ann Arbor: Ardis, 1976, 8–9.

———. "Ninety Years Later." *On Grief and Reason: Essays.* New York: Farrar, Straus and Giroux, 1995, 376–427.

———. *On Grief and Reason: Essays.* New York: Farrar, Straus and Giroux, 1995.

———. *A Part of Speech.* New York: Noonday Press, Farrar, Straus and Giroux, 1980.

———. "A Poet and Prose." *Less Than One: Selected Essays.* New York: Farrar, Straus and Giroux, 1986, 176–94.

———. "Torso." Trans. Howard Moss. *A Part of Speech.* New York: Noonday Press, 1980, 73.

———. *To Urania.* New York: Farrar, Straus and Giroux, 1988.

———. "Venetian Stanzas II." Trans. Jane Ann Miller and the author. *To Urania.* New York: Farrar, Straus and Giroux, 1988, 93–95.

———. *Watermark.* New York: Farrar, Straus and Giroux, 1992.

———. "A Writer Is a Lonely Traveler." *The New York Times Magazine,* October 1, 1972, 81–88.

Brodsky, Joseph, Pitkethly, Lawrence, Robards, Jason. *Joseph Brodsky: A Maddening Space.* New York: Inner Dimension, Mystic Fire Video, 1989.

———. *Brodsky's Poetics and Aesthetics.* Ed. Lev Loseff and Valentina Polukhina. London: Macmillan, 1990.

Bryson, Norman. *Looking at the Overlooked: Four Essays on Still Life Painting.* Cambridge: Harvard University Press, 1990.

Camus, Albert. "The Rains of New York." *Lyrical and Critical Essays.* Ed. Phillip Toddy. Trans. Ellen Conroy Kennedy. New York: Vintage Books, 1970, 182–86.

Carpenter, Bogdana. "Zbigniew Herbert's Lesson of Art." *CrossCurrents: A Yearbook of Central European Culture* 11 (1992): 127–38.

Cavanagh, Clare. "Lyrical Ethics: The Poetry of Adam Zagajewski." *Slavic Review* (Spring 2000): 1–15.

———. *Osip Mandelstam and the Modernist Creation of Tradition*. Princeton: Princeton University Press, 1995.

Caws, Mary Ann. *A Metapoetics of the Passage: Architextures in Surrealism and After*. Hanover and London: University Press of New England, 1981.

Cichy, Michał. "Opinie. O *W cudzym pięknie* Adama Zagajewskiego." *Zeszyty Literackie* 64 (1998): 159–61.

Clifford, James. *Routes, Travel, and Translation in the Late Twentieth Century*. Cambridge and London: Harvard University Press, 1997.

Coleridge, Samuel Taylor. "Biographia Literaria," *The Critical Tradition: Classic Texts and Contemporary Trends*. Ed. David H. Richter. New York: St. Martin's Press, 1989, 306–16.

Croix, Horst de la, Richard G. Tansey, Dianne Kirkpatrick. *Gardner's Art Through the Ages*, 2 vols. New York: Harcourt Brace Jovanovich, 1991.

Czytanie Herberta. Eds. Przemysław Czapliński, Piotr Sliwiński, and Ewa Wiegandt. Poznań: Wydawnictwo WiS, 1995.

Davydova, Elena. "Venetsia-Peterburg: Kniga Pavla Muratova v kulture serebrannogo veka." *Graduate Essays on Slavic Languages and Literatures* 8 (1996): 2–16.

Dedecius, Karl. "Uprawa filozofii. Zbigniew Herbert w poszukiwaniu tożsamosci." Trans. Elżbieta Feliksiak. *Poznawanie Herberta*. Ed. Andrzej Franaszek. Cracow: Wydawnictwo Literackie, 1998, 128–68.

Derrida, Jacques. *Given Time. Counterfeit Money*. Trans. Peggy Kamuff. Chicago: University of Chicago Press, 1992.

DiMauro, Giorgio. "Setting Maps into Motion: The Aesthetics of Wandering in Zbigniew Herbert's Essays." *The Other Herbert*. Ed. Bożena Shallcross. Special issue of *Indiana Slavic Studies* 9 (1998): 29–41.

Diment, Galya. "English as Sanctuary: Nabokov's and Brodsky's Autobiographical Writings." *Slavic and East European Journal* 8 (1993): 346–59.

Douglas, Charlotte. *Kazimir Malevich*. New York: Harry N. Abrams Publishers, 1994.

Eliot, T. S. *Selected Prose of T. S. Eliot*. Ed. Frank Kermode. London: Faber, 1975.

Fernandez, James W. "Reflections on Looking into Mirrors." *Semiotica* 30 (1980): 27–39.

Framing the Polish Home: Postwar Cultural Constructions of Hearth, Nation, and Self. Ed. Bożena Shallcross. Athens: Ohio University Press, 2002.

Franaszek, Andrzej. *Ciemne źródło. O twórczosci Zbigniewa Herberta.* London: Puls Publications, 1998.

Freedberg, David. *The Power of Images: Studies in the History and Theory of Response.* Chicago and London: University of Chicago Press, 1989.

Friedrich, Hugo. *The Structure of the Modern Poetry: From the Mid-Nineteenth to the Mid-Twentieth Century.* Trans. Joachim Neugroschel. Evanston: Northwestern University Press, 1974.

Frye, Northrop. *T. S. Eliot.* New York: Capricorn Books, 1972.

Gass, William. *On Being Blue: A Philosophical Inquiry.* Boston: David R. Godine, 1976.

Geissmar, Christopher. *Das Auge Gottes: Bilder zu Jakob Boehme.* Wiessbaden: Harrassowitz Verlag, 1993.

Goering, Laura. "Belyj's Symbolist Abyss." *Slavic and East European Journal* 4 (1995): 568–84.

Heidegger, Martin. *Poetry, Language, Thought.* Trans. and introduction by Hofstadter Albert. New York: Harper and Row, 1971.

Heller, Erich. *The Artist's Journey into the Interior and Other Essays.* New York: Random House, 1965.

Herbert, Zbigniew. "Akropol." *Twórczość* 1 (1969): 9–33.

———. "Akropol i duszyczka." *Więż* 4 (1981): 3–8.

———. "Among the Dorians." *Barbarian in the Garden.* Trans. Michael March and Jaroslaw Anders. Manchester: Carcanet, 1985, 18–29.

———. *Barbarian in the Garden.* Trans. Michael March and Jaroslaw Anders. Manchester: Carcanet, 1985.

———. *Barbarzyńca w ogrodzie.* Warsaw: Czytelnik, 1964.

———. "The Bitter Smell of Tulips." *Still Life with a Bridle. Essays and Apocryphas.* Trans. John and Bogdana Carpenter. New York: Ecco Press, 1991, 38–61.

———. "Brewiarz." *Epilog burzy.* Wrocław: Wydawnictwo Dolnośląskie, 1998, 11.

———. "Delta." *Still Life with a Bridle. Essays and Apocryphas.* Trans. John and Bogdana Carpenter. New York: Ecco Press, 1991, 3–17.

———. *89 wierszy.* Cracow: Wydawnictwo a5, 1998.

———. *Epilog burzy.* Wrocław: Wydawnictwo Dolnośląskie, 1998.

———. "Gerard Terborch: The Discreet Charm of Bourgeoisie." *Still Life with a Bridle. Essays and Apocryphas.* Trans. John and Bogdana Carpenter. New York: Ecco Press, 1991, 62–77.

———. "Home." *Still Life with a Bridle. Essays and Apocryphas.* Trans. John and Bogdana Carpenter. New York: Ecco Press, 1991, 139–43.

———. "Labirynt nad morzem." *Twórczość* 2 (1973): 7–40.

———. "Lascaux." *Barbarian in the Garden.* Trans. Michael March and Jaroslaw Anders. Manchester: Carcanet, 1985, 7–17.

———. "Memories of Valois." *Barbarian in the Garden.* Trans. Michael March and Jaroslaw Anders. Manchester: Carcanet, 1985, 163–80.

———. "Old Masters." *Report from the Besieged City and Other Poems.* Trans., introd. and notes John and Bogdana Carpenter. New York: Ecco Press, 1985, 10–11.

———. "Piero della Francesca." *Barbarian in the Garden.* Trans. Michael March and Jaroslaw Anders. Manchester: Carcanet, 1985, 148–62.

———. "Prayer of Mr. Cogito-Traveler." *Report from the Besieged City and Other Poems.* Trans., introd. and notes John and Bogdana Carpenter. New York: Ecco Press, 1985, 12–13.

———. "Próba opisania krajobrazu greckiego." *Poezja* 9 (1969): 23–30.

———. "The Price of Art." *Still Life with a Bridle. Essays and Apocryphas.* Trans. John and Bogdana Carpenter. New York: Ecco Press, 1991, 18–37.

———. "Revelation," trans. Bogdana and John Carpenter. *Postwar Polish Poetry.* Ed. Czeslaw Milosz. Berkeley, Los Angeles and London: University of California Press, 1983, 132–34.

———. "Siena." *Barbarian in the Garden.* Trans. Michael March and Jaroslaw Anders. Manchester: Carcanet, 1985, 50–79.

———. *Still Life with a Bridle. Essays and Apocryphas.* Trans. John and Bogdana Carpenter. New York: Ecco Press, 1991.

———. "A Stone from the Cathedral," *Barbarian in the Garden.* Trans. Michael March and Jaroslaw Anders. Manchester: Carcanet, 1985, 80–100.

———. "Study of the Object," trans. John and Bogdana Carpenter. *Postwar Polish Poetry.* Ed. Czeslaw Milosz. Berkeley, Los Angeles and London: University of California Press, 1983, 134–38.

——. "Węzeł gordyjski." *Więź* 6 (1981): 39–47.

——. *Wybór poezji. Dramaty.* Warsaw: Czytelnik, 1973.

Hillebrand, Bruno. *Ästhetik des Augenblicks. Der Dichter als Überwinder der Zeit-von Goethe bis heute.* Göttingen: Vandenhoeck and Ruprecht, 1999.

Hirsch, Ed. "Fidelity of Things." *The New Yorker,* December 23, 1991, 100–7.

Hirsch, Rudolf. "Edmund Husserl and Hugo von Hofmannsthal: Eine Begegnung und ein Brief," *Sprache und Politik: Festgaabe für Dolf Sternberger.* Eds. Friedrich Carl-Joachim and Benno Reifenberg. Heidelberg: L. Schneider, 1968: 109–15.

Huxley, Aldous. *The Doors of Perception and Heaven and Hell.* New York: Harpers and Row, 1990.

Iser, Walter. *Walter Pater: The Aesthetic Moment.* Trans. David Henry Wilson. Cambridge: Cambridge University Press, 1987.

Iwaszkiewicz, Jarosław. *Podróże do Włoch.* Warsaw: Państwowy Instytut Wydawniczy, 1977.

Jackowski, Antoni. *Pielgrzymowanie.* Wrocław: Wydawnictwo Dolnośląskie, 1998.

James, Henry. *Transatlantic Sketches.* Boston: Houghton, Mifflin, 1868.

Janacek, Gerald. "Brodski chitaet 'Stikhi na smert' T. S. Eliota." *Poetika Brodskovo. Sbornik statei.* Ed. L. V. Losev. Tenafly, N.J.: Hermitage, 1986.

Jongh, Eddy de, with assistance of Titia van Leeuwen, Andrea Gasten, and Hilary Sayles. *Still-Life in the Age of Rembrandt.* Auckland: Auckland City Art Gallery, 1982.

Kijowski, Andrzej. "Pielgrzym." *Twórczość* 5 (1963): 58–62.

Kirsch, Adam. "The Lucid Moment." *The New Republic* (March 1998): 38–44.

Kiślak, Elżbieta. "Podróż i doświadczenie historii." *Zdziwienia Kraszewskim.* Ed. Marta Zielińska. Wrocław: Ossolineum, 1990, 121–30.

Lemkhin, Mikhail. *Joseph Brodsky. Lenigrad. Fragments.* New York: Farrar, Straus and Giroux, 1998.

Lippard, Lucy R. *Ad Reinhard.* New York: Harry N. Abrams, 1981.

Lochnan, Katherine Jordan. *Whistler's Etchings and the Sources of His Etching Style 1885–1880.* New York and London: Garland Publishing, 1989.

Łukasiewicz, Jacek. *Poezja Zbigniewa Herberta.* Warsaw: Wydawnictwa Szkolne i Pedagogiczne, 1995.

Lyotard, Jean-Francois. "Newman: The Instant," *The Lyotard Reader.* Ed. Andrew Benjamin. Oxford: Blackwell, 1989.

The Lyotard Reader. Ed. Andrew Benjamin. Oxford: Blackwell, 1989.

Mac Fadyen, David. *Joseph Brodsky and the Baroque.* Montreal, Kingston, London: McGill–Queen's University Press, 1998.

Man, Paul de. "The Literary Self as Origin: The Work of George Poulet," *Blindness and Insight: Essays in Rhetoric in Contemporary Criticism.* Introd. Godzich Wlad. Minneapolis: University of Minnesota Press, 1983, 79–101.

Mandelstam, Osip. "Conversations about Dante," *The Complete Critical Prose and Letters.* Ed. Jane Gary Harris. Trans. Jane Gary Harris and Constance Link. London: Collins Harvill, 1991, 397–442.

Milosz, Czeslaw. Foreword to Mikhail Lemkhin, *Joseph Brodsky. Leningrad. Fragments.* New York: Farrar, Straus and Giroux, 1998.

——. *Modern Russian Poets on Poetry.* Ed. and introd. Carl R. Proffer. Selected and with a preface by Joseph Brodsky. Trans. Alexander Golubev, et al. Ann Arbor: Ardis, 1976.

——. "Opinie: O *W cudzym pięknie* Adama Zagajewskiego." *Zeszyty Literackie* 64 (1998): 165.

——. Preface to Adam Zagajewski, *Tremor.* Trans. Renata Gorczynski. London: Collins Harvill, 1987, 11–12.

——, ed. *Postwar Polish Poetry.* Berkeley, Los Angeles: University of California Press, 1983.

Nabokov, Vladimir. *Speak, Memory. The Portable Nabokov.* New York: Viking, 1971, 5–86.

Nichols, Ashton. *The Poetics of Epiphany: Nineteenth-Century Origins of the Modern Literary Movement.* Tuscaloosa and London: University of Alabama Press, 1987.

Nycz, Ryszard. " 'A closed sliver of the world': On the Writing of Gustaw Herling-Grudziński." Trans. Jolanta Dutkiewicz. *Sacrum in Polish Literature.* Ed. Halina Filipowicz. Special issue of *Renascence: Essays on Values in Literature* 47 (1995): 221–29.

——. " 'Every one of us is a stranger': Patterns of Identity in Polish Literature in the Twentieth Century." Trans. Tomasz Bieroń. *Framing the Polish Home:*

Postwar Cultural Constructions of Hearth, Nation, and Self. Ed. Bożena Shall-cross. Athens: Ohio University Press, 2002, 11–22.

————. "Poetyka epifanii a modernizm (od Norwida do Leśmiana)." *Teksty Drugie* 40 (1996): 20–38.

Ortega y Gasset, Jose. "On Point of View in Art." *Partisan Review* (August 1949): 822–36.

The Other Herbert. Ed. Bożena Shallcross. Special issue of *Indiana Slavic Studies* 9 (1998).

Paczowski, Bohdan. "Oko Brodskiego." *Zeszyty Literackie* 64 (1998): 127–36.

Patryk (pseud. Zbigniew Herbert). "Altichiero." *Zeszyty Literackie* 32 (1990): 143.

Poetika Brodskogo. Sbornik statei. Ed. L. V. Losev. Tenafly, N.J.: Hermitage, 1986.

Poliaki i russkie v glazakh drug druga. Ed. I. E. Adel'geim, B. V. Nosov, and V. A. Khorev. Moskva: Izdatelstvo "Indrik": 2000.

Polukhina, Valentina. *Joseph Brodsky: A Poet of Our Time.* Cambridge: Cambridge University Press, 1989.

Pops, Martin. *Vermeer: Consciousness and the Chamber of Being.* Ann Arbor: University of Michigan Press Research Press, 1984.

Postwar Polish Poetry. Ed. Czeslaw Milosz. Berkeley: University of California Press, 1983.

Poulet, Georges. *Mesure de l'instant.* Paris: Plon, 1968.

Poznawanie Herberta. Ed. Andrzej Franaszek. Cracow: Wydawnictwo Literackie, 1998.

Poznawanie Miłosza. Studia i szkice o twórczości poety. Ed. Jerzy Kwiatkowski. Cracow-Wrocław: Wydawnictwo Literackie, 1985.

Praz, Mario. *Mnemosyne: The Parallel between Literature and the Visual Arts.* Princeton: Princeton University Press, 1970.

Protzman, Ferdinand. "Justice Delayed?" *ArtsNews* (December 1998): 134–39.

Proust, Marcel. *The Captive.* Trans. C. K. Scott Moncrieff. New York: Albert and Charles Boni, 1929.

Rabasa, José. *Inventing America: Spanish Historiography and the Formation of Eurocentrism.* Norman: University of Oklahoma Press, 1993.

Reszty nie trzeba. Rozmowy z Josifem Brodskim. Ed. Jerzy Illg. Katowice: Książnica, 1993.

Richard, Jean-Pierre. *Microlectures.* Paris: Éditions du Seuil, 1979, 2 vols.

Richardson, John, ed. *G. Braque.* New York: New York Graphic Society, 1961.

Rilke, Rainer Maria. "Orpheus. Eurydice. Hermes." *Selected Works.* Trans. J. B. Leishman. New York: New Directions, 1967, vol. 2, 188–90.

———. *Selected Works.* Trans. J. B. Leishman. New York: New Direction, 1967.

Ruskin, John. *The Stones of Venice.* New York: Moyer Bell Limited, 1989.

Rymkiewicz, Jarosław Marek. "Krzesło." *Twórczość* I (1970): 50–88.

Sacrum in Polish Literature. Ed. Halina Filipowicz. Special issue of *Renascence: Essays on Values in Literature* 47 (1995).

Scammell, Michael. "Loyal Toward Reality." *The New York Review of Books* 14 (1998): 36–40.

Selected Prose of T. S. Eliot. Ed. Frank Kermode. New York: Harcourt Brace Jovanovich, 1975.

Shallcross, Bożena. "The Barbarian's Garden: Zbigniew Herbert and the Folly of History," *East European Politics and Societies* 1 (2000): 47–63.

———. "Morton Street 44," *Reszty nie trzeba. Rozmowy z Josifem Brodskim.* Ed. Jerzy Illg. Katowice: Książnica, 1993, 169–77.

Siemaszko, Piotr. *Zmienność i trwanie. O eseistyce Zbigniewa Herberta.* Bydgoszcz: Instytut Wydawniczy "Świadectwo," 1996.

Simmons, Sherwin W. *Kasimir Malevich's Black Square and the Genesis of Suprematism 1907–1915.* Ph.D. diss., John Hopkins University, 1979.

Sochoń, Jan. "Szare numinozum." *Zeszyty Literackie* 33 (1991): 124–29.

Sontag, Susan. Afterword to Mikhail Lemkin, *Joseph Brodsky. Leningrad: Fragments.* New York: Farrar, Straus and Giroux, 1998: 201–4.

Spieker, Sven. "Still Life as Fetish." *The Other Herbert.* Ed. Bożena Shallcross. Special issue of *Indiana Slavic Studies* 9 (1998): 61–78.

Sprache und Politik: Festgaabe für Dolf Sternberger. Eds. Friedrich Carl-Joachim and Benno Reifenberg. Heidelberg: L. Schneider, 1968.

Stala, Marian. "Contemporaneity and Reality: Toward a Reading of Zbigniew Herbert by the Artists of Generation 68." Trans. Katarzyna Owczarek. *The*

Other Herbert. Ed. Bożena Shallcross. Special issue of *Indiana Slavic Studies* 9 (1998): 121–35.

Sterling, Charles. *Still Life Painting: From Antiquity to the Twentieth Century.* New York: Harper and Row: 1981.

Szczęsna, Justyna. "Uwiedziony przez Boga." *Czytanie Herberta.* Eds. Przemysław Czapliński, Piotr Sliwiński, and Ewa Wiegandt. Poznań: Wydawnictwo WiS, 1995.

Tertz Abram. (Andrei Sinyavsky). *A Voice from the Chorus.* Trans. Kiryl Fitzlyon and Max Hayward. Introd. Max Hayward. New York: Farrar, Straus and Giroux, 1976.

Tyszczyk, Andrzej. "Herbert, Kant i Bóg." *Na Przykład* 4 (1998): 33.

Venclova, Tomas. "A Journey form Petersburg to Istanbul." Trans. Jane Miller. *Brodsky's Poetics and Aesthetics.* Eds. Lev Loseff and Valentina Polukhina. London: Macmillan Press, 1990.

Volkova, Marianna and Volkov, Solomon. *Iosif Brodskii v N'iu-Iorke.* New York: Cultural Center for Soviet Refugees, Inc., 1990.

Webb, Ruth. "Ekphrasis Ancient and Modern: The Invention of the Genre." *Word & Image: The Journal of Verbal/Visual Enquiry,* 15, no. 1 (1999): 7–18.

Wiegandt, Ewa. "Eseje poety." *Czytanie Herberta.* Eds. Przemysław Czapliński, Piotr Sliwiński, Ewa Wiegandt. Poznań: Wydawnictwo WiS, 1995, 212–28.

Wolfe, Thomas. *Of Time and River: A Legend of Man's Hunger in His Youth.* Garden City: Sun Dial Press, 1944.

Zagajewski, Adam. *Another Beauty.* Trans. Clare Cavanagh. New York: Farrar, Straus and Giroux, 2000.

———. "Bezdomny Nowy Jork." *Jechać do Lwowa.* London: Aneks, 1985, 22.

———. *Canvas.* Trans. Renata Gorczynski, Benjamin Ivry, C. K. Williams. New York: Farrar, Straus and Giroux, 1991.

———. "Changes in the East." *Two Cities: On Exile, History, and Imagination.* Trans. Lillian Vallee. New York: Farrar, Straus and Giroux, 1995, 220–23.

———. "The City Where I Want to Live." *Mysticism for Beginners.* Trans. Clare Cavanagh. New York; Farrar, Straus and Giroux, 1997, 55.

———. "Covenant." *Canvas.* Trans. Renata Gorczynski, Benjamin Ivry, C. K. Williams. New York: Farrar, Straus and Giroux, 1991, 21.

———. "W cudzym pięknie." *List. Oda do wielości.* Paris: Instytut Literacki, 1983. 25.

———. "Essentialist in Paris," *Two Cities: On Exile, History, and Imagination.* Trans. Lillian Vallee. New York: Farrar, Straus and Giroux, 1995, 177–84.

———. "Flamenco." *Solidarity, Solitude: Essays by Adam Zagajewski.* Trans. Lillian Vallee. New York: Ecco Press, 1990, 151–66.

———. "Fruit." *Canvas.* Trans. Renata Gorczynski, Benjamin Ivry, C. K. Williams. New York: Farrar, Straus and Giroux, 1991, 80.

———. *Jechać do Lwowa.* London: Aneks, 1985.

———. *List. Oda do wielości.* Paris: Instytut Literacki, 1983.

———. "The Moment." *Mysticism for Beginners.* Trans. Clare Cavanagh. New York: Farrar, Straus and Giroux, 1997, 40.

———. "Morandi." *Canvas.* Trans. Renata Gorczynska, Benjamin Ivry, C. K. Williams. New York: Farrar, Straus and Giroux, 1991, 19.

———. *Mysticism for Beginners.* Trans. Clare Cavanagh. New York: Farrar, Straus and Giroux, 1997.

———. *Solidarity, Solitude: Essays by Adam Zagajewski.* Trans. Lillian Vallee. New York: Ecco Press, 1990.

———. *Tremor.* Trans. Renata Gorczynski. Introd. Czeslaw Milosz. London: Collins Harvill, 1987.

———. *Two Cities: On Exile, History, and the Imagination.* Trans. Lillian Vallee. New York: Farrar, Straus and Giroux, 1995.

———. "Two Cities." *Two Cities: On Exile, History, and Imagination.* Trans. Lillian Vallee. New York: Farrar, Straus and Giroux, 1995, 3–68.

———. "A View of Cracow." *Tremor.* Trans. Renata Gorczynski. Introd. Czeslaw Milosz. London: Collins Harvill, 1987, 78.

———. "A View of Delft." *Tremor.* Trans. Renata Gorczynski. Introd. Czeslaw Milosz. London: Collins Harvill, 1987, 39.

Zaleski, Marek. "Nuda powtórzeń." *Res Publica* 5 (1998): 37–43.

Zdziwienia Kraszewskim. Ed. Marta Zielińska. Wrocław: Ossolineum, 1990.

Index

Abrams, M. H., 142
Abyss: black, 134, 135; images of the, 86, 88, 89, 90; negative, 136; and posthumous, 135; "prenatal" (Nabokov), 130; void, 104, 109, 119, 131, 134–35, 137. *See also* Nothingness
Acropolis, the, 44, 46, 65–66
Afterlife, the, 131, 167n28; Brodsky's 123–28; Brodsky's conception of, 123–25, 137; as confined space, 129; existence questioned, 139; journey to the underworld (*katabasis*), 125, 135, 165n5; netherworld, 126, 132–34; spatial arrangement of the underworld, 126, 132, 133, 134. *See also* Death
Agnosticism, 10, 97
Akhmatova, Anna, 114
Alberti, Leon Battista, 143
Albertina Museum (Vienna), 132
Alexander the Great, 67

Alpers, Svetlana, 70, 82
Altichiero da Zevio, 68–69
Amsterdam: Herbert in, 57, 141; Royal Museum, 77, 79, 89, 97. *See also* Holland
Annales (French school of thought), xv
Antiworld, antiuniverse, 104, 120
Apollinaire, Guillaume, "The Disappearance of Honoré Subrac," 111
Archaeological Museum (Herakleion), 74, 75
Architecture: Baroque, 166n20; Byzantine, 116; cathedral, 16, 17, 44, 50; Cracow, 9; Dutch, 51; Gothic, xv, 16, 34, 44, 49–50, 60, 66, 116; Greek temples, 44, 47–48; modernist, 116; Romanesque, xv, 16, 20; the sacred embodied in, 61, 99; Venetian, 116–17
Art criticism: by Brodsky, 131–33; ecstatic, 64–65, 156n5; by Herbert, *see* Herbert, Zbigniew

Aschenbach, Gustav, 104
Auden, W. H., 125
Augenblick, 65
Augustine, Saint: *Confessions,* 95
Avant-garde, rejection of, 138, 143

Bakhtin, Mikhail, 53
Baranczak, Stanislaw, xiv, 85, 145n2, 147n2
Baroque, Brodsky's use of the, 166n10
Barthes, Roland, 167n22
Baudelaire, Charles, 5; *The Parisian Prowler,* 18
Beja, Morris, 146n6, 155n2; *Epiphany in the Modern Novel,* xvi
Bellini, Giovanni, 114, 115
Bely, Andrey, 123
Benjamin, Walter, 8, 49
Berenson, Bernard, 28, 155n33
Bernstein, Leonard, 166–67n21
Bethea, David, 105, 123
Bidney, Martin, xvii, 127, 156n6
Binnenhof (The Hague), 74
Bishop, Elizabeth, vii, 5, 11, 30
Black: abyss, 134, 135; mirror, 134, 135–38, 143; paintings and backgrounds, 85–89, 91–92, 96, 98–99, 137–39. *See also* Color and light; Mirror motif; Nothingness
Blake, William, 25, 26
Boehme, Jakob, 58, 154–55n30
Bosch, Hieronymus: *Ascent to Heavenly Paradise,* 158n33
Brancusi, Constantin, 33
Braque, Georges, 161n4
Bredius, Abraham, 69
Brodkey, Harold, 160n3
Brodsky, Joseph, 79; as art critic, 131–33; black vision of, 99; as draftsman, 154n18; ekphrasis by, 128, 137, 142, 143; epiphanies of, xvii–xviii, 134; as exile, xiii–xiv, xv, 103–6, 110–14; and "great Perhaps," 123–24; metaphysics of, *see* Metaphysics; as Nobel laureate, 110, 146n11; post-Romanticism of, 142;

and prose vs. poetry, 105–7; sheds tears, 164n42; totalitarianism opposed by, xviii; in Venice, xiv, xv, 103–9, 110–15, 117–22, 126, 127–39, 139, 140, 143; as walker (*flâneur*), 8, 117–18, 127. WORKS: "After a Journey," 163n21; "Butterfly," 161n5, 162n19; "Flight from Byzantium," 126; "Footnote to a Poem," 124; "In Memory of Stephen Spender," 165n3; "In Praise of Boredom," 107; "In a Room and a Half," 110; "Lagoon," 163n22; *Less Than One,* 165n2; "Nature Morte," 130; "Ninety Years Later," 124, 129, 131; *On Grief and Reason: Essays,* 107, 165n3; "A Poet and Prose," 105; "To Please a Shadow," 165n2; "Torso," 136; "Venetian Stanzas (I and II)," 104, 105, 137; "Verses on T. S. Eliot's Death," 124, 125; *Watermark,* xix, 104–11, 114, 117, 121–22, 123–27, 129, 130, 132, 133, 136, 137; "A Writer Is a Lonely Traveler," 146n12; Wunderlust, 104
Brouwer, Adriaen, 80
Bruegel, Pieter the Elder: *The Artist and the Connoisseur,* 132
Bryson, Norman, 83–84
Burke, Edmund, 99
Byron, George Lord, 114

Camus, Albert, 21
Canal, Giovanni Antonio, 114, 115
Caravaggio, 78
Carmen (film), 24–25
Carpaccio, Vittore, 114
Carpenter, Bogdana, 54, 86
Cassirer, Ernst, 60
Cathars, the, 44
Cavanagh, Clare, 20, 132
Caws, Mary Ann, 157n26
Cazalis, Henri, 133
Cézanne, Paul, 65, 137
Chaos, 18, 25, 87

Charles, Prince of Wales, 117
Chartres Cathedral, 17
Chastel, André, 160n2
Christianity, 15–16, 129, 133, 135
Church of Notre Dame (Senlis), 49–50
Church of Saint Moise (Venice), 117
Church of Saint Pankras (Leyden), 56
Church of the Franciscans (Cracow), 10, 15
Clifford, James, 46
Clothing as metaphor, 112–13
Coducci, Mauro, 117
Coleridge, Samuel Taylor, 115
Color and light, xv, 10, 16; blue, significance of, 28–29, 30; in Dutch art, 24, 27–29, 52, 59–61, 80–81, 87–88; in Venice, *see* Venice; yellow associated with death, 166n16. *See also* Black
Communist regime, xiii, xiv, 5, 7, 49; censorship under, 147n2; travel restrictions, 46
Consorzio Venezia Nuova, 160n2
Consumerism criticized, 149n24
Corinthians, First Epistle to, 133, 135
Cracow, Zagajewski in, 8–10, 11, 21, 36
Creation, the, 15–16, 58, 82, 135
Creative Writing Program (University of Texas), 31
Cretan frescoes, 74–77
Cultural: deprivation, 7; discourses of culture, 80; obeissance, 16; and spiritual divide, 49; text 70
Cusanus, Nicolaus, 27

Dante Alighieri, 8, 125, 167n28; *The Divine Comedy,* 126
Darkness. *See* Black
Death, 136; cults of, 76–77, 81; Dutch burghers' fear of, 88; fascination with, 104; and nothingness, 97, 134; yellow associated with, 166n16. *See also* Afterlife, the
Derrida, Jacques, 80
Descartes, René, and Cartesianism, 131

Diment, Galya, 161n10
Dionysiac cult, 83
Disinheritance (exile), xiv–xv, 148n8. *See also* Travel
"Doodles" of Brodsky and Herbert, 146n10
Dostoyevsky, Fyodor, 66, 95; *Crime and Punishment,* 126, 166n16
Drugs. *See* Mescaline
Dust, symbolism of, 120–21, 130
Dutch visual tradition, 52–61, 80, 97; and cost of paintings, 82; Herbert's exploration of, 85–94; and realism, 53, 55, 56–57, 70, 82. *See also* Color and light; Vermeer van Delft, Jan

Eastern Orthodox Church, 57, 110
Echo, 162n18
Echoism, 106, 107–9, 127, 134, 163n24. *See also* Mirror motif
Eckhart, Meister, 136
Egyptian Book of the Dead, 76
Egyptian mysteries, 158n4
Ekphrasis: by Brodsky, 128, 129, 137; definition of, 148n17; by Herbert, *see* Herbert, Zbigniew; oldest known account of, 142; by Zagajewski, *see* Zagajewski, Adam; ekphrastic power, 23
Eleusian mysteries, 158n4
Eliot, T. S., 63, 66, 124–25, 137
Empedocles, 134
Encyclopaedia Britannica, 68
Epiphanies: Brodsky and, xvii–xviii, 134; definitions of word, xvi, 19, 25; epiphanic agent, 32, (irrelevance of agent) xvi, 156n4; epiphanic imagination, 20; epiphanic perception, 75; and epiphanic rapture, 63–65, 79, 80, 84, 146n9; epiphanic transformation, 29; and epiphanic travel, xiv–xviii, 64, 141, 145n3; epitomized in paintings, 158n4; and Heidegger, 155n2; of Herbert, *see* Herbert, Zbigniew; metaphysical,

Epiphanies (*cont.*)
95; modernist, in works of fiction, xvi, 64; movement related, 165n8; object-related, 33–39; patterns of, 127; principles inspiring, 83; Romantic roots of, 156n6; of Zagajewski, *see* Zagajewski, Adam
Ettinger, Pavel, 96
Evans, Sir Arthur, 74, 75
Everdingen, Caesar van, 150n8
Eye: 54; of constructivist, 34; dominance of 16; empirical, 61; journey of, 57, 61, 65, 86, 79; mechanical, 47; narrator's 52; poet's, 76, 142; traveler's 118, 164n32. *See also* God
Eye, the: of the beholder ("other"), 37, 53, 84; of God, 38–39, 58, 162n19; Herbert's "inner," 61, 94; journey of, 79; pupil of death, 93–94; and tears, 121–22; traveler's (Brodsky's) 107–8, 109. *See also* Vision

Fernandez, James W., 167n23
Fine Art Society (London), 118
Fischer, Pieter, 70
Flâneur. See Walking
Flemish art, 58, 83, 91
Fludd, Robert, 167n25
Form 72, 142; and formlessness, 25, 26–27, 87, 89, 90, 97
Frescoes: Cretan (Minoan period), 74–77; Lascaux Cave, 44, 45, 72–74, 76, 77, 79, 83; Renaissance, 44, 68; Siena, 95; Venetian, 128
Frick Museum (New York City), 22, 24, 29, 143
Friedrich, Caspar David, 94
Friedrich, Hugo, 133, 136
Fromentin, Eugène: *The Old Masters of Belgium and Holland,* 60
Frye, Northrop, 135

Gass, William, 27; *On Being Blue,* 29
"Generation 68," 147n2
Ghirlandajo, Domenico, 95
Gide, André, xiii

Giorgione, 114, 115
Girl Interrupted at Her Music (*The Music Lesson*). *See* Vermeer van Delft, Jan
God: eye of, 38–39, 58, 162n19; as form as well as formlessness, 27; and "great Perhaps," 123; immanence of, 39; as living presence, 15–16, (nonfigurative) 96–97, 99; man created in image of, 108; revelation of, 15, 78, (dark) 61, 96; transcendence of, 7; in visual tradition, 60, 96. *See also* Creation, the
Goethe, Johann Wolfgang von, 55, 74, 110; *Italian Journey, 1786–1788,* xv
Gogol, Nikolay, 103
Gombrowicz, Witold, 24, 25
Gordian knot, the, 67

Hagia Triada Sarcophagus, 75, 77, 81, 83, 84
Hals, Frans, 55
Hawthorne, Nathaniel, 18
Hazlitt, William, 114
Heaney, Seamus, 150n6
Heda, Willem, 80
Heidegger, Martin, 25, 155–56n2
Hepworth, Barbara, 48
Herbert, Zbigniew, xv, 8, 43, 120; as agnostic, 97; as art critic, 54–59, 64–70, 72–84, 97–99; as draftsman, 153–54n18; ekphrasis by, 52, 153n14, (of Torrentius) 69–72, 76–77, 79–80, 85–94, 98, 142–43; epiphanies of, 45, 63–65, 83, 99, 126–27, (in Crete) 75–80, 84, (at Lascaux) 72–74, 76; in exile, xiii–xiv, xv; influence of, 35, 161n8; metaphysics of, *see* Metaphysics; post-Romanticism of, 142; pseudonym of, 68; revelatory experiences of, xvii–xviii; totalitarianism opposed by, xviii; as traveler, 43–54, 64, 86, (to Europe and United States) 153n10, (in Greece) 67, 74–77, 81, 153n10, (in Holland) 51–

61, 141. WORKS: 126, 166n11; "The Acropolis," 65; "The Acropolis and the Little Soul," 46, 65; "Altar," 153n14; "Among the Dorians," 47–48, 49; "Apocryphas," 51, 52, 66, 86; *Barbarian in the Garden,* xix, 43, 44–46, 51–55 passim, 67, 79, 94, 155n33; "The Bitter Smell of Tulips," 155n1; "Breviary," 160n23; "Delta," 52, 53, 54, 55, 56, 57, 58, 59, 60; "The Epilogue of the Storm," 160n23; "Essays," 51; "Gerard Terborch: The Discreet Charm of the Bourgeoisie," 88; "The Gordian Knot," 156n14; "Home," 86–87; "The Labyrinth by the Sea," 64, 67; "Letter," 66; "Memories of Valois," 49, 51; "The Minor Creator's Problems," 159n20; "Mr. Cogito is examining his face in the mirror," 59; "Old Masters," 55; "The Prayer of Mr. Cogito-Traveler," 65, 152n5; "The Price of Art," 55; "Revelation," 92; "Siena," 94–96; *Still Life with a Bridle: Essays and Apocrypha,* xix, 43, 51–54, 55, 69, 70–71, 79, 86, 89–94, 155n1, n33; *A String of Light,* 153n14; *Study of the Object,* 92–93
Herling-Grudziński, Herbert and Gustaw, 152n2
Herzen, Aleksandr, 114
Hofmannsthal, Hugo von, 36
Holland: Herbert in, 51–61, 89, 96. *See also* Dutch visual tradition
Homer, 125, 135; *The Iliad,* 142; *The Odyssey,* 49
Horace, 125
Husserl, Edmund, 35, 36
Huxley, Aldous, 38, 143; "The Doors of Perception," 25–26
Huygens, Constantijn, 158n29; *Observations on Painting,* 69

Illness as theme, 166n15. *See also* Death
Illumination: dark, 134; epiphany and, 21; moment of, 20, 66, 75; poetics of, 74–84; in Zagajewski's prose writing, 7. *See also* Epiphanies; Vision
Ingarden, Roman, 35–36, 39
Intimism, 108
Italian painting, 83
Iwaszkiewicz, Jarosław, 95

James, Henry, 56, 154n28
Janacek, Gerald, 125
Jongh, Eddy de, 70
Joyce, James, xvi
Judaic law, 99
Jünger, Ernst, 12, 14–15

Kandinsky, Wassily, 28, 91
Kant, Immanuel, 98, 99
Khrushchev, Nikita, 46
Kijowski, Andrzej: "Pilgrim," 45
Kirsch, Adam, 6, 147nn3, 4
Kiślak, Elżbieta, 12
Knossos: frescoes, 75; labyrinth, 108
Kornhauser, Julian, 147n2
Krynicki, Ryszard, 147n2

Lascaux Cave. *See* Frescoes
Leeuwenhoek, Anton van, 67, 88
Léger, Fernand, 152n3
Leonardo da Vinci, 54; *Mona Lisa,* xv, 46, 72
Lermontov, M. Y., "Death of a Poet," 125
Lombardo, Pietro, 117
Lorenzetti, Ambrogio, 95
Lorrain, Claude, 136, 162n14
Lyotard, Jean-François, 98–99

Magritte, René, 87
Malevich, Kasimir, 87, 97, 99, 137–38, 143, 167n21; *Black Circle,* xix, 91–92, 93, 94; *Black Square,* xix, 91–92, 96, 139
Mallarmé, Stéphane, 85, 104, 133
Mandelstam, Osip, 105, 110, 114, 165n7

Mann, Thomas, 66, 114, 133

Maps. *See* Topography

Marcel, Gabriel, 125

Martini, Simone, 95

Meditation, wanderings as form of, 8

Memling, Hans: *Madonna with a Child,* 58

Merleau-Ponty, Maurice, 109

Mescaline, 25, 143

Metaphysics: Brodsky and, 106, 126, 137, 139, (Christian) 129, 135, (discussion of) 123, (metaphysical perspective) 104, 127; given visual form, xvii, 141–42; Herbert and, 59, 64, 73, 86, 90, 95, (metaphysical moment) 64; metaphysical journey, xvii; worldview, 97

Metropolitan Museum of Art (New York City), 37

Metsys, Quentin: *The Banker and His Wife,* 58

Mickiewicz, Adam, 6, 147n1, 147nn8, 9; *Pan Tadeusz,* 55

Microlecture, 106

Milosz, Czeslaw, 7, 31, 51, 161n8, 163n27

Milosz, Oscar de Lubicz, 126

Minimalism, 33, 86, 138

Minoan Book of the Dead, 76

Minoan frescoes, 74–77

Mirror motif, 57–59, 90–91, 104, 107, 108, 109–10, 114, 116, 133; black mirror, 134, 135–38, 143. *See also* Echoism

Modernism, xvi, 64, 91, 96, 97, 99; architectural, attacked, 117; postmodernism, 49; visual tradition, 133, 137

Moment: "aesthetic," 156n6; ephemeral, 79; epiphanic, *see* Epiphanies; frozen, 23; of illumination, 66, 86, 150n6, 159n17; intense 25; metaphysical, 64, 88, 150n6, 155–56n2, 159n17; revelatory, 125; of vision, 69, 94, 131

Mondrian, Piet, 91

Monet, Claude, 17

Montaigne, Michel Eyquem de, 8

Montsegur, 45

Movement, xiv, 20, 149n2; epiphanies connected with, 127; and imagination, 8; motion, xvii, 20, 95, 127; vision combined with, 134, 148n12. *See also* Passage; Travel; Walking

Munch, Edvard, 131

Muratov, Pavel: *Images of Italy,* 162n15

Music, 34, 108

Music Lesson, The. See Vermeer van Delft, Jan

Mystery (enigma), of the Acropolis, 65; arbitrary, 70, 83; mysterious, the, 66–76; *reductio ad mysterium,* 71; textual, 68; Torrentius's, 89; ultimate, 97; of work of art, 65

Nabokov, Vladimir, 130

Narcissus, 143

Native American artifacts, 49

Negativity, 94, 104, 113, 130; Brodsky's, 124; countenance, 97; mode, 91; negative aesthetics, 97, 99, 105; presentation, 99; revelation, 138; self-knowledge, 31; space, 48; theology, 97

Newman, Barnett, 99

New Wave movement, 6

New York City, Zagajewski in, 21–23, 25, 26, 38, 141

New Yorker, The, 165n3

Nichols, Ashton, 146n6

Nietzsche, Friedrich, 95, 156n7, 162n16

Nobel Prize (Brodsky), 110, 146n11

Nonexistence, 104, 161n4

Nothingness, 89, 90, 95, 161n5, 167n22; black representing, 138; Brodsky's, 161n5, (premonition of) 161n3; death and, 97, 134; epiphanic vision of, 135, 136; nothing, 97; primordial, 137; thingness vs., 120. *See also* Abyss; Form

Notre Dame Cathedral (Paris), 74
November Uprising (1830), 147n1
Nowosielski, Jerry, 160n27
Nycz, Ryszard, 31, 146n6, 156n4

Objects (and objecthood): artifacts as living, 44; Brodsky's, 166n14; enigmatic, 81; genesis of, 93; Herbert's, 79–80; inanimate, 17; inventory of, 36; living, 44; material, xviii; materialization of, 36; nonobjective image, 92, 139; nothingness, 93, 119, 136–37; object erasing mirror, 137; object-related epiphanies, 33–39; order of, 56; and phenomenology, 35–39; poetry of, 35; representation of, 151n23; stereotyped image of, 85; subject-object split, 109, 131; thingness of, 33–34, 35, 80, 90, (Dutch focus on) 53, (vs. nothingness) 120; (things) elemental image of things, 33; utensils, 79–80; Zagajewski's, 33–37, 39
Olis, Jan, 157n19
Orpheus, 125
Ortega y Gasset, José, 98
Ostade, Adriaen van, 145n5
Ostroumova-Levedeva, A. P., 163n28
Ozerov, V. A., 125

Paestum: Herbert visits, 44, 45, 47–48
Palladio, Andrea, 117
Paris, 6, 14–15, 17–18, 30–31, 32
Pascal, Blaise, vii
Passage: aporetic path, 128; between end and beginning of time, 130; between thingness and nothingness, 90; Brodsky's 132, 134–35; death and rites of, 136; emotional, 33; epiphany as, xvii; "homeward/inward," 32–33; intertextual, xv; kinetic, 20; paired with vision, 142; to rapture, 84; and revelation, xvii, (Brodsky) 126 (see also Epiphanies); textual, 146n7; from visible to invisible reality, 141. See also Travel

Pater, Walter, 154n19, 156n6
Patryk (Herbert's pseudonym), 68. See also Herbert, Zbigniew
Paul, Saint, xvii, 135
Perception: epiphanic, xiv; revelatory, xiv; "transfiguring perceptual power," xiv. See also Vision
Perlina, Nina, 163n28
Petersburg, 103, 107, 110–11
Phaistos disc, 68, 69, 70
Phenomenological view, 36–37, 59
Photography, 47
Piazza del Campo (Siena), 94
Piazza di San Marco (Venice), 108
Picasso, Pablo, 19
Piero della Francesca, 68, 74, 152n2; The Baptism of Christ, 159n17; Flagellation, 66
"Pilgrim" as term, 45–46. See also Travel
Pissarro, Camille, 17
Plato and Platonism, 107; neo-Platonic ideas, 18
Poland: in 1980s, 5–6; free elections, 30; regains independence, 149n24; rhetorical device in literature of, 55
Political activism, 6; Zagajewski withdraws from, 7
Polukhina, Valentina, 104, 135, 166n14
Proust, Marcel, 19, 28, 114
Pushkin, Aleksandr, 125, 162n18

Rabasa, José, 14
Rabelais, François, 123
Rapture: elation, 121; capacity for, 45; epiphanic, see Epiphanies; happy consciousness, 29
Realism. See Dutch visual tradition
Redentore, Il (Venice), 117
Redon, Odilon, 131, 138
Régnier, Henri de, 114, 134, 165n9
Reinhardt, Ad, 138
Relativism, 10
Rembrandt van Rijn, 21, 55

Renaissance art and architecture, 44, 68, 116, 117, 118

Revelation: description is, 6; (revelatory) experience, 78. *See also* Epiphanies

Reynolds, Sir Joshua: *Journey to Flanders and Holland,* 54

Richard, Jean-Pierre, 106

Rilke, Rainer Maria, 15, 34. WORKS: "Orpheus. Eurydice. Hermes," 124, 128–29, 131–32; *Weltinnenraum,* 11

Rio de Janeiro, 163n21

Romanticism, 6, 60, 64; and post-Romanticism, 142

Roman xenia (artistic form), 83–84

Rosicrucians, the, 70, 167n25

Rousseau, Jean-Jacques, 8, 21; burial place of, 49

Royal Museum (Amsterdam), 77, 79, 89, 97

Ruisdael, Jacob van, 72

Runge, Phillip Otto: *Repose during the Flight,* 60

Ruskin, John, 119, 136, 164n37; *The Seven Lamps of Architecture,* 116; *The Stones of Venice,* 116–17

Russian: Orthodox culture, 110, 129; tradition of travel writing, 126

San Giorgio Maggiore (Venice), 117

Sansovino, Andrea, 117

Sartre, Jean-Paul, 15

Saul, the conversion of, 78

Saura, Carlos: *Carmen* (film), 24, 25, 143

Schelling, Friedrich von, 86

Schopenhauer, Arthur, 32, 56, 82

Schulz, Bruno, 19

Schwob, Marcel, 154n19

Senlis: Herbert visits, 45, 49–50

Sickert, William, 118

Siena: Herbert in, 94–96

Sinopoli, Giuseppe, 160n2

Sochoń, Jan, 97

Solidarity movement, 5, 153n10

Sontag, Susan, 110, 166n15

Soviet Union, 103, 110. *See also* Communist regime

Spender, Stephen, 125

Stalin, Joseph, 46

Stazione Termini (Venice), 117

Sterling, Charles, 83

Still life genre, 33; in Dutch art, 56, 157n19, (black background used in) 88 (*see also* Black); Herbert's analogy to, 52–53, 142–43; origin of, 83–84; Schopenhauer's view of, 82; "thingness" in, 80; Zagajewski on objects in, 34

Styles, *see* Architecture; Dutch visual tradition; Minimalism; Modernism; Romanticism; Still life genre; Suprematism

Suprematism, 91–92, 138

Swedenborg, Emanuel, 126

Szczęsna, Justyna, 97

Tears as aesthetic response, 121–22

Templars, the, 44

Terborch, Gerard, 87–88

Theophany, 64; biblical, xvii

Thing (form), 89. *See also* Form

Thingness of objects. *See* Objects (and objecthood)

Thoreau, Henry David, 141

Thoré-Bürger, Théophile, 68, 69

Tiepolo, Giovanni Battista, 115

Tintoretto, 115

Titian, 114

Tolstoy, Lev, 165n8

Topography, 11–14, 43; in Dutch art, 56

Torrentius, Johannes, 61, 68, 69–72, 142; *Still Life with a Bridle,* xix, 77–84, 85–87, 89–94, 97–99

Totality: of God's creation, symbolized, 82; of knowledge, Herbert and, 57–58; of vision, 135; Zagajewski's search for, 7, 11, 13, 17

Tourism. *See* Travel

Transcendence: blue representing, 28;

of God, 7; Herbert and, 64, 95; and phallic allusions, 29; and visual tradition, 60, 136, 137

Travel, 141; artists' provincialism vs., 55; Brodsky in Venice, *see* Brodsky, Joseph; epiphanic, xiv–xviii, 64, 141; and the *flâneur*, xviii (*see also* Walking); Herbert as traveler, *see* Herbert, Zbigniew; imaginary, 16; "pilgrim" as term, 45–46; Russian journeys and literature about, 114, 126; and tourism, 17, 45, 47, 48–49, 51; to the West, xv, xvi, 12, 13, 31, 49, (banned) 46; Zagajewski on, 14, 16–18 (*see also* Zagajewski, Adam)

Tsvetayeva, Marina, 105; "New Year's Greetings," 124

Turner, J. M. W., 59, 114, 118, 119

Underworld. *See* Afterlife, the

University of California (Los Angeles), 153n10

University of Michigan (Ann Arbor), 103

University of Texas (Houston), 31

Utrillo, Maurice, 152n3

Van Eyck, Jan, 74; *Portrait of Giovanni Arnolfini and His Wife, Giovanna Cenani,* 58, 91

Van Gogh, Vincent: *Old Shoes,* 155n2

Van Goyen, Jan, 58; *Landscape with Objects,* 57; *The View of Leyden,* 56

Vasari, Giorgio, 143

Velásquez, Diego Rodríguez de Silva y, 21

Venclova, Tomas, 126

Venice: architecture of, 116–17; Brodsky in, *see* Brodsky, Joseph; color and light in, 112, 113, 114–16, 118–20, 128, 129, 130–32; as "labyrinth," 127; Ruskin in, 116–17, 119; visual tradition of, 114–21; Whistler in, 118–19

Vermeer van Delft, Jan, 7, 11, 24, 28,

55, 143; discovery of, 68; Picasso quoted on, 19; point of view imagined (by Herbert), 66–67. WORKS: *Girl Interrupted at Her Music (The Music Lesson),* xix, 22–24, 25, 27–30, 32–33, 38; *The Little Street,* 32; *View of Delft,* 32; *Woman Holding a Balance,* 32; *A Young Woman with a Water Jug,* 37–38

Villa of the Mysteries, 83–84

Virgil, 125, 135

Vision: artistic, metaphysics and, 141–42; color and, 28; dual (blindness/insight), 21; duration of perception, 65; eidetic, 39; epiphany and, xvii; Herbert's apocryphal type of, 44; objectless, 143; "open door" of perception, 25–26; symbols representing perception, 60; topography and, 11–14; travel paired with, 142; type of, for narrator, 13; Vermeer's, Huxley's view of, 26. *See also* Epiphanies; Eye, the; Illumination; Mirror motif; Topography

Visual tradition. *See* Dutch visual tradition; Venice

Vivaldi, Antonio, 109

Walking (as *flâneur*), xviii, 8–10, 14–15, 16–17, 18, 117–18, 127

West, travels to. *See* Travel

Westhof, Clare, 131

Whistler, James Abbott McNeill, 75, 118–19; *Nocturnes* and *Nocturne: Palaces,* 118

Winckelmann, Johann, 156n5

Wolfe, Thomas, 64

Woolf, Virginia, 64

Wordsworth, William, 127

Wyspianski, Stanislaw, 10, 15–16

Xenia (Roman artistic form), 83–84

Yalta agreement, 31

Yourcenar, Marguerite, 154n19

Zagajewski, Adam, 99; in Cracow, 8–10, 11; ekphrasis by (of Vermeer's work), 11, 22–33 passim, 38–39, 142, 143; epiphanies of, 19–39, 126–27, 143, ("minor") 145n3; as exile, xiii–xiv, xv, 6, 13, 30–31; in New York City, 21–23, 25, 26, 141; post-Romantic style of, 142; totalitarianism opposed by, xviii; as walker (*flâneur*), 8–10, 16–17; weds Maria Wodecka, 146n11. WORKS: 126, 166n11; *Another Beauty,* xviii, 6–7, 8–9, 12, 15–16, 33, 37, (quoted) 9, 11, 18, 20, 31, 32, 35, 36, 39; "Covenant," 37; "Essentialist in Paris," 12; "Flamenco," 6, 7, 21, 24–25, 28, 29, 32, 33, 143; "Homeless New York," 29, 38; "Morandi," 34; *On Exile, History, and the Imagination,* xviii; *Solidarity, Solitude: Essays by Adam Zagajewski,* xviii, 6, 21; "Spring Thunderstorm," 12, 14; *Two Cities* (collection and title essay), 12, 36; "A View of Cracow," 11; "A View of Delft," 11